More Praise for *Th*

"[Hansen] displays a remarkable lightn[...]
ingly comprehensive account casts worl[...]
—*Publishe[...]*

"*The Year 1000* is a tour de force and offers many new ways of thinking about the past."

—*The Spectator* (UK)

"An informative and entertaining romp around the world of a thousand years ago, on everything from Viking longboats to camel caravans in Central Asia. Anyone who thinks that globalization is something new in life needs to read this book!"

—Ian Morris, author of *Why the West Rules—for Now*

"Outstanding . . . a lively and engrossing book that describes in fascinating detail how trade enriched the world. [Hansen] displays the delightful exuberance of an author deeply in love with her subject."

—*The Times* (London)

"The myth of the 'European Middle Ages' dissolves in the ocean currents and trade winds of this stimulating account. . . . Bolstered by facts and enlivened by intriguing theories, Hansen's book presents a world of objects, ideas, people, animals, and know-how constantly on the move."

—Barbara H. Rosenwein, author of *A Short History of the Middle Ages* and *Generations of Feeling*

"Daring . . . A smart, broad-ranging survey of the global Middle Ages that is learned, thought-provoking—and perfectly tuned to our times."

—*London Sunday Times*

"A whole new way of looking at the world. If you have the idea that medieval history was a time when there were few connections between those who inhabited different places on the map, this book will reorient you in the most stimulating way possible. . . . Brilliant."

—Rana Mitter, author of *Forgotten Ally*

"As Valerie Hansen shows in this fascinating book, much of the inhabited globe already had complex systems of long-distance trade more than a millennium ago."

—*The Telegraph* (UK)

"What makes *The Year 1000* so special is that it is the result of the author's unique fusion of firsthand, on-site investigations around the world and intensive research in far-flung libraries, archives, and museums. What's more, all of this energetic, scholarly activity is combined with a compelling argument for a new hypothesis concerning the origins of globalization, a topic that could hardly be more pertinent to our own age."

—Victor H. Mair, editor of *The Columbia History of Chinese Literature* and coauthor of *The True History of Tea* and *Sacred Display*

"No one has told this story better or has been able to combine the latest scholarly research with such an exciting and accessible narrative. This is how world history should be written."

—Stuart B. Schwartz, author of *All Can Be Saved: Religious Tolerance and Salvation in the Iberian Atlantic World*

"Offers timely proof that globalization has a point of origin and a long history . . . Although Hansen doesn't quite have us wishing we could turn back the clock, she offers in three hundred vivid pages the kind of deep texture that makes an age come alive."

—Paul Freedman, author of *Out of the East: Spices and the Medieval Imagination*

"Elegantly written and meticulously researched . . . a whirlwind world tour that challenges the notion of a more recently hyper-connected globe."

—Sarah Parcak, author of *Archaeology from Space: How the Future Shapes Our Past*

"Rich and fascinating . . . Hansen shows how people, goods, and ideas traversed vast spaces. Ranging by sea and land across six continents, she seeks out exciting and unexpected connections, showing that globalization is by no means new to our own time."

—David Abulafia, author of *The Discovery of Mankind* and *The Great Sea*

Also by Valerie Hansen

The Silk Road:
A New History with Documents

The Open Empire:
A History of China to 1800

Negotiating Daily Life in Traditional China:
How Ordinary People Used Contracts, 600–1400

Changing Gods in Medieval China, 1127–1276

Voyages in World History (with Kenneth R. Curtis)

THE YEAR
1000

WHEN EXPLORERS CONNECTED THE WORLD—
AND GLOBALIZATION BEGAN

Valerie Hansen

SCRIBNER

New York   London   Toronto   Sydney   New Delhi

Scribner

An Imprint of Simon & Schuster, Inc.

1230 Avenue of the Americas

New York, NY 10020

First Scribner trade paperback edition April 2021

SCRIBNER and design are registered trademarks of The Gale Group, Inc.,
used under license by Simon & Schuster, Inc., the publisher of this work.

For information about special discounts for bulk purchases,
please contact Simon & Schuster Special Sales at 1-866-506-1949
or business@simonandschuster.com.

The Simon & Schuster Speakers Bureau can bring authors to your live event.
For more information or to book an event, contact the Simon & Schuster Speakers Bureau
at 1-866-248-3049 or visit our website at www.simonspeakers.com.

Maps by David Lindroth Inc.

Manufactured in the United States of America

3   5   7   9   10   8   6   4   2

Library of Congress Cataloging-in-Publication Data

Names: Hansen, Valerie, 1958– author.
Title: The year 1000 : when globalization began / Valerie Hansen.
Other titles: One Thousand
Identifiers: LCCN 2019045048 (print) | LCCN 2019045049 (ebook) |
ISBN 9781501194108 (hardcover) | ISBN 9781501194115 (paperback) |
ISBN 9781501194122 (ebook)
Subjects: LCSH: One thousand, A.D.
Classification: LCC D123 .H37 2020 (print) |
LCC D123 (ebook) | DDC 909/.1—dc23
LC record available at https://lccn.loc.gov/2019045048
LC ebook record available at https://lccn.loc.gov/2019045049

ISBN 978-1-5011-9410-8
ISBN 978-1-5011-9411-5 (pbk)
ISBN 978-1-5011-9412-2 (ebook)

For Jim,
who went everywhere
and read everything

Contents

Author's Note

To reach the broadest possible audience, I've followed a few guidelines. Keep foreign names and words to a minimum. Use the most familiar spellings and drop most diacritics. Refer to modern countries and regions and avoid bogging down the reader with place names no longer in use. Convert historic measurements and units into both English and metric measures. Write endnotes that provide sufficient information to locate the sources.

Prologue

The street is packed with customers buying pearl necklaces from Sri Lanka, ornaments carved from African ivory, perfumes preserved with stabilizers from Tibet and Somalia, vials crafted from Baltic amber, and furniture made from every imaginable aromatic wood. The smell of foreign incense permeates the air. A shop around the corner sells expensive and high-tech products alongside versions modified for local consumers. Depending on the holiday, Hindu, Muslim, or Buddhist worshippers join the throngs. Later, when you drop by a friend's place, she offers you a cool drink with an unusual fragrance. The family shows off their latest acquisitions: a fine table made of Javanese sandalwood displaying an intricately carved rhinoceros horn. Many of the knickknacks look imported, testifying to your friend's cosmopolitan taste.

This city, with its many connections to distant places, sounds like any important modern metropolis, but this is what the Chinese city of Quanzhou was like in the year 1000. Halfway between Shanghai and Hong Kong on the China coast, and directly facing Taiwan, Quanzhou was then one of the largest and wealthiest ports in the world.

All the products for sale were common trade goods of the day. For centuries, the Chinese had been importing fragrant woods such as sandalwood from present-day Java and India and aromatic tree resins including myrrh and frankincense from the Arabian Peninsula. The Chinese burned imported incense to perfume the air, steamed their clothes with imported aromatics to give them

1

a pleasant fragrance, and flavored medicines, drinks, soups, and cakes with imported spices.

A vigorous export trade financed these imports, and the most technologically sophisticated Chinese product was high-fired pottery. Low-cost competition came from Middle Eastern potters who mixed imitation glazes that resembled the glossy Chinese ceramics but weren't fired at the same high temperatures. With the opening of new routes, craftsmen who'd been the only suppliers for their countrymen suddenly found themselves competing for market share with manufacturers on the other side of the globe.

The year 1000 marked the start of globalization. This is when trade routes took shape all around the world that allowed goods, technologies, religions, and people to leave home and go somewhere new. The resulting changes were so profound that they affected ordinary people, too.

In the year 1000—or as close to it as archeologists can determine—Viking explorers left behind their home region of Scandinavia, crossed the North Atlantic, and arrived on the island of Newfoundland on the northeast coast of Canada, a region where no Europeans had traveled previously. (No one had crossed into the Americas since a wave of migrations from Siberia to the west coast of the Americas more than 10,000 years earlier.) The Vikings connected preexisting trade routes across the Americas with those of Europe, Asia, and Africa—a landmass we'll refer to as Afro-Eurasia. For the first time in world history an object or a message could travel all the way around the world.

Unlike the Norse, the other key players in the year 1000—the Chinese, the Indians, and the Arabs—were not European. The longest maritime route in regular use connected China with the Persian Gulf cities of Oman and Basra, the port closest to Baghdad. This, the Persian Gulf–China route, combined two pilgrimage pathways: one for Muslims going from China to Mecca, the other for East Africans also performing the hajj. Most of the traffic traveled from the Arabian Peninsula to the ports on China's southeast coast, but some goods continued all the way to the ports along the East African coast.

Prologue

The agents of globalization in 1000 included the Vikings of Northern Europe as well as the inhabitants of the Americas, Africa, China, and the Middle East. Trading goods for commodities they'd never seen before, these explorers opened up land and sea routes that marked the true beginning of globalization. The new pathways these traders and voyagers pioneered allowed multiple kingdoms and empires to brush up against each other, causing goods, people, microbes, and ideas to move into new regions. The different parts of the world came into contact with each other for the first time, and today's globalized world was the ultimate result.

True, people living in a few regions—Rome, India, China—knew well before 1000 that other societies existed. A well-documented sea route linked the Roman empire with the west coast of southern India in the first centuries AD, but that trade eventually died out. On the other hand, the overland and maritime Silk Roads, which formed around AD 500, created lasting cultural and trade ties among India, China, and the countries of Southeast Asia and were still in use in 1000. Still, these two trade networks, as sophisticated as they were, took in only one part of the world. The expansion of regions occurring in the year 1000 affected the entire globe.

To be sure, this wasn't globalization in one current sense of the word. Ordinary people weren't able to travel virtually anywhere, walk into a store, and buy goods from almost any country.

Nonetheless, the changes around the year 1000 constituted globalization in the most fundamental sense. What happened in one place profoundly affected the residents of other distant regions. New pathways bound together different parts of the globe, and trade goods, people, and religions all moved along those pathways. The ongoing demand for slaves in Constantinople (modern Istanbul), Baghdad, Cairo, and other cities resulted in the forced movement of millions of people from Africa, Eastern Europe, and Central Asia—hundreds of years before the transatlantic slave trade began.

Globalization profoundly affected those who never left home. Once a ruler converted—and many did around 1000—many of their subjects adopted the new faith as well. People living on both the Southeast Asian mainland and the islands gave up their traditional occupations to work full-time to supply Chinese consumers, both rich and poor, with spices and fragrant woods. As foreign merchants increasingly benefited at the expense of local businessmen, the world's first anti-globalization riots and attacks on the newly wealthy broke out in cities such as Cairo, Constantinople, and Guangzhou.

The materials that survive from 1000 do not provide exact numbers for the goods and peoples that moved around the world at that time. That's why we're going to pay so much attention to other kinds of evidence. We will track trade goods as they moved along different pathways and see which types of people and information followed them. We're interested in people who wrote about their actual journeys, as well as those who recorded what they heard from others because they are our main witnesses to the massive transformation that occurred after 1000.

These exchanges of the year 1000 opened up some of the routes through which goods and peoples continued to travel after Columbus traversed the mid-Atlantic. But the world of 1000 differed from that of 1492 in important ways. First, the travelers who encountered each other in the year 1000 were much closer technologically—unlike in 1492, when firearms and cannon enabled the Europeans to defeat almost everyone they met.

In the year 1000, the major players were also different. Some parts of the world, such as China and the Middle East, flourished while others—Europe in particular—lagged behind. In fact, the world of 1000 looks much more like our world today in which the Chinese, the Arabs, and the Americans are all genuine rivals to the Europeans.

The events set in motion by the year 1000 were a significant point in humanity's evolution, and they've produced both good and bad effects. The blazing of global pathways caused fertilization and infection, intellectual enrichment and cultural fragmentation, the spread of new technologies and the extinction of traditional crafts. The pathways encouraged *both* fraternization and conflict. They opened some people's eyes to possibilities they'd never glimpsed but also hastened the subjugation of those who were less able to fend off domination.

This book is the first to recognize these events as "globalization." Globalization always produces winners and losers, and it did so in 1000, too, when the world changed fundamentally. We're still feeling the effects now, and we need to understand the long-term legacy of that year.

The story seems terribly familiar, but when we go back to the year 1000, we realize how different the setting was. Most obviously, industrialization hadn't yet occurred. There was neither steam power nor electricity. Power came from people, animals, water, and wind.

Political units back then were also different: warbands, tribes, kingdoms, and empires. None were nation-states that could force all of their citizens to serve in the army and pay taxes (these took shape only in the nineteenth century).

This book explains who developed the networks in the world's major regions and how these networks became interlaced. As peoples living in different regions established contact with each other around the year 1000, they set the stage for the next phase of globalization in the 1500s when the Europeans reshaped existing networks to suit their own interests. But the Europeans didn't invent globalization. They changed and augmented what was already there. If globalization hadn't yet begun, Europeans wouldn't have been able to penetrate so many regions so quickly.

Globalization was always fraught: as soon as people realized that they weren't alone on this planet, they faced new dangers. The people who experienced globalization for the first time had to strategize, and they did so from different vantage points.

When individuals encountered unfamiliar peoples—as they did all over the world around the year 1000—they assessed the risks: Were the strangers going to kill them? Were they going to capture them? They had to judge their relative standing: If a fight broke out, who would win? Who had better technology? What if the strangers knew how to read and write? These individuals had to make reasoned decisions about what to do, and their decisions have much to teach us.

Some reactions were hasty and ill considered: the Vikings, for example, sometimes killed sleeping indigenous peoples before they had a chance to exchange a single word.

Other reactions were spontaneous and, to tell the truth, bizarre. When Amerindians attacked a Viking settlement and the Norse leaders called for a retreat, one pregnant but feisty Viking woman named Freydis couldn't keep up with her male companions. She found herself alone and facing a band of indigenous warriors. She pulled her naked breast out of her shirt and "slapped" it with a sword. The startled Amerindians dispersed immediately, if we can believe what the saga says.

Other responses in the year 1000 are more instructive: some brave souls swallowed their fears and reached out to the peoples they'd never seen before. They established trading relationships.

Often the places with the fewest natural resources ended up exporting their own people as slaves. No single place provided most of the world's slaves. The richest urban centers imported slaves from poorer regions that had few exportable commodities besides human labor: West and East Africa, Central Asia, and Northern and Eastern Europe. (So many slaves came from Eastern Europe that our word "slave" is derived from "Slav.")

People with nothing to trade sometimes became successful middlemen. They were critical to the pioneering of new trade routes. Surprisingly, people from a society with lesser technology were sometimes able to best a people with better technology because they assimilated new ways more quickly.

One of the fastest ways to advance one's own society was to convert to the religion of a more developed society, a decision not always based on religious conviction. One ruler living in modern Ukraine (his name was Prince Vladimir) aspired to strengthen his kingdom and looked to his immediate neighbors for models. Like many other monarchs, he chose a religion that offered him the greatest chance to consolidate power and form alliances with powerful neighbors. Prince Vladimir's major source of information was the reports presented by envoys he dispatched to visit other rulers. Working as spies, they returned with news of his neighbors.

Vladimir chose Christianity, specifically Eastern Orthodox Christianity as practiced in the Byzantine empire, from a very short list. He weighed the pros and cons of Judaism, Islam, Roman Christianity, and Byzantine Orthodoxy. He rejected Judaism because the Jews had lost Jerusalem. He crossed off Islam because it banned drinking. He rejected Roman Christianity without explaining why. He opted for Byzantine Orthodoxy because the magnificent Hagia Sophia cathedral in the Byzantine capital of Constantinople represented a technological marvel, just as impressive in its day as the latest skyscraper is today.

As other leaders selected religions for their realms in the years immediately leading up to and following the year 1000, the number of world religions shrank. One such religion, Manichaeism, which had been popular in the region we now know as Iran and which emphasized an ongoing struggle between good and evil, disappeared entirely because it couldn't compete with more established religions or attract the same level of patronage.

No major new religions arose after the year 1000 except for Sikhism, Baha'i, and Mormonism, along with a few others. Those that did were remixes, combining elements of religions already firmly in place by 1000.

Other rulers made decisions similar to Vladimir's choice of Byzantine Orthodoxy. The result was a dramatic expansion around the year 1000 of the number of worshippers who professed allegiance to the major religions. Northern and Eastern Europe became Christian, the realm of Islam expanded east into Central Asia and south into North India, and Buddhism and Hinduism both spread into Southeast Asia. We live in a world shaped by the interactions of the world in the year 1000: 92 percent of today's believers subscribe to one of the four religions that gained traction then.

Indeed living in a world shaped by the events of the year 1000, we're wrestling with exactly the same challenges that people faced for the first time then: Should we cooperate with our neighbors, trade with them, allow them to settle in our countries, and grant them freedom of worship when they live in our society? Should we try to keep them out? Should we retaliate against the people who become wealthy through trade? Should we try to make new products that copy technologies we haven't yet mastered? Finally, will globalization make us more aware of who we are, or will it destroy our identity?

This book's goal is to address those questions.

CHAPTER ONE

The World in the Year 1000

Strangely, no new technology caused this burst of interregional travel around the year 1000. As in earlier times, people moved overland primarily by walking or riding animals or carts, and they traversed water in canoes, sailboats, or wooden ships. Trade among different regions increased in the year 1000 because a surplus in agriculture led to population growth and allowed some of the populace to stop farming full-time, to produce goods for markets, and to become merchants.

The place in the world with the highest population in the year 1000, as now, was China. Its population reached some 100 million. Throughout history, the Chinese have made up between one quarter and one third of the people living on the globe. The economy boomed during the Song dynasty (960–1276), as Chinese merchants and ships traded with both Southeast Asia and South India, where localities growing rice also supported burgeoning populations.

The populations of grain-growing areas in the Middle East and Europe weren't as high as those in Asia but were still significant. From 751 to about 900 the Abbasid empire controlled a large swath of territory from North Africa in the west all the way to Central Asia in the east.

Unification under the Abbasids facilitated the movement of many crops across the empire. Some, like sorghum, originated in West Africa; others, like rice, came from India. The cultivation of tropical plants from Iran and India transformed life all over the Abbasid realm by encouraging farmers to work throughout the summer (something they previously hadn't done). This change brought sustained prosperity to the Islamic heartland in the early years of the Abbasid caliphate.

After 900, though, the empire broke apart into regional dynasties, each ruled by a different military leader. The caliph in Baghdad remained the nominal head of the Islamic community (Muslims continued to mention him in their Friday prayers all over the former Abbasid territory), but the empire was no longer united. Nevertheless, the population of the former Abbasid lands continued to grow, reaching an estimated 35 to 40 million in the year 1000.

The population of Western Europe also rose as the residents adopted far-reaching changes in agriculture, which the British historian R. I. Moore has called "cerealization." They planted more and more land with wheat and barley. In northern France and England, cultivators first recognized that raising the same crop in a given field year after year lowered its fertility, so they allowed one third to one half of their land to lie fallow.

After 1000, farmers began alternating their crops. One popular rotation was turnips, clover, and grain, which helped retain nutrients and soil quality. This practice, so important for raising agricultural yield, spread only slowly (it was already well known in China). At the same time, other innovations also increased output: horse-drawn plows, water mills, windmills, and iron tools that could dig deeper into the soil than wooden tools. Before cerealization, most of the land in Western Europe was not under regular cultivation; afterward much of it was.

In addition to raising population, these changes contributed to the rise of settled communities in Europe. Before the growing of grain became widespread, many farmers in Western Europe had been itinerant, moving from place to place to work the land and raise livestock. This continued to be true of farmers in Scandinavia and Eastern Europe, who followed their herds of pigs, goats, sheep, cattle, and horses. But first in France, England, and Germany, and later in Eastern and Northern Europe, farmers began to build houses and settle down in villages, thanks to crop rotation and other agricultural advances.

Europe's population nearly doubled, from less than 40 million in 1000 to 75 million in 1340 (before the Black Death struck in 1347). This increase in population coincided with the Medieval Warm Period, which began in 1000, peaked around 1100, and had ended by 1400. Because climate historians do not yet know whether the warming trend occurred all over the world, they now refer to this period as the Medieval Climate Anomaly. Ongoing research suggests that while some regions, such as Europe, experienced an increase in temperature, others became colder.

The distribution of people across Europe changed, too. The population of Southern and Eastern Europe—Italy, Spain, and the Balkans—increased by 50 percent. But because of improved agricultural techniques, the growth in Western and Northern Europe—the region of modern France and Germany—was far greater: there the population skyrocketed by a factor of three, so that nearly half of Europe's people lived in Northern and Western Europe by 1340.

The Chinese population shift resembled Europe's but was in the opposite direction: the Chinese moved south of the Yangzi River to rice-growing areas at precisely the same time Europeans moved north, away from the Mediterranean and toward the North Sea. In 742, 60 percent of the population of 60 million lived in northern China, where they grew wheat and millet; by 980, 62 percent lived in southern China, where they cultivated rice, a much more productive crop than the northern grains.

In contrast to China's emperor, no single monarch ruled Europe in the year 1000. In Eastern Europe, the Byzantine empire was the most prosperous power, but its military strength was rapidly declining. Although the Byzantine army grew increasingly weaker, forcing the emperor to depend on mercenaries or foreign armies, Constantinople (modern Istanbul) was the most advanced city in Europe. When Western Europeans visited, they couldn't believe the beauty of its promenades or the sophistication of its buildings, particularly the magnificent cathedral of Hagia Sophia.

In Western Europe, Charlemagne had unified modern-day France and Germany, but after his death in 814, his kingdom split into three. In the 900s, King Otto I of Germany, his son Otto II, and grandson Otto III—the three are known as the Ottonians—were the most powerful rulers in Western Europe. Otto controlled the territory of Germany and Rome but not the entire Italian Peninsula, much of which belonged to the Byzantine empire. Otto's power allowed him to appoint the pope. In turn, the pope crowned Otto I emperor of the Holy Roman Empire in 962, a position that his son and grandson succeeded to as well.

Otto III chose Pope Sylvester II (999–1003) to head the Roman church. One of the best-educated men of his day, Sylvester knew how to do a little algebra, a mathematical technique that Europeans learned from the Islamic world (the word "algebra" derives from the Arabic word *al-jabr*, which referred to the manipulations necessary to balance two sides of an equation).

The year 1000 occurred during the reign of Sylvester II, yet the year didn't mean much to Europeans because very few people used a calendar that counted years starting at the birth of Jesus. Such calendars had existed since the 500s, but this system of dating gained ground slowly, winning official acceptance by the church only in 1500. Most people referred to the year by the reign of the ruling king or pope, calling the year 1000, for example, the second year of Sylvester's reign.

Few Christians believed that Christ would return to earth in the year 1000. Various itinerant preachers and church reformers claimed to be the messiah and led uprisings, but their movements occurred in different centuries, none near the year 1000.

Of all the agrarian empires in the world in the year 1000, scholars know the least about the Maya in Mesoamerica. Sometime before 600, the Maya had already begun the extensive use of irrigation to cultivate corn, which they grew in raised fields in the original heartland in modern-day Mexico, Belize, Guatemala, El Salvador, and Honduras. The Maya peaked sometime around the year 700, when their total population numbered in the millions. (A 2018 estimate suggests 10–15 million.) The Maya city of Tikal, in modern Guatemala, one of the largest between 600 and 800, had some 60,000 residents. At the end of the 700s, multiple cities collapsed and were abandoned, possibly because of overfarming, possibly because of environmental change. After 830, very little new construction took place. A prolonged drought occurred between 1000 and 1100, causing a precipitous decline in population, as well as mass migration to the northern Yucatan, where the new city of Chichén Itzá arose.

Although the written record in Mayan glyphs stops before the year 1000 (the last inscription on a stone monument dates to 910), the Maya in Chichén Itzá experienced a revival, extending their trade contacts north to the Mississippi Valley and the Four Corners region (where Colorado, New Mexico, Arizona, and Utah meet), and south to Panama and Colombia. The Chichén Itzá metropolis contains an enormous ball court as well as a sophisticated astronomical observatory. The city was so impressive in the year 1000 that many neighboring rulers sent envoys laden with gifts to visit the Maya ruler.

What was the world's population in the year 1000? Ballpark estimate: around 250 million. We know a lot more about societies that conducted censuses (think China) than we do about societies that didn't keep records, and societies that practiced agriculture had much larger populations than itinerant herding societies. Asia, home to China, Japan, India, and Indonesia—all major rice producers—made up the lion's share of the world's population (more than 50 percent, or approximately 150 million people), and Europe was next with about 20 percent. Africa may have accounted for another 20 percent, leaving 10 percent or less in the Americas (Oceania's population never reached one percent of the world's total).

A world population of 250 million represented a turning point in history. When explorers set off from their home countries to go to neighboring territories, they were more likely to run into people than in earlier periods when populations were lower.

In the different locations around the world where agricultural production boomed and population increased, some people were able to stop farming and live in cities. European cities between 1000 and 1348 weren't the world's biggest: Paris had a population of 20–30,000 and Islamic Córdoba 450,000, both lower than the Song dynasty capitals of Kaifeng and Hangzhou, each with at least one million.

As cities grew, so did the number of enterprising merchants. The unusual objects they procured in distant lands whetted the desire for more. Traded goods were most often lightweight objects such as feathers, furs, beautiful textiles, and medicines. Precious metals were an important exception; people were willing to carry them across huge distances.

In these same societies, agricultural surpluses also supported large literate bureaucracies. All had their own writing systems. The largest bodies of sources about the world in the year 1000 are in Latin, Old Icelandic, Greek, Arabic, Persian, Sanskrit, and Chinese. Because of the written record, we know more about people in these heartlands, and their immediate neighbors, than we do about places that had no writing systems.

This book doesn't cover isolated parts of the earth about which there are no records or that didn't engage in trade with neighboring regions. This was true of Australia, some of sub-Saharan Africa, and multiple areas in the Americas. In some of these places, inhabitants engaged in hunting and gathering, with intermittent farming. They planted seeds in the spring and returned in the fall to harvest them without tending them in the summer. In recent years some have argued that life as a hunter-gatherer was far better than working as a farmer cultivating crops in a field. That may indeed have been the case. But hunter-gatherers didn't produce sufficient surplus to support significant population growth. Nor did writing arise in any of these societies, meaning that we know little about them except what we can learn from archeology. Many believe that writing first arose in large agrarian empires because rulers needed to keep track of their subjects and record their taxes.

Still, the areas that had little contact with outsiders weren't all the same. In West Africa, the city of Jenne-jeno has prompted scholars to rethink their underlying assumption that only settled agrarian societies could give rise to cities. There, the locals were pastoralists who moved with their herds most of the year

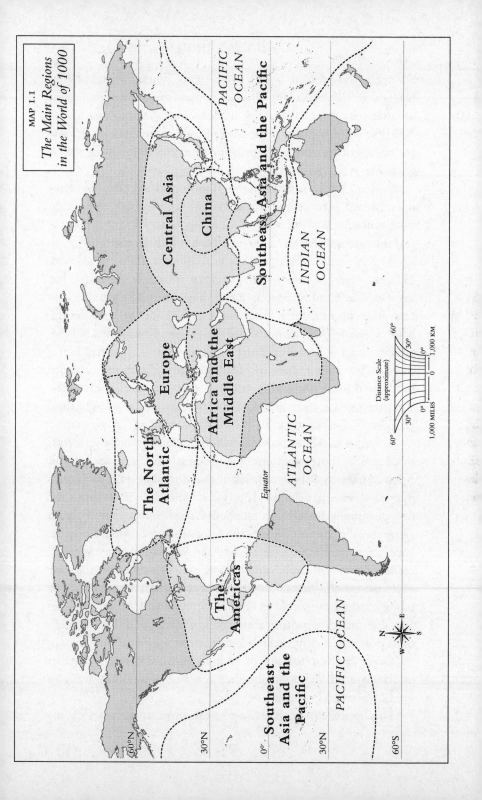

MAP 1.1
*The Main Regions
in the World of 1000*

but spent the rainy season in Jenne-jeno, when the population reached as high as 20,000. The site contains an enormous deposit of broken pottery 26 feet (8 m) deep that dates to as early as 300 BC, when a major settlement already existed. Interestingly, the only written records about Jenne-jeno are from outsiders who started to write about the city around the year 1000.

Similar large settlements certainly existed in the less-documented parts of the world, but we know about them only from archeological excavations. In many places like the Americas and sub-Saharan Africa, archeology is our only source.

Writers all over Eurasia in the year 1000 lived in a world very different from our own—where every corner of the earth has been explored and mapped in detail. They were interested in distant places and recorded what they knew about the lands on the edge of the known world. Classical authors writing in Chinese, Greek, and Latin had all described quasi-human entities living there. Many later authors recorded glimpses of creatures without heads, or missing limbs, or possessing other strange characteristics. Early travelers in circa 1000 had only minimal knowledge of their neighbors—and a seemingly inexhaustible well of fearlessness.

Accounts in Arabic provide the most detail about the residents, trade goods, routes, and customs of many preliterate societies in Afro-Eurasia. A Persian official in the Abbasid postal and intelligence service named Ibn Khurradadhbih (820–911) wrote the first geography book that described the different countries lying along specific routes as well as the goods they produced. Aptly, he entitled his work *The Book of Routes and Realms*. Subsequent geographers writing in Arabic and Persian used the same title for their observations of different places, writings of crucial importance to understanding the world in the year 1000. The Chinese also had a long tradition of writing about foreign places, and their descriptions provide equally valuable information.

To judge the reliability of such accounts, the best method is to compare one report with other available sources and form an opinion about whether it rings true.

This approach allows us to test the different theories claiming that certain travelers reached the Americas before Columbus. Some are utterly credible and have received widespread scholarly support; others, utterly unfounded, have triggered profound skepticism. While, for example, the evidence for the Viking voyages to Newfoundland is ironclad, the case for the Chinese beating Columbus to the Americas is speculative.

The idea that the Chinese arrived first is, to some, both appealing and intriguing: what if they had? It's certain that the Chinese navy led by Admiral Zheng He voyaged to Southeast Asia, India, the Arabian Peninsula, and the East African coast in the 1400s.

Yet there is no credible evidence to indicate that Admiral Zheng He's fleets sailed beyond the Cape of Good Hope to the Americas, Australia, or to the North and South Poles—all claims put forward by Gavin Menzies's book *1421*. The book enjoyed enormous success—it has outsold every other book on Chinese history—yet it seems no serious scholar of Chinese history accepts its findings. The book's problems are so many that one prominent scholar of the Ming dynasty made a complaint to the book's publishers for marketing the book as nonfiction.

Muslim explorers also arrived in the Americas before Columbus, or so claimed Turkey's president Recep Tayyip Erdogan in a 2014 speech. His evidence? Christopher Columbus recorded seeing a mosque in Cuba. In actuality, though, Columbus wrote in his diary, "One of them [the local mountains] has another little hill on its summit, like a graceful mosque." Clearly Columbus was describing a mosque-shaped hill, not an actual mosque.

One professional historian has made a similar claim about al-Biruni, a brilliant Central Asian polymath born in 973 and who died sometime after 1040. He was famous for his researches into the calendar, astronomy, geography, and India. Claiming "Biruni Discovers America," S. Frederick Starr contends that al-Biruni realized that there was a continent on the opposite side of the globe from Afro-Eurasia. This is not accurate.

Al-Biruni didn't know that the Americas existed. But he did recognize that the earth was a sphere, knowledge passed down from the ancient Greeks to scholars writing in Arabic. Al-Biruni also understood that people lived on only a fraction of the earth's surface. It was too cold for humans to live at the North Pole and too hot south of the equator. He suspected that most of the opposite side of the globe, which was completely unknown to the residents of Afro-Eurasia, was taken up with water, but he was a sufficiently rigorous thinker that he didn't rule out the possibility of some inhabited lands. Still, Al-Biruni never discovered a continent, much less one named America.

Except for al-Biruni and other leading scholars in the Islamic world, few people alive in the year 1000 conceived of the entire globe. The most complete map of the world—one that showed most of Afro-Eurasia but nothing in the Americas—was made in 1154 by al-Idrisi, a cartographer based in Sicily, Italy, one of the Islamic portals into Europe. Working in the court of King Roger II, al-Idrisi, a native of Ceuta, Morocco, crafted a world map on a silver disk more than two yards (2 m) in diameter and accompanied it with a complete list of the latitudinal and longitudinal coordinates of all the places shown. Not surprisingly, the original map was destroyed (probably melted down for the value of the silver), but al-Idrisi's list of places, accompanied by short descriptions of each locality, survives intact, as do maps made on the basis of the information he collected. One of these appears on the cover of this book.

Starting in 1000, as Europeans learned Arabic and translated Arabic texts, more knowledge entered Europe from the Islamic world. Euclid's geometry was translated from an Arabic translation of the original Greek into Latin, and Fibonacci introduced Arabic numerals (which were much more convenient than Roman numerals).

The transfer of knowledge wasn't limited to intellectual fields. Europeans also learned how to play new games. Chess, which was first created around 600 in India, spread throughout the Islamic world and became popular in Europe around 1000. The game taught the basics of military strategy; players learned that it was wiser to move with multiple infantry, or pawns, than alone. As chess entered Europe, some of the pieces took on new identities;

the elephants became bishops because craftsmen mistook the elephants' two tusks for two points on a bishop's mitre hat. Some chess pieces were made from elephant ivory, but more were from walrus ivory, which entered Europe in large quantities at the time the Vikings were most active in the North Atlantic.

Modern travelers accustomed to airplanes, trains, cars, and ships tend to exaggerate the difficulties of travel in earlier periods. We wonder how people could traverse thousands of miles on foot and forget that most people could walk 20 miles, or 32 km, a day, and for long periods. People in the year 1000 were used to this—one envoy went on foot more than 2,500 miles, or 4,000 km, between 1024 and 1026.

The historian who records this long trip doesn't mention how the envoy managed it, but we can suppose that he—and most of the explorers in this book—received help from local guides, no matter how difficult the terrain. During the 1990s, villagers helped one research group get over a difficult section of the Himalayas, showing them multiple routes that didn't appear on any map. Depending on the time of year, and the amount of snow, these routes posed varying levels of difficulty. There was even a gradual, flat route suitable for use by pregnant women.

Data about the speed with which people could travel on foot survives from multiple places and times. If couriers were running individual legs of a journey, and they did not have to carry anything, a team could achieve extraordinary speeds, up to 150 miles (240 km) in a single day, as the Spaniards reported for the Inca in the early 1500s.

Of course, soldiers bearing their own food and weapons traveled more slowly. The rates of travel for ancient armies, including those of Persian ruler Xerxes, Alexander the Great, and Hannibal—and even that of the more modern Queen Elizabeth I of England—ranged between 10 and 20 miles (16–32 km) per day. Even now, U.S. Army guidelines define a normal rate for a march at 20 miles per day. Anything more rapid qualifies as a forced march.

Riders on horseback could go faster: a modern rider in Mongolia can cover 300 miles in a single day if he frequently changes mounts, and in the past, Mongol soldiers could sustain speeds of 60 miles (100 km) per day for a few days during intense campaigns.

Good roads could also increase speeds dramatically. Many types of roads existed in the year 1000. In the most advanced societies, like China, dirt roads and bridges over rivers were common, and movement was straightforward. In others, few roads existed, and explorers had to find their own paths.

Conditions of overland travel also determined how far people could carry bulk goods. Around the year 1000, the residents of Chaco Canyon in New Mexico regularly hauled corn 90 miles, or 150 km, and, on an occasional basis, transported large timbers from 170 miles (275 km) away (Chaco had no trees). They went even farther to obtain luxury goods such as macaw feathers.

In the year 1000, distances across land weren't absolute. Temperature, terrain, and the presence of obstacles could speed up or slow down journeys.

The same was true of boat travel, whether by river or on the ocean. The rate of travel varied, and surprisingly, sailing or rowing times were usually no faster than going overland. Of course, it was much easier to sit on a boat than to walk overland.

Viking ships were famed for their flexible, lightweight construction, speed, and ability to land in shallow waters. Replicas have attained maximum speeds of 17 mph (27 kph) when sailing, but these are difficult to sustain for more than short periods. Considerably slower, Polynesian double canoes fitted with triangular sails attain speeds about half that in normal winds. Even today, well-built traditional sailboats average 10 mph (16 kph), while America's Cup contestants reach speeds five times that.

Rowboats or canoes are much slower, going around 7 mph (11 kph). It is difficult to row faster than that except in a short burst, but rowboats can travel in any direction, while sailboats can't go directly into the wind. Rowing was crucial to the success of the Vikings. They could sail near the coast, row up close to shore, raid, and then make a quick escape, regardless of the direction the wind was blowing.

Ocean currents shaped the journeys sailors made in the year

1000 just as they do today. Mariners could make faster progress if they rode the ocean's regular surface currents, called gyres, which are determined by wind patterns, gravity, heat from the sun, and the speed of the earth's rotation. The gyres in the Northern Hemisphere—the North Atlantic Gyre and the North Pacific Gyre—flow clockwise, while those in the Southern Hemisphere go counterclockwise.

Because of the clockwise direction of the North Atlantic Gyre, the trip across the North Atlantic to Canada was much more difficult than the return leg. Hugging the coast, the Vikings took the slower cold-water Greenland Current to Iceland and Greenland, and from there they caught the Labrador Current to Canada. The trip had its hazards. The Greenland Current encounters the much warmer Gulf Stream at Cape Farewell, the southern tip of Greenland, and the resulting fog and winds frequently blow boats off their course.

This is probably what happened to a Viking sailor named Bjarni Herjolfsson in 985 or 986, who set sail from Iceland for Greenland, where he hoped to find his father, who had just moved to a new settlement launched by Erik the Red.

Bjarni and his men sailed three days from Iceland to Greenland. Then, the sagas report, "the wind dropped and they were beset by winds from the north and fog; for many days they did not know where they were sailing." When the skies cleared, he and his men sighted land, but Bjarni had heard enough about Greenland to know what it looked like, and this was not it. After visiting two other places, they changed course and returned safely to Greenland. Bjarni and his men never set foot on land, but their report inspired Leif Erikson, the first Viking credited with arriving in the Americas, to retrace their steps in 1000. That's when he touched down in northeastern Canada.

When they voyaged back to Scandinavia, the Vikings could catch the Gulf Stream, which is part of the North Atlantic Gyre. Sailing on the Gulf Stream is like taking a fast-moving river through a sluggish ocean. It travels north along the east coast of the Americas and then veers out into the Atlantic around Newfoundland. Reaching the British Isles, it continues north into Europe. It moves at more than 100 miles (160 km) in a day, and its width—visible because it is a different color from the surrounding water—is some 40 miles (70 km) across.

The distances across the Pacific were much greater than those across the Atlantic: at its widest point, between Indonesia and Colombia, the Pacific Ocean stretches 12,000 miles (20,000 km), versus 4,000 miles (6,400 km) for the Atlantic. Even Japan and California are 5,500 miles (8,800 km) apart. Early sailors took advantage of the North Pacific Gyre to continue their expansion across the Pacific in double canoes bearing sails; like the Vikings, they did not use any navigational instruments. Departing from Samoa, they reached the Society Islands in around 1025, and it took them two and a half centuries longer to reach Hawaii, Easter Island, and New Zealand.

In fact, if the conditions are right, one can cross the Pacific drifting on ocean currents with no sail at all, as fourteen unfortunate Japanese sailors discovered. On December 2, 1832, their wooden fishing vessel, some 50 feet (15 m) long, set off from Nagoya on the east coast of Japan and headed for Tokyo. A powerful storm blew them off course, and the mastless ship was carried along first by the Kuroshio Current and then the North Pacific Current, both part of the North Pacific Gyre.

The ship came ashore some fourteen months later, in January 1834, in the town of Ozette, Washington. Only three sailors survived by collecting rainwater, fishing, and capturing the occasional bird. Because they had no source of vitamin C, the men were vulnerable to scurvy, which killed their eleven companions.

Prevailing winds facilitated some journeys and made others difficult. As any experienced sailor knows, boats can go much faster with the wind pushing from behind. Seasonal weather patterns had considerable impact in certain regions. Best known are the monsoon winds, which are caused by the movement of air flowing toward the ocean when the Eurasian landmass heats up as spring approaches and then flowing back in the opposite direction six months later. By the year 1000, navigators knew precisely the feel and the timing of the winds that could take them between the Indian and Pacific Oceans.

As the great historian of Arab seafaring George F. Hourani (1913–1984) has noted, "This sea route, from the Persian Gulf to Canton [Guangzhou], was the longest in regular use by mankind before the European expansion in the sixteenth century, and it merits attention as a remarkable achievement." Ships going on the Persian Gulf–China route traveled almost twice as far as Columbus; if you add the leg from Basra, in Iraq, to Sofala, Mozambique, the route was three times as long as Columbus's.

Around the year 1000 the Indian and Pacific Oceans witnessed an intensification of trade among Arab, Indian, Southeast Asian, East African, and Chinese ports. No mariner went east of the Philippines, because the Chinese believed all the ocean's waters converged into a dangerous whirlpool there from which no ship could return.

There was an element of truth to this belief. The Indonesian Throughflow carries warm water from the Pacific Ocean to the Indian Ocean; the direction of flow is predominantly southward through the Indonesian archipelago and then westward into the Indian Ocean. These currents collide and move in all directions around the islands of Southeast Asia, causing the level of the oceans to rise one and one half feet (46 centimeters) higher than anywhere else on the planet. The currents are so swift and vast that scientists had to create a new unit, the sverdrup, which has a value of one million cubic meters per second, to measure the flow. The direction of the current makes it easy for boats and other objects floating in the ocean to go south and west into the Indian Ocean, but much more difficult for anything to move northward.

Because it was easier to go south, humans traveled to Australia by boat early on, some 50,000 years ago, but almost no one went north. Accordingly, there was very little subsequent contact between Australia and Indonesia or the landmass of Southeast Asia until at least 1300 or 1400. In fact, the Chinese first went to Australia in search of sea slugs, which are also known as trepang, sea cucumbers, or bêche-de-mer. Chinese consumers loved sea slugs so much that their fishermen first overfished the waters around Guangzhou and then moved south along the Southeast Asian coast to Vietnam and from there to Indonesia and finally to the north coast of Australia around 1400.

In the year 1000, most sailors navigated by dead reckoning, meaning that they depended on the naked eye and their knowledge of the movements of the sun, moon, and stars to choose their course. The important exceptions were Muslim navigators who used sextants, and the Chinese, who were making magnetic shipboard compasses just around the year 1000.

Skilled Polynesian and Viking mariners were able to set their course by careful observation of waves, seaweed, birds' flying patterns, and the contours of land. Mau Piailug, a Micronesian who studied the traditional Polynesian system of navigation, taught it in the 1980s to Steve Thomas, then an avid navigator, and later the host of the television show *This Old House*. When the weather was clear, he used the stars to navigate, Mau explained, and when the sky was cloudy, he used the shapes of the waves to determine his course.

Like the Polynesian explorers, the Vikings used no instruments. Why did they travel to new places in the year 1000? Social structure, specifically the dynamics of warbands, played a key role because ambitious chieftains sought out new territory. The famous epic *Beowulf*, written in Old English, explains how such groups functioned. (The sole surviving manuscript dates to 1000, and the story is set a few centuries earlier.) The young Swedish prince Beowulf goes to Denmark to help a neighboring king, whose realm is threatened by a monster named Grendel. Accompanying him are some twenty young male companions who fight at his side and voyage with him to distant lands in search of rare treasures. In turn, he rewards his followers with gifts, often silver armbands, plundered from their enemies. The men in Beowulf's warband don't war all the time; sometimes they hang out and enjoy the pleasure of each other's company.

Warband members weren't all male; such groups sometimes included a few women, and often the leader's wife. Women could

lead warbands, too; the breast-baring Freydis eventually commanded her own ship to go to the Americas, as the saga passed
down by her descendants relates. Nor were warbands made up of
people from the same place; people from different countries or
who spoke various languages often joined together. Small warbands might have twenty or so members, but they could grow
to 100–200 people. Warband leaders who succeeded in attracting
even larger followings could end up as princes or kings.

The real-life experience of the Viking Erik the Red illustrates
how warband leaders led their men outside of their home regions
to new territories. In 980, after being found guilty of murder in
Iceland, Erik was exiled for three years. Already banished from
Norway, he set off for new territory, in his case Greenland, which
had been sighted sometime around 900. When the three years
ended, he returned to Iceland to recruit followers who set sail
in twenty-five ships for Greenland. Eleven ships were blown off
course and never seen again. Fourteen vessels arrived, and their
occupants established the Eastern Settlement. Erik's son Leif, and
the other Vikings who traveled across the North Atlantic to Canada, also headed their own warbands.

Let us begin our global journey with the one certain moment
of contact between Europe and the Americas before 1492: when
the Vikings landed on Newfoundland in 1000. From there we'll
travel around the world, following the routes described by written sources and reconstructing others on the basis of archeological
finds.

In 1000, Viking explorers closed the global loop. For the first
time an object or a message could have traveled across the entire
world. True, we do not know—yet!—of any item that did so. But
because the Viking voyages to Canada in the year 1000 opened up
a route from Europe to the Americas, it is fact—not supposition—
that a network of global pathways took shape in that year. And so
we begin our history of globalization then.

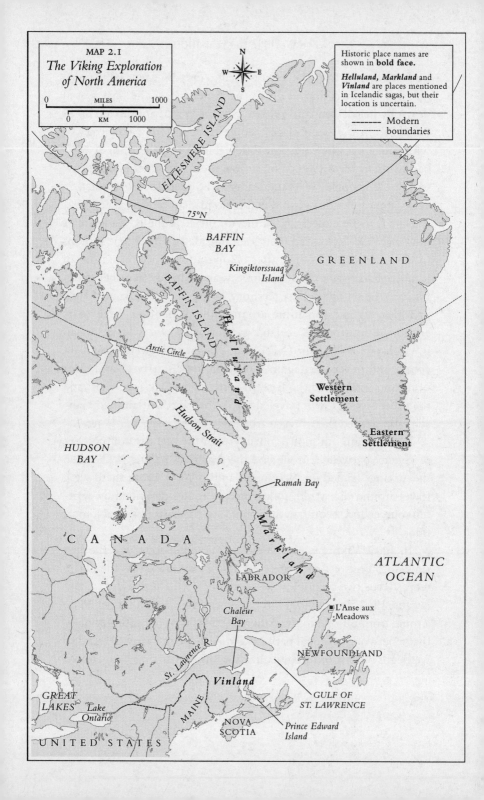

MAP 2.1
The Viking Exploration of North America

MILES
0   1000

KM
0   1000

Historic place names are shown in **bold face.**

Helluland, Markland and *Vinland* are places mentioned in Icelandic sagas, but their location is uncertain.

—————— Modern
- - - - - - - boundaries

ELLESMERE ISLAND

N
W   E
S

75°N

BAFFIN BAY

Kingiktorssuaq Island

GREENLAND

BAFFIN ISLAND

Helluland

Arctic Circle

Western Settlement

Hudson Strait

Eastern Settlement

HUDSON BAY

Ramah Bay

C A N A D A

Markland

ATLANTIC OCEAN

LABRADOR

■ L'Anse aux Meadows

Chaleur Bay

St. Lawrence R.

NEWFOUNDLAND

Vinland

GULF OF ST. LAWRENCE

GREAT LAKES

Lake Ontario

MAINE

NOVA SCOTIA

Prince Edward Island

U N I T E D   S T A T E S

CHAPTER TWO

Go West, Young Viking

The Vikings made three separate voyages to the Americas, the sagas tell us. The first occurred in the year 1000, when Leif Erikson led the men in his warband to the lands that Bjarni Herjolfsson had sighted earlier. Blown off course, Bjarni described three different places—he never set foot on any of them—before reaching the Greenland settlement founded by Leif's father, Erik the Red. Purchasing Bjarni's ship some fifteen years later, Leif set off from Greenland with his warband to find a place that he could rule on his own.

Leif and his followers first landed on a place "like a single flat slab of rock from the glaciers to the sea," which they called Helluland, meaning "Stone-slab land." This was probably Baffin Island, between northeastern Canada and Greenland. They then proceeded to a "flat and forested" land, "sloping gently seaward," with "many beaches of white sand." This Leif called Markland, or "Forest land"—most likely the Labrador coast of northeastern Canada, still known for its dazzling white beaches. Both places were too cold and too barren for human habitation.

Their third destination was much more inviting. At low tide, the ship carrying Leif and his men ran aground, and "their curiosity to see the land was so great that they could not be bothered to wait for the tide to come in," so they jumped off the ship to explore the region. They found a fertile land with plentiful grass and fish. Building booths, or short wooden structures covered with cloth at night for sleeping, they named their first settlement Leifsbudir, "Leif's booths," and the island Vinland, or "Vineland."

Scholars still debate where they landed. After spending the winter in Vinland, Leif and his men returned to Greenland without encountering any indigenous peoples.

A few years later, Leif's brother Thorvald decided to go to Vinland on a second expedition. Choosing not to accompany him, Leif offered Thorvald the use of his ship and of the buildings he and his men had built at Leifsbudir. Unlike Leif, Thorvald did meet inhabitants of the new continent, and for him the encounter turned out to be fatal. He and his men caught sight of three "hide-covered boats" with nine men hiding below them.

Whenever the indigenous peoples appear in the sagas, they are always paddling "hide-covered boats," or canoes. Although birchbark canoes were common throughout the northeast regions of present-day Canada and the United States, the peoples living in Maine and Nova Scotia covered their canoe frames with moose hides.

Unprovoked, Thorvald's men killed eight of the men under the boats, perhaps to test if they were spirits or live human beings. Humans could be killed with iron weapons, but spirits couldn't. The ninth man escaped and returned with reinforcements who shot at the Vikings with bows and arrows. An arrow pierced Thorvald's chest and killed him. One saga identifies the killer as a one-footed being, or a uniped, a creature believed to inhabit distant lands. And so Thorvald's men returned to Greenland without him.

The third Viking expedition to Vinland was led by an Icelander named Thorfinn Karlsefni, a man related by marriage to Leif. Because of Thorvald's killing, Karlsefni and his men had every reason to be fearful when they looked out and saw, paddling toward them, strange men in "nine hide-covered boats" waving wooden poles, "that made a swishing sound as they turned them around sunwise," or clockwise.

Wondering if the poles might indicate their peaceful intentions, Karlsefni ordered his men to lift up a white shield to welcome the strangers, who then came closer. "They were short in height with threatening features and tangled hair on their heads.

Their eyes were large and their cheeks broad." This encounter was brief. The two sides simply observed each other and then parted.

When the indigenous people returned in the spring, they came in a larger group. "It looked as if bits of coal had been tossed over the water, and there was a pole waving from each boat." This time, the two groups exchanged goods: for the "dark pelts" of the locals, the Norse offered lengths of cloth woven from sheep's wool and dyed red. The local peoples wanted swords and spears, but Karlsefni and his second-in-command, Snorri, forbade the trade of any weapons.

As they exchanged furs for cloth, the locals bound the lengths of red wool around their heads, and when supplies began to run out, the Norse started to cut shorter and shorter pieces, some no "wider than a finger's width," but still the locals offered full pelts for the scraps. Then a noise interrupted the trading. "A bull, owned by Karlsefni and his companions, ran out of the forest and bellowed loudly." The sound frightened the inhabitants, who jumped into their boats and went south.

The description of the trade of red cloth for fur pelts comes from *Erik the Red's Saga*, an oral epic composed in Old Icelandic named for Erik, a glorious ancestor of the family whose history the saga recounts. Orally transmitted, the saga had multiple, unknown authors. It puts the number of Norse present in the new land at 140; in the summer a group of 100 or so remained at Leif's original base camp Leifsbudir, it claims, while Karlsefni and Snorri were out exploring with 40 men.

A second saga, the *Greenlanders' Saga*, also has no known author, and it provides an account in which similar events occur in a different order. The bull bellows before the two groups trade, and the Norse present fresh milk and dairy products in place of red cloth. The second saga reports that Thorfinn Karlsefni led a group of sixty men and five women, less than half the figure given in *Erik the Red's Saga*. It also informs us that the warbands included not just Scandinavians but also captured prisoners of war or purchased slaves, typically from Germany or France.

Not composed merely for entertainment, the sagas glorified

the accomplishments of ancestors, whose descendants listened to these tales about their family's past. *Erik the Red's Saga* recounts the deeds of Erik and his sons Leif, Thorvald, and Thorstein, as well as his daughter Freydis. The men are heroes, but Freydis is aggressive and frequently bad-tempered. Named for the Norse goddess Freya, she is a force unto herself. The modern audience can't help liking her; even though she lies and occasionally murders, she displays an unusual spunkiness, as when she slaps her breast with a sword in defiance of the indigenous attackers.

The *Greenlanders' Saga* switches the focus to Thorfinn Karlsefni and his wife, Gudrid, since they were the ancestors of the bishop Björn Gilsson (d. 1162) in whose honor the saga was composed. Karlsefni's wife, Gudrid (her name has the same root as "God"), is as virtuous as Freydis is wayward.

The two sagas, which are known as the Vinland sagas, describe events occurring before the population of Scandinavia was Christianized, a centuries-long process that began in the 900s as the rulers of Denmark, then Norway and Iceland, officially converted to Christianity. Before the coming of Christianity, the Norse had worshipped a pantheon of gods, headed by Thor, the powerful deity who ruled the sky and controlled thunder, wind, rain, and the harvest. Other important deities were Freya, the powerful goddess of fertility, and Odin, the god of war.

At the time they were worshipping these deities, the Norse had already begun to expand outside the Scandinavian heartland of modern Norway, Sweden, and Denmark. In those lands, people spoke either Latin or Old Icelandic (a language that developed into modern Icelandic, Norwegian, Swedish, and Danish). Since Roman times, the Scandinavians used an alphabet of angular letters called runes. In the 1100s some shifted to using the Roman alphabet with a few additional letters, while others continued to use runes, particularly on tombstones because they were easier to carve onto stone.

Some Scandinavians ventured to new places because farmland was largely limited to southern Denmark and Sweden, where residents cultivated such grains as barley, rye, and oats, and such vegetables as peas and cabbage. Because arable land was in short supply, most Scandinavians also tended herds of cows, oxen, pigs, sheep, and goats. Those living closer to the Arctic Circle (including the ancestors of today's Sami peoples in Lapland) fished, herded reindeer, and hunted walrus.

The Norse lived on small farms. Most people married late, only after they'd accumulated sufficient wealth to buy their own land, and, before that, worked for more established landowners. The persistent shortage of land, coupled with limited opportunities to improve one's social position, prompted some of the Norse to turn to plundering. Some Scandinavians didn't go on a single raid while others went on just one—gaining enough loot to buy a farm. And still others looted and plundered their entire lives.

This is the original meaning of the word "viking": to raid or to engage in piracy, with the noun form meaning "raider" or "pirate." In fact, few sources from 1000 refer to the Norse as Vikings. For this reason, this book will refer to those from modern Denmark, Norway, and Sweden as Scandinavians or Norse and reserve the word "Viking" only for active raiders.

In most books, the Viking Age begins with the 793 attacks on the Northumberland monastery of Lindisfarne on the east coast of the United Kingdom. But recent excavations of a Viking burial in Salme, Estonia, demonstrate that the Vikings raided Salme even earlier, between 700 and 750.

The first Viking boats had no sails. The builders used axes and wedges to hew planks, or strakes, from oak and pine tree trunks, overlapped them slightly, and nailed them onto a curved frame with small iron nails called clinkers. The resulting straked hulls could give a little when dashed onto rocks. These vessels could both be rowed long distances and go ashore in shallow waters, so they were well suited to travel within Scandinavia, and the introduction of the square sail around 750 allowed Viking ships to go longer distances. (Mediterranean sailors had known about the sail for thousands of years; the technology came late to Scandinavia.)

The Vikings wove square sails from wool or linen, which they could rotate, but they couldn't angle the square sails as close to the wind as today's triangular sails. Still, modern replicas of Viking ships sail into the wind more directly than previously thought possible.

Buried hoards show how far the Vikings ventured. One group of objects, from the Swedish island of Helgö about 20 miles (32 km) west of Stockholm, contains the head of an Irish bishop's staff, an Egyptian ladle, a Carolingian sword pommel, a Mediterranean silver dish, and most surprising of all, a small bronze statue of the Buddha, 4 inches (10 cm) high, which was made in northern Pakistan around the year 500. These goods arrived in Sweden several centuries after the introduction of the sail.

In the centuries before the coming of Christianity, the Norse repurposed ships to make graves for the dead, whom they buried with lavish goods. Such burials reveal much about the construction of Viking ships. Two intact boats found near Oslo with nearly all their grave goods (but not any precious metals because they were stolen) are particularly informative about construction techniques. Wood usually, but not always, disintegrates when buried in the ground. If, however, no oxygen comes into contact with the wood, as can happen in deep mud, then wood can survive for centuries with little damage.

The two vessels are housed today in the Viking Ship Hall at Bygdøy, a lovely suburb a short ferry ride away from the Oslo harbor. Hewn from oak planks and buried in 834, the intricately carved Oseburg ship held rare textiles, including imported silks, and was buried with a wooden cart. A high-ranking chieftain probably used the boat as a pleasure craft on inland waters before burying it.

The Gokstad ship, dating to 890, contained the skeletons of two peacocks and two goshawks—long-tailed hawks used for hunting. The bodies of twelve horses and six dogs were also buried near the ship, evidence of the importance of these animals to the deceased. With a keel hewn from an oak tree more than 80 feet long running along its bottom, the Gokstad ship (76 feet, or 23.24 m) measures slightly longer than the Oseburg ship (71 feet, or 21.58 m) and was suitable for ocean journeys. The Gokstad ship was the more typical vessel—with only one decorative carving on the rudder. Sixteen overlapping strakes are visible on the boat's exterior.

The Vikings built different types of ships depending on their purpose. Warships had to be long and narrow, while boats that carried cargo were shorter and broader. When traveling inland on rivers, the Norse switched to their lightest vessels, allowing them to portage their ship from one river to the next.

Around 1000, the Norse vessels grew even larger, with the longest measuring over 100 feet (30 m). These ships made it possible for the Norse to go to more distant waters. Piles of refuse in Scandinavian towns from this time contain increasingly large quantities of cod bones, a fish imported from Iceland, showing how common long-distance ocean voyages were.

The Norse sailed to Iceland in such boats in the 870s and to Greenland around 900. The first permanent settlement on Greenland came in the 980s when Erik the Red led his followers there after his period of exile ended. The Norse established two settlements on Greenland: the Eastern Settlement was larger than the Western. Everyone who went on to North America departed from one of these two settlements.

The two sagas describe these voyages of 1000, but they were recorded after the Christianization of the region. Living in Christian times, the authors believed that their ancestors were Christian, but the stories they inherited describe pre-Christian behavior. The storytellers retroactively put a Christian spin on what were clearly pagan acts. Even Karlsefni's virtuous wife, Gudrid, is involved; at one point she refuses to sing a pre-Christian warlock song but agrees when a "wise woman," who has special powers, specifically asks her to do so. The Christian rewrite requires her to protest before she can engage in this type of singing, which, though not Christian, was certainly quite common in pre-Christian times.

Much to the frustration of historians, the material in the sagas cannot be firmly dated. A bard reciting a saga or a later copyist could always have inserted new material.

The contents of the *Greenlanders' Saga* and *Erik's Saga* sometimes overlap and sometimes conflict. Barring the discovery of new evidence, we'll never know for sure which is earlier. We *are* certain of the dates of the earliest surviving manuscripts. *Erik the Red's Saga* was recorded shortly after 1264, and the *Greenlanders' Saga* was copied into a larger compendium in 1387. It's likely that they were first composed in 1200, some 200 years after the events they describe.

Because a source close in date to the actual events is more likely to be accurate, some historians dismiss all the information from the sagas as too late to be reliable. These scholars view the sagas as more reflective of Icelandic society in 1200 and 1300 than what came before. They think it unlikely, for example, that Freydis actually slapped her breast with a sword. They suggest that the bard or scribe who included the incident must have had a reason linked to the time of writing: perhaps the goal was to emphasize Freydis's courage in contrast to the cowardice of her male companions. Or perhaps Freydis's descendants wanted to emphasize her accomplishments.

Some scholars of Icelandic literature deny that any of the events in the sagas ever occurred because they believe that any work describing real-world events has less literary merit. They want to stress the creativity of those who composed the sagas so that they can make the case for them as genuine works of world literature.

Yet another group of scholars is even more extreme in their denial that the Vinland sagas can teach us anything about North America. They assert that the sagas have no historic value at all because they simply repeat recurring literary phrases about unfamiliar peoples. These deniers are convinced that the saga authors had no idea where Vinland was located; they maintain that Vinland was most likely to have been in Africa, because that is where unipeds lived according to other Norse sources.

But if you accept the anecdote soup theory, these objections don't matter. This theory holds that the bards composed the sagas by selecting different items from a preexisting set, or soup, of orally transmitted anecdotes and presented them in the order that made for the most gripping narrative. This explains why the two sagas agree about the main events of the encounter between Karlsefni's band and the indigenous peoples but present them in a slightly different order.

The naysayers who challenge the Vinland sagas forget two crucial points: the sagas contained sufficiently accurate information to serve as a guide to the only verified Viking site in all of North America, at L'Anse aux Meadows. And, as we'll see below, the sagas' description of the indigenous peoples and how they indicated their desire to trade matches up nearly perfectly with what Jacques Cartier experienced on his first trip to the region in the 1530s. If we approach the sagas carefully, they have a great deal to teach us about North America in 1000.

The sagas used the word "Skraeling," a derogatory term meaning "wretches," for the peoples they encountered. Today, scholars prefer Amerindian as a broad term referring to all the indigenous peoples living in the Americas; Americans call these peoples Native Americans, and Canadians refer to them as the First Nations.

Three different peoples resided in the northeastern corner of North America in 1000 at the time of the Norse voyages. The Dorset peoples had been living in northern Greenland and the eastern Canadian Arctic since about 2000 BC. One Dorset object was found at L'Anse aux Meadows: a round soapstone object with a slight depression in the top. In the 1960s the first excavators thought the object was an Icelandic stone pivot for a door, but more recent researchers identify it as characteristically Dorset. It may point to contact or trickle-trade with the Dorset, meaning that one group traded it with their neighbors, who traded it with theirs, and so on until it reached l'Anse aux Meadows. Or it may have been an item that the Norse picked up from an abandoned Dorset site.

Sometime around AD 1000, a new group of people, called the Thule, displaced the Dorset because they were better adapted to Arctic conditions. The Thule migrated from Alaska, all the way across northern Canada, and their descendents, today's indigenous Greenlanders, refer to themselves as the Inuit ("the people") and reject the label Eskimo ("eaters of raw flesh") as pejorative.

Before and after the Norse occupation, different indigenous groups occupied the area around the site of L'Anse aux Meadows, but no archeological evidence of Amerindian occupation in the year AD 1000 has yet surfaced. This is why archeologists don't know precisely which group the Norse might have met. It is most likely that the Norse encountered a third group of indigenous peoples, called the Ancestral Beothuk or the Ancestral Innu. The Beothuk lived on Newfoundland but died out in the early 1800s; the Innu still live on the Labrador coast today. These groups deposited some artifacts at L'Anse aux Meadows in the twelfth and thirteenth centuries.

After 1500, the peoples of the region formed the Wabanaki Alliance, which included the Mi'kmaq, the Penobscot, the Maliseet, and the Passamaquoddy. Wabanaki is an Eastern Algonquian word for "Peoples of the Dawnland," meaning the easternmost regions, where the sun comes up. The Wabanaki spoke different Algonquian languages, and in the 1500s their trading networks extended all the way from northern Labrador south through Maine and west to the Great Lakes. They lived by hunting sea animals, particularly seals who migrated each year from the Canadian mainland to Newfoundland. The Wabanaki traded certain commodities, such as objects made from the distinctive translucent silicate chert that came from Ramah Bay in northern Labrador.

Much of what we know about the Wabanaki comes from later descriptions, particularly those by the French explorer Jacques Cartier (1491–1557), who arrived in Quebec in July 1534. Hugging the coast, Cartier learned, it was possible to travel by boat from the St. Lawrence River to Chaleur Bay, and to carry canoes overland anywhere the rivers were too shallow. The fertility of the region struck Cartier: "The land along the south side of it [Chaleur Bay] is as fine and as good land, as arable and as full of beautiful fields and meadows, as any we have ever seen; and it is as level as the surface of a pond."

On his first voyage to Chaleur Bay, Cartier met two groups of Mi'kmaq Amerindians in "some forty or fifty canoes." We can be confident that they were Mi'kmaq because Cartier recorded some phrases they uttered, which have since been identified as the Mi'kmaq language. When the first group of Mi'kmaq arrived, "there sprang out and landed a large number of people, who set up a great clamor and made frequent sign to us to come ashore, holding up to us some skins on sticks." Even though Cartier and his men had the impression that they were friendly, the French refused to get out of their boats and come on land. When the Mi'kmaq pursued them, the French shot off two cannon. The Mi'kmaq still shadowed them, prompting the French to fire two muskets. Only then did the Mi'kmaq disperse.

The Mi'kmaq returned the next day, "making signs to us that they had come to barter with us; and held up some skins of small value, with which they clothe themselves. We likewise made signs to them that we wished them no harm, and sent two men on shore, to give them some knives and other iron goods, and a red cap to give to their chief." Just like the Skraelings who met the Norse some 500 years earlier, the Mi'kmaq desired red textiles. Unlike the Norse, the French were willing to trade metal knives because they possessed other more powerful weapons.

After the French gave their gifts, Cartier records that the Mi'kmaq "sent on shore part of their people with some of their skins; and the two parties traded together. They showed a marvelously great pleasure in possessing and obtaining these iron wares and other commodities, dancing and going through many ceremonies, and throwing salt water over their heads with their hands. They bartered all they had to such an extent that all went back naked without anything on them; and they made signs to us that they would return on the morrow with more skins." The overlap with the account in Erik's Saga—the noise, the sticks, the skins, the promise to return the next day—provide unusual confirmation of the Vinland sagas' reliability. It also reveals strong continuities between the Skraelings of 1000 and the Mi'kmaq of 1534.

When Annette Kolodny, a professor of American literature and culture at the University of Arizona, investigated whether modern Amerindians living in northeastern Canada remember the Norse, she found that they didn't. One of her interview subjects,

Wayne Newell, a Passamaquoddy elder living in Indian Township, Maine, did tell Kolodny that "red was a spiritual color" for his people and that the tale of the Skraelings' noisemakers "reminded him of homemade flutes or whistles whirled on the end of a string, a noisemaker he too had made as a child."

Although in the sagas the fur-trading encounter was peaceful, Karlsefni senses that the Skraelings pose a threat and builds a wooden palisade around his dwelling to protect his wife, Gudrid, and their infant son, Snorri, the first baby born to Europeans in the Americas and named for Karlsefni's co-leader. At the start of the second winter, the Skraelings return to trade. As Gudrid sits inside with her son, "a shadow fell across the doorway and a woman entered, rather short in stature. . . . She was pale and had eyes so large that eyes of such size had never been seen in a human head."

She asks Gudrid, "What is your name?"

Gudrid replies, "My name is Gudrid and what is yours?"

The woman replies, "My name is Gudrid."

This conversation makes sense when we remember that people who didn't share a common tongue often repeated each other's sentences back to one another. The visitor mysteriously disappears.

Then a Norsemen kills some Skraelings who were stealing weapons, and they run away. Karlsefni urges his men to prepare for the next attack because he is wonderfully prescient (remember: he's the ancestor in whose honor the saga was composed).

Sure enough, three weeks later the Skraeling return and attack in large numbers, "as thick as a steady stream." This time they're yelling, waving their poles counterclockwise, and hurling objects. The two leaders, Karlsefni and Snorri, "saw the natives lift up on poles a large round object, about the size of a sheep's gut and black in color, which came flying up on the land and made a threatening noise when it landed." This was a ballista, a skin filled with rocks, which was launched from a wooden structure. A nineteenth-century description reports that a ballista used by the Algonquians could sink a boat or a canoe: "brought down among a group of men on a sudden, it produced consternation and death."

And, indeed, after the ballista lands, Karlsefni and his men decide to abandon camp and go upriver. Always quick to speak her mind, Leif's spunky sister Freydis berates them: "Why do you flee such miserable opponents, men like you who look to me to be capable of killing them off like sheep? Had I a weapon I'm sure I would fight better than any of you." Pregnant and moving slowly, she reluctantly follows Karlsefni out of the settlement until she retrieves a sword from a Norse corpse and turns back to fight the Skraelings.

This is when she smacks her breast with the sword. Do we accept this as an actual event? Or the invention of a gifted bard to glorify his ancestors? To me, the display is so unusual that it seems plausible, but there is no way to be certain that it actually happened.

In the confusion one of the locals picks up an axe from the corpse of a Norseman. He tries chopping a tree, as do each of his companions. They consider the axe "a real treasure," the saga reports, but when one of his companions tries to cut a stone with it, demonstrating his unfamiliarity with metal tools, the axe snaps in two. Disappointed, the man throws it away.

In hand-to-hand combat, the iron and steel weapons of the Norse gave them a slight advantage but certainly didn't guarantee victory, especially when they were outnumbered. After all, two Norsemen had died in the battle, fewer than the "many" casualties among the locals, but enough to give Karlsefni pause. *Erik's Saga* is succinct: Karlsefni's "party then realized that, despite everything the land had to offer there, they would be under constant threat of attack from its prior inhabitants. They made ready to depart for their own country."

The sagas, as we know, date to the thirteenth and fourteenth centuries, but some sources mentioning the existence of Vinland date to before then. The most detailed early account of the Norse voyages is in Latin and dates to 1076, when a German historian of Christianity named Adam of Bremen completed his *History of the Archbishopric of Hamburg*. This book, a history of a North German region administered by one bishop, describes the ongoing Christianization of Scandinavia, Iceland, and Greenland. Adam's straightforward account includes some dubious nuggets like this about Greenland: "the people there are greenish from the salt water, whence, too, that region gets its name." Adam's statement illustrates the kinds of misinformation circulating at the time, much like the claim by Erik the Red, in the hope of attracting settlers, that Greenland was actually green.

Adam also records his conversation with the king of the Danes, Svein Estrithson (ruled 1046–1074), who "spoke also of yet another island of the many found in that ocean. It is called Vinland because vines producing excellent wine grow wild there." Here is yet more proof, from a source recorded less than a century after Leif's first voyage, that the Viking voyages actually occurred. Adam of Bremen continues, "Beyond that island," the king explained, "no habitable land is found in that ocean, but every place beyond it is full of impenetrable ice and intense darkness." So Vinland marked the end of the world known to the Danes.

But where precisely was Vinland?

For centuries readers of Adam of Bremen and the Vinland sagas wondered if the Norse voyages were real, and if they were, where Leif and Karlsefni had actually gone. Analysts scrutinized the descriptions in the *Greenlanders' Saga* of Leif's landings at Helluland, Markland, and Vinland.

A significant clue to Vinland's location: the hours of daylight in this mysterious land were noticeably longer than in Greenland: "In the depth of winter," the *Greenlanders' Saga* explains, "the sun was aloft by mid-morning and still visible at mid-afternoon," information that places Vinland anywhere between New Jersey and the Gulf of St. Lawrence.

In 1960, the Norwegian diplomat Helge Ingstad and his wife, the archeologist Anne Stine Ingstad, decided to explore the Canadian coast to see if they could locate where Leif Erikson had journeyed. Sailing down the east coast of Canada, they found a close match between the beaches of Labrador and the description of Markland in the *Greenlanders' Saga*: "The land was flat and forested, sloping gently seaward, and they [Leif and his men] came across many beaches of white sand."

The Ingstads reasoned that anyone sailing south of Markland/

Labrador, as the Vikings had, would reach the island of New-foundland. When they landed at the village of L'Anse aux Mead-ows, on the northern tip of the island, they asked the locals about possible Viking sites. A villager led them to some grassy mounds on a beach, which turned out to be the collapsed remains of sod buildings with wooden frames. The villagers believed them to be the abandoned dwellings of Amerindian peoples.

There was only one way to find out who had lived in the sod dwellings: by digging. Although the Ingstads justifiably receive credit for the discovery, some earlier readers of the sagas had pro-posed L'Anse aux Meadows as a likely Viking site. But they never put their theories to the test by excavating. Over the course of eight summers, between 1961 and 1968, the Ingstads excavated eight structures. Initially the Ingstads weren't certain if the struc-tures were European or Amerindian.

The most telling evidence of the Norse presence at L'Anse aux Meadows wasn't a single item—any given object could have been trickle-traded across long distances by the indigenous peoples—but a workshed attached to a larger building that contained slag, an anvil, a large stone, and iron fragments, all signs of an active smithy. The shed also had a large fireplace, which shipwrights used to heat water so that they could steam planks into the correct shape before nailing them onto their boats. In another room, which was a lean-to, archeologists found many fragments of iron nails.

Some metalworking took place in North America in the year 1000, but no one anywhere else on the continent was working iron. So when archeologists found iron being worked at L'Anse aux Meadows, they knew that outsiders were doing the smelting.

Archeologists also uncovered traces of a wooden structure. Not connected to the walls, this was most likely a boatbuilding frame like those in use in western Norway even today. The vessel under construction measured no more than 25 feet (8 m) long, a typical length for Norse boats used on inland waterways. On the tip of Newfoundland, L'Anse aux Meadows was the ideal location for a repair center for ships setting sail across the North Atlantic to return to Greenland.

One find was distinctively Scandinavian, confirming that the residents of the eight structures were definitely Norse: a straight bronze pin with a ring at the end of it. As happens so often, the archeologists uncovered the pin on the final day of their last season in 1968. In her memoirs, Anne Stine Ingstad described the discovery: "We let out a holler because we immediately knew that here was evidence that nobody could deny—a bronze ring-headed pin indisputably like those from the Norse Viking period." Used to fasten a cloak at the neck, it matched those from Norse sites in Ireland and Scotland dating to between 920 and 1050. Other objects also pointed to the Scandinavian presence: a quartzite tool for sharpening needles and a weight used to twist raw wool fibers (called a spindle whorl), but these weren't as convincing to non-experts as the bronze cloak pin.

The needle sharpener and spindle whorl indicated that women were present at the site, but in lower numbers than men. The main building had a small bedroom for the warband leader and his spouse, who probably needed a few women to help her with domestic chores. There was a much larger adjacent room for the men in his retinue, who weren't entitled to bring their wives. This is why the gender balance was so uneven.

The Ingstads were sure that L'Anse aux Meadows was the location of Leifsbudir, the settlement where Leif's men had landed and originally built houses. There was, however, a major problem with their identification: the absence of wild grapes on Newfoundland.

The sagas leave no doubt why Leif chose the name Vinland. At one point, one of Leif's men, a German named Tyrkir the Southerner, claims to have made an important discovery when exploring on his own. When he tells Leif, he speaks in German, "with his eyes darting in all directions and his face contorted. The others understood nothing of what he was saying." What was going on? Was he drunk? When Tyrkir switches at last to Norse, he reports finding "vines and grapes," which he recognizes from his childhood in Germany. This is why Leif, with his father's instinct for marketing, names the new land Vinland.

Interestingly, the text identifies Tyrkir as an older man, probably a slave who knew Leif as a child. It was common for slaves to raise children, and Tyrkir could have been such a slave brought to Greenland to take care of the offspring of Erik the Red.

Tyrkir's story undermined the Ingstads' claim that the Leifsbudir village was located at L'Anse aux Meadows: wild grapes don't grow as far north as Newfoundland. The northernmost limit for wild grapes is the southern shore of the Gulf of St. Lawrence. Even if the climate had been a degree or two warmer in the year 1000, wild grapes still wouldn't have flourished on Newfoundland. The Ingstads offered an ingenious solution. Proposing that the *vin* in Vinland has a short "i" vowel and meant "wheat," not "grapes" (*vìn*, with a long "i" vowel), they chose to disregard Tyrkir's claim to have found grapes and defined Vinland as "the land of meadows."

The late Professor Erik Wahlgren (1911–1990), who taught Scandinavian literature at UCLA, came down hard and persuasively against their argument; a generic name like "land of meadows" conveys nothing, he reasoned, while "land of grapes" would entice future settlers. Since Vinland had grapes, he concluded, L'Anse aux Meadows could not be Vinland.

A related question: where in North America did the Norse go? *Erik's Saga* refers to Straum Island ("Stream Island," or "Strong Current Island"), where Leifsbudir was located and where Karlsefni spent the first winter, as well as a much more inviting land to the south called Hope or Tidal Lake.

The discovery of three butternuts and one piece of twisted wood from a butternut tree trunk, called a burl, at L'Anse aux Meadows confirms that the Norse voyaged farther south because the northern limit for butternuts then was about what it is today: some 600 miles (1,000 km) south of the northern tip of Newfoundland and to the north of Maine. The archeological discovery of butternuts matches the mention of wild grapes in the sagas; both are crops that don't grow in Newfoundland but flourish farther south. These discoveries showed that the Norse certainly had a settlement at L'Anse aux Meadows, and they went farther south, too.

No one knows why the two sagas refer to so few locations in Vinland. Surely the Norsemen went to many more places along the east coast of Canada and possibly the northeastern United States. Perhaps as the sagas were told and retold, some place names were dropped, a common phenomenon in oral history.

We know that L'Anse aux Meadows was a Norse site because of the cloak pin and other irrefutable archeological evidence, yet the sagas don't mention a boat repair station, which L'Anse aux Meadows most certainly was.

There is good reason to believe that L'Anse aux Meadows wasn't the main Norse camp in the Americas. Unlike typical Norse settlements in Iceland and Greenland, the site had no agricultural fields nearby and couldn't have supplied the residents with food. The site produced evidence of a few pigs, but the highest number of bones came from seals and whales. Worse still, there was no place nearby to graze herds, and the Scandinavians always traveled with large herds. Remember the sagas' account of the settlers' bull whose bellowing so frightened the Skraelings.

The small size of the L'Anse aux Meadows site, combined with the presence of butternuts at the site as well as mentions of wild grapes in the sagas, suggests that the Vikings' main settlement lay somewhere to the south. After careful study of all the evidence and the geography of the coastline, Professor Wahlgren suggested that Leif's original settlement at Leifsbudir was located on Passamaquoddy Bay facing Grand Manan island, just on the U.S. side of the Maine border with New Brunswick. And the lead archeologist for many years at L'Anse aux Meadows, Birgitta Wallace, locates Leifsbudir to the north of Passamaquoddy at Chaleur Bay, partially because of the uncanny similarities between *Erik's Saga* and Cartier's diary. Others who refuse to pinpoint a precise location concur that the evidence places Vinland somewhere in Maine or Nova Scotia.

Why did the Norse abandon Vinland? The sagas blame the fear of attack. They also indirectly suggest that the Norse failed to find any truly valuable trade goods besides lumber.

The Norse departed the site of L'Anse aux Meadows in an

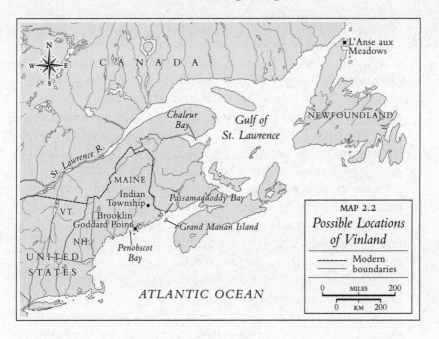

MAP 2.2
*Possible Locations
of Vinland*

------- Modern
----------- boundaries

orderly fashion, removing all items of value and leaving behind only a few items including the one cloak pin, presumably dropped by accident, and the Dorset soapstone object, which was too heavy to carry back.

On their way home, the Norsemen had several hostile encounters with indigenous peoples. At one point, they killed five men who were asleep near the coast, simply because the small size of the group indicated that they must have been "outlaws." At Markland/Labrador the Norse captured two young boys after their adult companions, a man and two women, ran away and escaped.

The line between adoption and slavery was a fine one. Karlsefni may have intended to adopt the two boys; he and his men taught them their language. But nothing prevented Karlsefni from selling the boys on his return to Greenland, in which case they, too, would have become commodities. Because slaves were a major Scandinavian export, we can assume that Karlsefni was aware of the profits to be made from slaving. But, as far as we know, the Norse never sold Amerindian slaves in Europe.

After the Norse dismantled their colony and returned to Greenland, the trade between Scandinavia and the Americas continued on a limited basis. The Scandinavians periodically returned to Labrador to gather lumber because of the persistent shortage of timber on Greenland and Iceland. Iceland originally had trees, but the first settlers cut them down to make houses, and they didn't grow back. Even today hardly any trees grow on Iceland.

After the first winter in Vinland, when Leif sailed home, he spotted some fifteen shipwrecked Norwegians on a reef near Greenland, where they'd been stranded, most likely blown off course in a storm. Leif unloaded the lumber that he was carrying from the Americas to Greenland to make room for them. After he had delivered them to safety, he returned to the reef to pick up the lumber, a sure sign of the wood's value.

With the notable exception of a single Norse penny, no archeological evidence of the later trade survives in the Americas. Found at the Goddard site, a large summer settlement in the town of Brooklin, which faces Penobscot Bay, Maine, the penny was mainly silver with some copper and lead. It was minted between 1065 and 1080, after the Norse had left Canada.

How did the penny travel to Goddard, Maine? Most likely the Norse brought it with them to somewhere on Baffin Island, Labrador, or Newfoundland when they came to cut down trees. It was then trickle-traded from one place to the next by the locals until it arrived in Goddard Point, so far the southernmost location where archeological evidence of the Norse has surfaced. (The famous Kensington "Viking" runestone in Minnesota is definitely a forgery.)

Limited archeological evidence from Greenland points to continuing contact between Greenland and the Americas after 1000. Two arrowheads found on Greenland also came from the Americas: one worked from translucent Ramah chert was found in the Norse cemetery at Sandnes, in the Western Settlement, while the other, made from quartz, surfaced on the estate from which Thorfinn Karlsefni departed for the Americas in the 1000s, Brattahlid in the Eastern Settlement. Furs seldom survive underground, especially after a thousand years, but textiles preserved in ice from the Greenland site of the Farm Beneath the Sand, south of the Western Settlement, contain the fur of brown bear and bison, both animals native to North America. These finds indicate that fur must have been exported to Greenland from the Americas.

The Norse decision to abandon their settlements in North America was due to a modern problem: they suffered a trade imbalance. True, Vinland may have offered the Norse useful commodities such as lumber and rare furs and some curiosities such as arrowheads, but the European mainland offered more valuable trade items: manufactured goods, particularly swords, daggers, and other metal objects, in addition to the always necessary flour and salt. The ongoing need for these items contributed to the decision of the Norse colonists to abandon their settlements in the Americas and move back to Greenland, where they remained for another 400 years.

Whenever the Norse arrived in a new place, they looked around their environment, and Greenland was no exception. The impulse to explore took the Norse far north into Greenland, even though they continued to live in their original two communities on the south coast of the island—the Eastern and Western Settlements.

At least two expeditions probed the northern reaches of Greenland. One group traveled as far as the 75th parallel, above the Arctic Circle, and kept going for three additional days past that point, as we learn from a description of a copied (but now lost) letter written in 1266.

A second group of three men traveling in the 1330s reached Kingiktorssuaq Island in Baffin Bay, off the west coast of Greenland at the 72nd parallel. They carved a text in runes on one stone, which they added to three piles of cairn stones. Danish explorers discovered these in the early 1800s. An ivory figurine of a Norseman with a cross on his chest found on Baffin Island in the Canadian Arctic dates to this time. Crafted from walrus ivory, he stands under 2 inches (5 cm) tall. It, too, suggests that the Norse explored the northern reaches of Greenland.

The Norse began to abandon their settlements in Greenland in the 1300s, partially because the climate was cooling as the Medieval Climate Anomaly came to an end and the Little Ice Age began. More significant, the Thule residents of Greenland adapted to the cold climate better than the Norse. The Thule possessed multiple technologies that the Norse never adopted.

The Thule, for example, wore thick fur clothing and used toggling harpoons for hunting seals and whales. The Inuit also knew how to dig holes in the ice in winter and catch ring seals, a crucial skill that eluded the Norse. Dogs and tools such as a feather or a light bone pin helped the Inuit to detect seals breathing under the ice. Because the ringed seals never migrated, they were a year-round food source. Separate drag-floats, which were made by inflating sewn-up sealskins, allowed the Inuit to hunt large sea mammals such as whales. When the hunters speared a whale with a harpoon, they could track it until the animal died. All these technologies helped the Inuit to move along northern pathways from Alaska across Arctic Canada and to Greenland between AD 900 and 1200.

The Norse population in Greenland peaked at over 2,000 people in 1300 and then began to decline precipitously just as the Thule population moved south from their settlements in northern Greenland. One year-by-year history of Iceland, entitled the *Icelandic Annals*, has the following entry for 1379: "Skraelings

This sketch of a rare wooden figurine, thought to be Inuit handiwork and made around 1300, portrays a European missionary who came to the Americas before Columbus.

Amelia Sargent

attacked the Greenlanders, killing eighteen of them and carrying off two boys into captivity." Here "Skraelings" refers to the seal-hunting Thule, and "Greenlanders," indicates the Norse. A wedding certificate for a Scandinavian couple from the Hvalsey church shows that the Norse were still on Greenland in 1408. Two years later, the *Icelandic Annals* report the return of a lone Icelander from Greenland. After 1410, the historical record contains no further mention of the Norse residents of Greenland.

Even though the Norse left Greenland, the knowledge of Vinland was never lost. Adam of Bremen's conversation with the Danish king circulated in a few Latin manuscripts in the 1200s and 1300s, just as the Vinland sagas were gradually assuming their current form, and his book survives in multiple manuscripts. Adam's testimony offers a glimpse of how information about distant peoples was passed down through the ages: he recorded what the king of Denmark told him about Vinland, but the account of Vinland received little notice in subsequent centuries. It was just another account of a dangerous place on the edge of the world, like so many others in medieval times.

Compared to other encounters around the year 1000, the one between the Norse and the Amerindians had limited long-term impact. A few conversations, occasional exchanges of goods, perhaps some incidents of hand-to-hand combat—this was the extent of contact between the Norse and the Amerindians.

Knowing that the Amerindians died en masse when exposed to European germs after 1492, one can't help wondering whether the Amerindians suffered a similar fate around 1000. Neither saga mentions the indigenous peoples falling ill as a result of meeting the Norse. On one occasion, though, the Norse mysteriously fell sick, possibly after eating tainted whale meat.

In fact, the Amerindians also didn't suffer from disease immediately after 1492. It took several decades, until the 1520s, before they began to perish in large numbers. The brief period of contact—just the ten years that the Norse lived in L'Anse aux Meadows—was probably too short for the Norse to introduce any diseases to the indigenous peoples of North America.

By 1492, European knowledge of Greenland and Vinland was already fading. In that year, a papal letter describes Greenland as "an island near the edge of the world. . . . Because of the ice that surrounds the island, sailings there are rare, for land can only be made there in August when the ice has receded. For that reason, it is thought that no ship has sailed there for the last eighty years, and no bishop nor priest has been there."

Still, Adam of Bremen's account circulated within a small circle of scholars who could read Latin. In 1590, almost a century after Columbus's first voyage, an Icelandic schoolteacher named Sigurdur Stefansson drew a map to support Iceland's claim to have discovered the Americas before Columbus.

Norway, Britain, and Ireland stand as separate pieces of land on the eastern edge of his map. A single landmass along the northern and western edges of his map contains Greenland, Helleland (an error for Helluland), Markland, and Skralinge Land (a new place name that Stefansson coined), which is connected by a long narrow inlet to the Vinland Promontory. This depiction of the Vinland Promontory as a sharp point provided a crucial clue to the Ingstads to look for a Norse settlement near the northern tip of Newfoundland.

Stefansson's map revived the memory of the Norse voyages to the Americas in 1000, which raise many of the same challenges posed by globalization today. What happens if weapons technology is unequal and hostilities break out? What are the consequences of trade imbalances? If one side has more people, what can the other side do to compensate? And, finally, why is it so difficult to learn from the other side, even if it has mastered a demonstrably useful skill?

When the Norse encountered the Amerindians in the Americas, they had the advantage of metal tools. But the Norse decided to withdraw, perhaps because of the ferocity of the Amerindians, perhaps because the Norse could not easily obtain the supplies they needed to survive. Similarly, the Norse gradually retreated from Greenland just as the Thule migrated in from Alaska. The Norse encounter with the Amerindians in the Americas and with

In 1590 an Icelandic schoolteacher made a map showing the Vikings' understanding of the Americas in the year 1000. It is the earliest surviving Norse depiction of North America.

the Thule in Greenland typify the more evenly balanced encounters of 1000, so different from those after 1500 when superior guns and cannon almost always allowed the Europeans to prevail.

Because they created a new pathway westward, the Scandinavian voyages across the Atlantic were important. Pioneering new routes around 1000, the Norse were active in a huge swath of territory stretching from L'Anse aux Meadows in the west to the Caspian Sea in the east. They opened a route to the far north of Greenland, and they may have traveled to other destinations farther south.

The Norse voyages to the Americas teach us something else important about globalization: their voyages did not start trade in the Americas. As the next chapter will show, the Amerindians they encountered were already trading across long distances. Ultimately the Norse voyages were most significant because their explorations connected preexisting trade networks on both sides of the Atlantic and so kicked off globalization.

CHAPTER THREE

The Pan-American Highways of 1000

In the year 1000, the largest city in the Americas was probably the Maya settlement of Chichén Itzá, with an estimated population of some 40,000. Situated about 50 miles (80 km) from the sea, it lies near the northern coast of the Yucatan Peninsula, Mexico. Arguably the world's best-preserved city from the year 1000, Chichén Itzá daily draws thousands of tourists. The main attraction is the Castillo, a stepped pyramid standing 100 feet (30 m) tall, with perfectly balanced staircases on its four sides. Huge crowds come each year on March 21 and September 21 to see an astonishing feat of engineering. Around 3 p.m., the sun's rays create a pattern of shadows that forms the image of a serpent on the north face of the pyramid. Over the course of an hour, the serpent's body stretches to meet its stone head at the bottom of the stairs in a perfectly choreographed light show designed 1,000 years ago.

Also impressive is the ball court, measuring some 500 by 200 feet (150 x 60 m). Much larger than a football field, and dating to about 1000, it is the largest Maya ball court anywhere in Mesoamerica, the region comprised of central and south Mexico, Belize, Guatemala, El Salvador, Honduras, Nicaragua, Costa Rica, and Panama. Modern visitors often start their tours at the ball court because it's right by the entrance.

Divided into two teams, ball game players bounced a rubber ball on their hips, elbows, and knees. The object was to get the ball

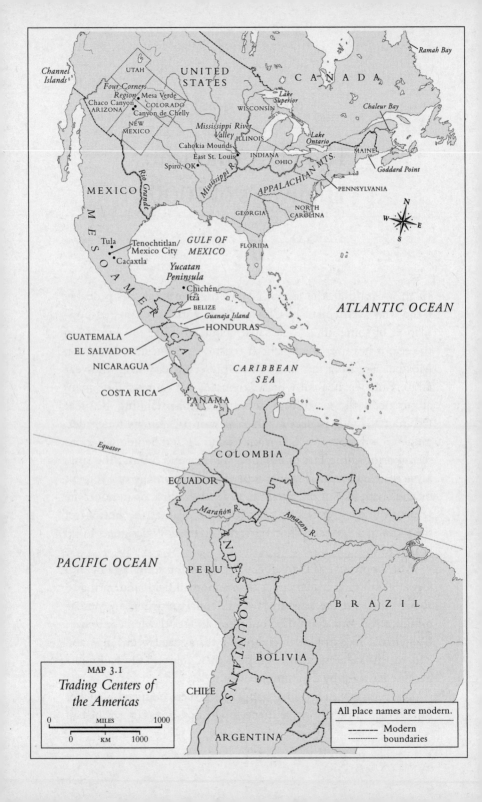

MAP 3.1
Trading Centers of the Americas

0   MILES   1000

0   KM   1000

All place names are modern.

-------- Modern
---------- boundaries

through one of the stone rings on either side of the field. The 8-inch (20 cm) balls were made by gathering liquid latex from rubber trees, allowing it to coagulate, and forming it into balls. Rubber trees were indigenous to the Americas. Ball makers added sap from morning glory flowers to give the rubber in the balls more bounce. The Spanish had never seen anything like rubber, and they marveled at how quickly and unpredictably the balls moved.

Perhaps to portray the independent movement of the balls, Maya artists depicted them with skulls inside. One such ball appears in a relief on the walls of the Chichén Itzá ball court, which shows a member of the losing team with his head cut off and placed on the ground; six snakes spurt from the blood gushing out of his neck. The gods of the Maya required frequent and large offerings of blood. Even rulers were expected to draw stingray spines through their penises to satisfy this demand.

A short walk from the ball court brings you to the Temple of the Warriors, with 200 columns outside. Their facades show gift bearers and warriors for whom the temple was named by archeologists from the Carnegie Institution of Washington, D.C., between 1925 and 1934. Clearing the temple of rubble and trees, these archeologists also recovered multiple wall paintings, all rapidly deteriorating, from fragments lying on the floor. Today you can view them only in black-and-white drawings or watercolor reproductions done by the Carnegie Institution team. Because visitors aren't allowed to enter any of the structures at Chichén Itzá, it's impossible to see the walls on which these murals were originally painted.

Many wall paintings at the Temple of the Warriors depict conquest. From ninety different fragments, the Carnegie Institution scholars reconstructed a giant mural, depicting an army invading a village. Invaders had gray skins; the defenders, light skins with black horizontal stripes. Their shields were also different, presumably to help the viewer keep the two sides straight.

We aren't absolutely certain who the attackers shown in the Chichén Itzá murals are. The aggressors are most likely the Toltecs, a people who came to Chichén Itzá from the central Mexican city of Tollan (modern-day Tula), 50 miles (80 km) northwest of Mexico City, as we learn from two later sources, both recorded after contact with the Spaniards. A Toltec account reports that a king named Feathered Serpent (Topiltzin Quetzalcoatl in the Toltec language, Nahuatl) left Tula in 987, went to the Gulf Coast, and then set off in a raft. By a remarkable coincidence, a Maya record tells of the arrival of a man also named Feathered Serpent (K'uk'ulkan in Mayan) in Chichén Itzá in that same year. It must have been the same man, and he became the ruler of Chichén Itzá.

Across a doorway in the Temple of the Warriors is a truly unusual painting. Although it's on the same wall that shows the conquest of a village, it depicts people totally unlike the warriors in other murals because they are so lifelike.

With yellow hair, light eyes, and whitish skin, one victim has his arms tied behind his back. A second has beads woven into his blond hair, as is common for captives in other Maya paintings (both are shown in the color plates). Yet another, also with beads in his hair, floats naked in the water as a menacing fish, mouth open, hovers nearby. The artist has used Maya blue, a pigment that combines indigo with palygorskite clay, for the water. These unfortunate prisoners of war have all been thrown into the water to drown.

Who were these light-skinned, blond-haired victims?

Could they have been Norsemen captured by the Maya?

The first scholars who wrote about these paintings didn't think so. Ann Axtell Morris, the meticulous conservator, also a member of the Carnegie Institution team, who did a full set of watercolor copies of the murals in the 1920s, wasn't sure of the identity of the people with yellow hair but suspected that the artist used the color scheme to "emphasize a difference of tribe, or even of race." Writing in the 1940s, one scholar offered an extreme solution: he proposed that the victims wore yellow wigs with beads so that their hair would match that of the sun god to whom they were being sacrificed. Working long before the Ingstads discovered the Norse site at L'Anse aux Meadows, this generation of scholars had no reason to think that the sacrificial victims might be Scandinavian.

But, nowadays, thanks to the excavation at L'Anse aux Meadows, we can be certain that the Norse were in North America in the year 1000. The Ingstads' discovery casts the murals from the Temple of the Warriors in a whole new light. These unusual murals might actually depict Scandinavians and their ships. Two eminent Maya scholars who hold this view—the archeologist Michael D. Coe and the art historian Mary Miller—note that no other Maya mural shows captives with blond hair and light skin.

The timing coincides perfectly with the Norse voyages. Multiple Norse ships crossed the North Atlantic in the late 900s and early 1000s, departing from Scandinavia, Iceland, or Greenland, and voyaging to Canada and possibly Maine. This is precisely when these paintings were done (the Temple of the Warriors was built just after 1000).

Skeptics note that Maya artists portrayed warriors using different color schemes and therefore dismiss the blond hair of the captives as artistic convention. They also wonder if the original pigments changed color in the thousand years before the watercolor copies were made.

We might also doubt the identification of painted warriors as Norse: no Scandinavian artifacts have yet been found in the Yucatan. This isn't as serious an objection as you might think; the archeological record is far from complete. Many things we know from written documents have left no archeological traces at all. People who google archeology and the Battle of Hastings are usually shocked to learn that archeologists may have only recently uncovered the first casualty from the 1066 battle that gave England to William the Conqueror.

Given the state of archeological testing available today, we can't be certain that the Norse were at Chichén Itzá: only a diagnostic artifact like the bronze pin from L'Anse aux Meadows or genetic evidence showing Scandinavian DNA would clinch the case. Such evidence may someday surface. For now, though, we have to conclude that the Vikings could have arrived in the Yucatan, which would have been the farthest point south that they went in the Americas.

If the Norse did reach Chichén Itzá, how did they get there? They could certainly have been blown off course and then captured. One battle scene from the Temple of the Warriors shows a blond-haired victim alongside two wood-colored boats, one with a carved prow, the other decorated with shields and sinking at an angle.

We learn more about these unusual boats from a mural in a different building in Old Chichén, one called Las Monjas, meaning "nuns" and, by extension, "nunnery." (The Spaniards assumed that any building with a large courtyard nearby had to be a nunnery, but the Maya had no nunneries.) Built before 950, the Las Monjas Nunnery contains murals that may have been painted slightly later. One of these paintings has no people with blond hair, but it shows a boat with clearly delineated planks, or strakes. The Las Monjas artist depicted the strakes as cut into sections that don't run the full length of the ship. Although many published drawings of Norse boats don't make this clear, the planks on Norse boats were almost always shorter than the full length of the boat. Limited by the size of available oak and pine trees, the length of strakes ranged between 5 and 20 feet (1.5–5 m) on the Norse vessels, some 100 feet (30 m) long.

The use of strakes indicates that the Las Monjas boat cannot be a local craft because the Maya, like most of the peoples living in the Americas, made their canoes by burning and hollowing tree trunks. Only one Amerindian people ever made boats with sewn planks, the Chumash, who used them to voyage to the Channel Islands from Santa Barbara, California. The men in the Las Monjas boat appear to be Maya warriors who have captured a Scandinavian vessel from its original owners. Although the boat painting from Las Monjas has received less attention than the Temple of the Warriors mural of the blond-haired warriors, in fact, its sharply outlined strakes offer even more persuasive evidence of Norse presence at Chichén Itzá.

Winds frequently prevented Norse ships from reaching their destinations. When Erik the Red set off for Greenland with twenty-five ships, only fourteen arrived; "some were driven back, and some were lost at sea," the *Greenlanders' Saga* reports. Remember also that Leif Erikson carried the crew of a shipwrecked boat to Greenland before returning to pick up the American lumber that he unloaded to make room for them. A Norse boat could have been blown off course in a storm, been pulled across the ocean by the currents of the North Atlantic Gyre, and come to rest on the coast of the Yucatan Peninsula. It might have been a grueling voyage, but it wasn't impossible, even if the boat was damaged and the crew couldn't row. Remember the journey across the Pacific of the Japanese fishing vessel that ended up in Washington state with just three survivors.

Voyagers from Africa may have also been blown across the Atlantic. When a Spanish friar named Alonso Ponce, who traveled along the Yucatan coast in 1588, arrived in the town of "Xequechakan" (then pronounced "shekechakan," but now Hecelchakán in the Mexican state of Campeche), he asked how the town received its name. The locals explained: "In ancient times seventy *Moros* [black Africans] reached the coast in a vessel that must have been through a great storm." Their experience shows that, once winds took a boat into the mid-Atlantic, ocean currents could carry it all the way to the Yucatan Peninsula.

The locals continued, "Among these was one whom the rest obeyed and respected, whom they called Xequé." Xequé? The locals explained that it meant "lord" or "chief," surely a variant of the Arabic word "sheikh," a convincing detail given that the Maya didn't know any Arabic. When the Moors asked to go home, the locals brought them to a port near "a savannah and unpopulated country," for which the word in Mayan was "chakan." And so the town came to be known as Xequechakan, explained Ponce's informants.

Ponce's account provides another kernel of important information. When the Moors, he tells us, first arrived, "the Indians, having pity on them, sheltered them, and were good hosts to them." But once the locals had shown the visitors the way home, the Moors turned on their hosts and murdered some of them. "The Indians, having seen this, then notified the nearby people who came with their arms and killed the unfortunate Moros, and with them their chief and leader." Their experience suggests that anyone shipwrecked on the Yucatan Peninsula could have met a similar fate.

If the Norse reached the Yucatan Peninsula, it was probably by sea. It is also possible, though much less likely, that they were enslaved elsewhere and brought to the Yucatan on foot. Let us start our exploration of possible routes from Goddard Point, Maine, where the Viking penny was found, and proceed overland to Chichén Itzá. The most likely route to Mexico from Maine ran through the Mississippi Valley. It would have been a long and difficult journey, and no evidence survives of anyone—or any object—making the entire trip. Still, we are certain that an extended network of pathways across North America had taken shape by 1000, and goods, people, and information traveled along them as globalization began.

Goddard Point is located next to a beach on the central Maine coast. It is a rich archeological site with a refuse heap, called a midden, measuring about 12 inches (25 cm) at its deepest point. When Maine state archeologists excavated there in 1979, the original context had been destroyed. They could date materials only on the basis of comparisons to similar artifacts or by using carbon 14 testing. The earliest material in the midden dated to 2000 BC, but 90 percent of the material recovered—a total of 25,000 artifacts—came from the period AD 1000–1600.

The midden contained surprisingly few seashells, indicating that the locals—unlike most coastal peoples—didn't consume much shellfish. The large quantity of bones from seals and sturgeon showed that they were the main elements in the local diet. And cross sections of seventeen teeth from harbor seal, gray seal, and sea mink revealed even more: the seals and sea mink had been killed between June and October. The takeaway? Clearly each summer Amerindians feasted on seals and sea mink at the site.

Archeologists found thirty tools and over 100 flakes of chert from Ramah Bay in northern Labrador, which had been trickle-traded southward. (Chert is a type of flint that can be used to start fires or to make tools.) Ramah Bay chert has other attributes besides its unusual translucence. Its high silica content causes it to fracture with clean and predictable breaks, making it the ideal material for crafting projectile points to attach to arrows, spears, and other types of weapons. Finds of Ramah chert in places far from Labrador date to at least 2000 BC, showing that the long-distance exchange of this material began early.

In addition to Ramah Bay chert, the Goddard Point site produced ten minerals including other cherts, rhyolites, and jaspers from all across the northeastern U.S. and Canada. This unusually large amount of nonlocal material—other contemporary sites had many fewer imported artifacts—shows that Goddard Point was an important node on a trading network stretching all the way from the Atlantic coast to Lake Ontario and Pennsylvania.

After 1000, this region was home to the Late Woodland peoples, who planted maize in the spring and returned to harvest it in the fall. The Woodland peoples moved on circuits collecting various plants and hunting different animals, prompting one scholar to call them "mobile farmers." (The Algonquians, who traded red cloth for furs from Jacques Cartier at Chaleur Bay, were Woodland peoples.)

Any group traveling from the northeast into Ohio and on to the Mississippi River Valley would have realized only gradually that they were leaving one region and entering another. As they moved closer to where the Missouri converged with the Mississippi, they would have noticed that the locals were regularly eating corn. For the residents of the Mississippi Valley, corn was the major staple in their diet, and they cultivated it intensively, tending the fields year-round.

Small villages would have looked much the same as in the northeast: a few small houses clustered together. But after the intensified cultivation of corn began around 900, larger settlements began to appear in the Mississippi Valley with open plazas and high dirt mounds with ridges, sometimes with temple buildings on them.

Beans came to the Mississippi Valley around the year 1000, further contributing to population growth. (The three crops that formed the core of the Amerindian diet—corn, beans, and squash—weren't regularly planted together until 1300.) The residents didn't depend solely on cultivated crops such as corn, beans, and goosefoot (a vegetable also called lamb's quarters); they also hunted deer and other animals.

Population growth led to an increase in village size. One of the largest settlements was located at the Cahokia site in the town of East St. Louis, Illinois. The settlement at Cahokia expanded so dramatically in 1050 that the lead archeologist writing about the site, Timothy R. Pauketat, refers to the changes of that year as the Big Bang. After the Big Bang, some 20,000 lived in the city or nearby suburbs, making Cahokia the largest urban complex in the continental U.S. before 1492 and half the size of contemporary Chichén Itzá.

At its peak, the city of Cahokia stretched over an area of 5–6 square miles (13–16 sq km). At the center of the city stood an enormous mound, called Monks Mound, which was 100 feet (30 m) tall. To the south, the residents used earth to create the flat, even surface of the Great Plaza, which measured 900 feet by 1,200 feet (275 x 365 m).

Monks Mound contained various food remains, broken pottery vessels, and tobacco seeds, all left over from the feasting that typically accompanied the construction of mounds. The different mounds, which are the distinguishing feature of the regional Cahokia archeological culture, are so large that individual families couldn't build them. The organization of a larger labor force is one of the signs that Cahokia was a city.

An additional 200 mounds were distributed throughout the site. They originally had ridges along the top, but many lost their characteristic outline in the centuries after 1250 when Cahokia was abandoned and later farmers plowed and planted them. In addition to the mounds, the Cahokia site had an extensive fence made from vertical wooden poles, six circular observatories surrounded by more poles, and thousands of dwellings.

The most distinctive Cahokia artifacts are called chunkey stones. Living on in different Amerindian languages spoken in Indiana, Wisconsin, North Carolina, and Florida, the word was recorded by Lewis and Clark in the early 1800s. Because of this nineteenth-century research, we know how the game was played. A chunkey stone, about the size of a hockey puck, was round with an indentation on one side. Players rolled the stones on the ground and threw 9-foot-long (2.75 m) spears, aiming at the indentations to stop the chunkeys. The closer the spear landed to the rolling stone, the more points the player received. The stakes were high. The defeated sometimes lost their lives. More than a pastime, chunkey created loyalties between rulers and ruled.

Cahokia was clearly a hierarchical society. One earthwork at the site, Mound 72, contained two men's bodies. One lay on top of 20,000 shell beads, and the other rested immediately below it on a wooden stretcherlike frame. Because the beads covered an area 6 feet (1.8 m) long in the shape of a bird, archeologists concluded that they must have once decorated a garment, most likely a cape, worn by the man on top. Buried near the two men was one group of seven adults whose bodies were intact, most likely the kin of the ruler or other prominent people.

Mound 72 had multiple mass graves, one with 200 victims. One pit contained a group of four individuals, with their heads and hands cut off. One held fifty-three women, fifty-two between the ages of fifteen and twenty-five, with one woman—could she have been a senior wife?—in her thirties. In yet another pit lay thirty-nine victims who'd been clubbed and possibly buried alive. Who were these unfortunates? Surely prisoners, slaves, or members of some other underclass who ended up as sacrificial victims.

However you understand the identities of those in these different pits, it's clear that the two men with the bead cape outranked them. The pair were also buried with a large copper-covered rod, a two-bushel heap of mica, 700 arrows, a chunkey spear, fifteen chunkey stones, and multiple conch-shell beads more than an inch (2.5 cm) in diameter.

Some of these goods, like the arrows and chunkey stones, could have been made locally, but others had arrived via long-distance trade. The mica, a flaky mineral that catches the light, came from the Appalachian Mountains of North Carolina, while the copper's source was Lake Superior. Earlier Amerindian societies had also traded copper and shells, but the Cahokians imported noticeably larger numbers of conch and whelk shells from the Gulf of Mexico. Pottery vessels, characteristic of Cahokia ceramics, holding intact shells inside, have been found in sites north of Cahokia, which served as a transshipment center for goods on their way north.

At first, archeologists didn't think the Cahokia trade networks extended beyond the continental U.S. But to their surprise, one item of certain Mexican origin—a tool used for scraping that was made of unusual greenish-gold obsidian—surfaced at Spiro, Oklahoma, a site where the inhabitants began to build mounds and plant corn intensively around 1250. Obsidian is a glassy volcanic rock that makes an excellent cutting tool, and was especially prized in societies that didn't use metal knives. For all its sharpness, obsidian is brittle and shatters easily. X-ray spectrometer analysis of the scraping tool from Spiro showed that it was from near Pachuca, Mexico. This obsidian was so unusual that it, like Ramah chert in the northeast, was traded over a wide area including Guatemala and Honduras.

Archeology rarely tells us exactly how or in what way one society influenced another. Scholars have long wondered whether the Cahokians and the Maya had any direct contacts; after all, the intensive cultivation of corn, which originated in Mexico, underlay the Big Bang of 1050, and the open plazas and mounds of Cahokia and its satellites resemble those of Maya cities.

Careful examination of corpses from Cahokia produced a surprise: several individuals, some buried in Mound 72, had front incisor teeth with one to four notches on the bottom edge, which would have been visible whenever they opened their mouths. Since only Mesoamericans altered their teeth in this way, it's likely that either some Mesomericans visited Cahokia or that some Cahokians visited the Maya region, had their teeth notched, and returned to Cahokia. Another sign of possible contact with the

Maya: ceramics with traces of chocolate in them, but archeologists haven't yet ruled out the possibility of modern contamination.

Information from after 1492 reinforces the impression of extensive contact between Cahokia and the Maya region. Nineteenth-century observers recorded the origin myths of different Amerindian groups, many of which claimed descent from a pair of male twins or a ruler and his alter-ego half-brother. These beliefs echo the Maya myth of the hero twins from the famous Maya oral epic entitled Popol Vuh, itself written down only in the 1550s. The pair of male bodies at the top of Mound 72 appear to have been twin rulers, and the falcon-shaped bead cape suggests that Cahokia residents credited their rulers with the ability to fly.

These ties between Cahokia and the Maya world point to a pathway that followed the Mississippi River to the Rio Grande and crossed the Gulf of Mexico to the Yucatan Peninsula.

A different route to Chichén Itzá was known to the people of Chaco Canyon, an advanced agricultural community with close ties to the Maya. Chaco Canyon is located in New Mexico in the Four Corners region. Living at the same time as the Cahokia residents, the Ancestral Puebloans built three much visited UNESCO World Heritage sites: Mesa Verde, Chaco Canyon, and Canyon de Chelly, which tourists flock to simply because, with canyon walls soaring 1,000 feet (300 m) above, they are all so beautiful.

These sites contain many unsolved puzzles. Everyone grants that the Puebloan road system is a marvel of engineering, but no one knows why the Ancestral Puebloans designed it as they did. Two roads, each 30 feet (9 m) wide, lead some 30 miles (50 km) north and south from Chaco Canyon. Not always visible on the ground, these roads consistently appear in aerial photographs. Wherever one of these roads runs into a hill or a large rock, it goes straight over it. Puzzlingly, builders didn't remove the obstacles. Instead they constructed ramps, steps, and staircases as part of the roads. So abrupt are the vertical rises and descents that it's hard to imagine that the roads were built for transportation. Did they have a symbolic meaning? Did they reflect a belief that you had to walk in a straight line when performing rituals?

The Ancestral Puebloans mastered building with precisely cut stone. At Canyon de Chelly they used the same technique as the Maya to make walls, which they covered with plaster. Embedding large chunks of sandstone in mortar made from mud, builders faced the wall's two sides with carefully chosen flat rocks in what is called core-and-veneer construction.

Chaco had great houses with hundreds of residents, large kivas (round, underground storage rooms), and expansive plazas. Its total population of only a few thousand was considerably smaller than Cahokia's 20,000. The largest great house at Chaco is the Pueblo Bonito, where tree-ring dating shows that construction began in 860 and ended in 1128. After that year, the Puebloan peoples migrated elsewhere.

The Pueblo Bonito complex, with 800 different rooms, contains multiple stone structures of several stories. Scholars debate the purpose of the great houses: were they trading posts? Or the residences of the rulers and their families? Whatever the answer, they were certainly designed to impress, as they still do today.

Chaco Canyon was home to peoples from different regions, skeletal analysis has shown. One group lived in the great houses like Pueblo Bonito while the other lived in communities of small houses, which were quite different architecturally. The residents also had different styles of burial. It seems most likely that the site was home to indigenous peoples as well as migrants from southwestern Colorado, who moved there in the late 800s or early 900s. The presence of a single skeleton with deliberately notched teeth at Pueblo Bonito points to the presence of visitors from the Maya region. Typically in globalization, the movement of peoples followed the initial exchange of trade goods. And as the trade increased, merchants moved to wherever their new customers lived and formed expat communities there.

The Ancestral Puebloans were master traders with ample supplies of something the Maya loved: turquoise. They traded the turquoise to obtain tropical birds with bright feathers, such as parrots and macaws, whose brilliant red feathers decorate surviving tapestries. Sometimes they brought in just feathers while at other times they shipped live birds whose feathers they could pluck. The Ancestral Puebloans respected macaws so much that they gave them formal burials. Yet excavated macaw skeletons indicate that the birds were poorly nourished and didn't receive sufficient sunlight, a sign that as much as the Ancestral Puebloans esteemed the birds, they still caged them.

About ten years ago at Chaco Canyon, investigators discovered another surprising import from Mesoamerica: chocolate. Archeologists found some pottery fragments from broken storage jars dating to 1000–1125 in a garbage midden. Not knowing their original contents, the scientists used high-performance liquid chromatography to identify chocolate's telltale chemical signature, theobromine. The absorption of the chocolate into the pottery fragments indicates that the chocolate was in liquid form before it dried. (Chocolate was first domesticated in Ecuador about 1900 BC.) The processing of chocolate was a complex, multistep process: once cultivators opened the pods, they had to germinate the seeds (otherwise they wouldn't taste like chocolate), dry them for one or two weeks in the sun, roast them (for the same reason), and remove the useless shell.

Although Hershey Chocolate funded this research, the chocolate the Maya consumed—and exported to the Chaco site where it was found in jars—tasted nothing like a Hershey bar. The Maya drank their chocolate unsweetened and spiced with chili peppers; they frothed it by pouring it from one cup to another and then back again, just like tea vendors in India's train stations. Chocolate's role as a stimulant made it perfect for ceremonies. Archeologists believe that ritual experts from the Maya region accompanied the chocolate beans north so that they could teach the Ancestral Puebloans how to prepare these chocolate beverages, which makes perfect sense. Once the trade reached a certain volume, someone had to manage it, and expats could teach locals how to make chocolate.

The finds of chocolate, macaws, and other tropical birds show that trade pathways connected Chaco with Chichén Itzá more than 2,000 miles (3,600 km) away. Of course, some of the peoples

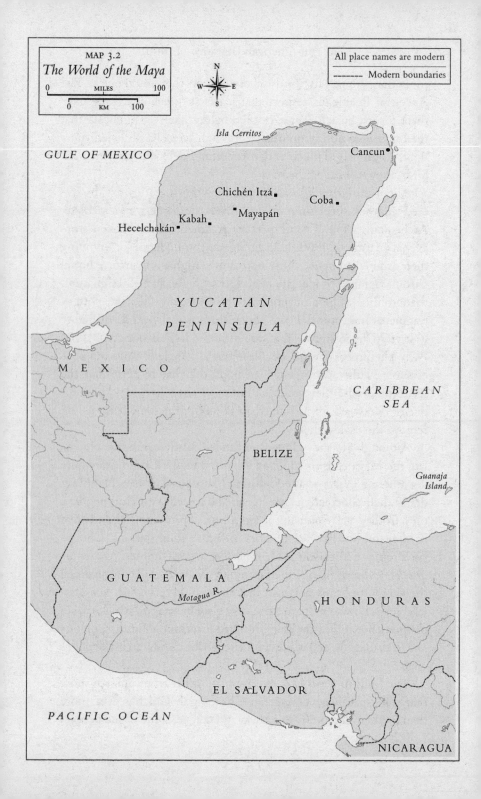

MAP 3.2
The World of the Maya

0   MILES   100

0   KM   100

N
W   E
S

All place names are modern

------ Modern boundaries

Isla Cerritos

GULF OF MEXICO

Cancun•

Chichén Itzá ■

Coba ■

■ Mayapán

Kabah ■

Hecelchakán ■

Y U C A T A N

P E N I N S U L A

M E X I C O

C A R I B B E A N
S E A

BELIZE

*Guanaja
Island*

G U A T E M A L A

Motagua R.

H O N D U R A S

EL SALVADOR

PACIFIC OCEAN

NICARAGUA

traveling to the Maya center covered much shorter distances. Sometime around 1000 the Toltec peoples migrated from Tula, some fifty miles northwest of Mexico City, to Chichén Itzá, either crossing the Gulf of Mexico in boats or traveling overland.

We know about their journey because the city's architecture changed after their arrival. Two distinct architectural styles coexist at the site: the earlier style dates to before 950 and the later after 950. Before the arrival of the newcomers, the most typical construction method for walls in Old Chichén was core-and-veneer, just as in Chaco. While structures in Old Chichén possess features identical to other Maya cities in the region, buildings in New Chichén, such as the Temple of the Warriors, display strong Toltec architectural influence.

Scholars call this style "international." The international style includes many elements from Tula, such as buildings with columns and wall paintings divided into bands. Interestingly, buildings at the Toltec homeland of Tula also absorbed Maya elements, suggesting a two-way flow of influence between the two cities. Also new at Chichén Itzá were chacmool sculptures, reclining figures whose stomachs served as platters for offerings to the gods.

Some fifty inscriptions in the Mayan language indicate that Old Chichén was built between 864 and 897. And then, just as in the Maya heartland to the south, the inscriptions come to an abrupt halt.

The end of Mayan-language inscriptions at Chichén Itzá coincided with a crisis throughout Maya lands between 800 and 925, the period called the Terminal Classic. The rulers of the multiple Maya kingdoms had always fought with one another, but the intensity of the fighting sharply escalated. The systematic cultivation of maize depletes nitrogen in the soil and caused an overall decline in soil fertility just as urban populations rose to dangerously high levels. Starting around 900, prolonged drought hit, and cities throughout the region shrank—either because residents fled or because they died.

The slowdown in construction in Chichén Itzá coincided with

the decline of the Maya heartland, but after that the city bounced back. Major buildings like the Castillo and the Temple of the Warriors were built between 950 and 1100.

Could climate change account for the collapse and then rebirth of Chichén Itzá? As we have seen, 900 marked the beginning of population growth for both the Cahokia and Chaco cultures, and some have linked these developments to the Medieval Climate Anomaly, which began in Europe around 950 and continued until 1250. Scholars don't yet know what types of climate change the Americas may have experienced when Europe was experiencing the Medieval Warming Period. But the collapse of Maya society in its tropical lowland heartland and the hiatus in building in Chichén Itzá between 900 and 950 point to a prolonged period of little rainfall.

When Chichén Itzá emerged from the difficult period, the rulers launched a massive building campaign. Like the residents of Chaco, the Maya constructed an elaborate road system of raised, utterly straight roadways whose purpose couldn't have been purely for transportation. The Maya never used the wheel for travel, even though they knew about it and made some wheeled toys. Some have wondered if the lowland tropical forest terrain wasn't suitable for wheeled transport, but people living in similar areas, such as Southeast Asia, made extensive use of the wheel. Whatever the reason, the Maya clearly intended their roadways for foot traffic.

A road of crumbled white limestone 900 feet (274 m) long connects New Chichén with a sinkhole pool just north of the city. The Yucatan Maya word for such a road was *sakbeh*, meaning "white road," and by extension the Milky Way. The Maya believed that the Milky Way connected earth to the realm of ancestors and gods and that walking long distances made rituals more effective. One of the longest white sakbeh roads runs from Coba for over 60 miles (100 km) through the Yucatan jungle. Curiously this road ends at a point 12 miles (19 km) southwest of Chichén Itzá, not in the city itself.

The geology of the entire Yucatan Peninsula took shape some 65 million years ago when an asteroid crashed into the Gulf of

Mexico. (The collision covered the atmosphere in so much ash that many of the earth's animals, including all dinosaurs, became extinct.) The resulting shock waves in the Gulf pelted the giant limestone formation of the Yucatan Peninsula with enormous waves. As a result, the region has millions of underground tunnels and pools. When the ceilings of underground tunnels collapse, they form sinkholes filled with water, called cenotes, which connect to form networks hundreds of miles long.

The Sacred Cenote at Chichén Itzá is a large oval, measuring 187 feet (57 m) across at the widest point. The earliest description of the cenote comes from Bishop Diego de Landa, one of the most observant of the early Spanish friars in the mid-1500s. (He was also responsible for the destruction of hundreds of Maya books, of which only four survive today.) Landa reported that the Maya tossed sacrificed human beings into the cenote in hopes of bringing rain and that "they also threw in many other offerings of precious stones and things they valued greatly," because the Maya believed that cenotes and underground caves served as portals to the divine world.

Some 300 years later, Landa's report attracted the attention of an aspiring archeologist named Edward Herbert Thompson. Visiting the site for the first time in 1885, Thompson returned in 1904 with sufficient funding to dredge the Sacred Cenote. The first skeleton exhumed by the dredge confirmed Landa's reports of human sacrifice. Some of the skeletons were from young females (physical examination can't determine if a skeleton was a virgin), and others were from adult males and children. Many of the jade and metal objects found in the cenote had been hacked into pieces, presumably destroyed during rituals before being thrown away.

After three years of dredging, Thompson wanted to retrieve the smaller objects that slipped through the dredge's metal teeth. He took a break to learn how to dive and returned to Chichén Itzá, where he rigged up a pump to supply himself with air. Then Thompson suited up, jumped into the water, and descended to layers of muck so thick that he couldn't see anything even with a submarine flashlight. At one point, Thompson forgot to adjust the valves as he was coming up. Suffering permanent hearing loss, he never dove again.

Although controversial (his techniques certainly didn't meet modern standards for scientific excavation), his dredging recovered a huge amount of material, now held at Harvard. The oxygen-starved waters of the cenote preserved materials, such as textile fragments, copal tree resin, and rubber, which perish in most contexts. (Such an oxygen-starved environment also preserved the textiles and bird feathers in the buried Viking ships.) The Maya burned copal, which gave off a pleasant fragrance, and rubber, which produced a dark, pungent smoke. Both heightened the sensory experience of ritual.

The significance of the finds from the Sacred Cenote isn't the evidence of human sacrifice among the Maya—this is well known today even if it came as news to Thompson—but rather what they reveal about Chichén Itzá's trade ties to other places. In addition to confirming Maya exchanges with the residents of Chaco Canyon to the north, the finds also make it possible to pinpoint when the Maya began to trade with their neighbors to the south.

Before 900 the Maya hadn't made any luxury goods from metal. All their most valuable goods were made of lustrous green jade (technically jadeite) from the Motagua River Valley in Guatemala. The Maya prized the deep hues of macaw and quetzal feathers and Spondylus shells. The most important trade goods of the time appear in a painting of a merchant god done between 700 and 800 in a temple at Cacaxtla, Mexico: sea turtle shells, books, textiles, rubber, and salt, which the Maya harvested on the Yucatan coast.

Maya legends have it that the Merchant God L (assigned the letter "L" pending later decipherment) was the enemy of the Maize God, who returned with the summer rains to vanquish God L for another year. God L was said to travel at night—because this was a cooler time to travel? To evade thieves? To avoid scrutiny? All seem possible, as all fit the shady persona of the deity. Maya rulers associated themselves with agriculture, which they saw as pure. They avoided portraying themselves as engaged in mercantile pursuits, even though in actuality they greatly prized goods from foreign lands and personally participated in long-distance trading trips.

If we could update this painting of the Merchant God L on the basis of the Sacred Cenote finds, we'd have to add items made of metal because the Maya began after 900 to import gold and copper goods from Costa Rica, Panama, and Colombia.

No major cities on the scale of Chichén Itzá or Cahokia ever arose in Central America. Living in villages of a thousand inhabitants at most, the residents of Central America made their living by fishing and hunting local animals and cultivating crops like manioc, peach palm, and maize on an occasional basis. They also engaged in trade, using massive dugout canoes, carved from hardwood trees native to the rainforest, to travel up and down the Pacific and Caribbean coasts.

The Sacred Cenote at Chichén Itzá contained small metal bells made of copper and gold as well as elaborately decorated flat disks of gold, on which Maya artists portrayed sacrificial victims whose hearts had been removed. The southern limit for goods found in the Sacred Cenote was Colombia. No item made farther south in South America has ended up in the Sacred Cenote or anywhere else in Mexico, indicating that no direct trade occurred between the Andean cultural areas and the Maya before 1492.

Although no one traded physical goods, metalworking craftsmen brought the know-how for making those goods northward from South America along the Pacific coast to western Mexico. The Andes had a long metallurgical tradition. Starting around 2000 BC, Andean metalworkers in Peru extracted ores from rocks they found in streambeds—first gold, then copper, and finally silver. (They never worked iron.) As they refined their metalworking techniques over thousands of years, they learned how to pound, fold, pierce, and solder together sheets of metal. Andean metallurgists managed to pass their skills to others, who eventually conveyed these techniques to craftsmen in Yucatan, who crafted the metal objects in the Sacred Cenote.

The metalworkers also brought the lost-wax casting technique;

it, too, originated in the Andes. Metalworkers began by crafting the item they wanted in beeswax, built a clay mold around the beeswax, fired it, and poured molten metal into the mold. The wax melted away, hence the term "lost wax." The locals used the lost-wax technique to produce small bells, many of which were found in the Sacred Cenote at Chichén Itzá. Bells occupied some 60 percent of western Mexican metal production. The inhabitants treasured bells because whenever their rulers wore them and walked, the bells tinkled, creating a sound worthy of royalty. This exchange of know-how constituted—to use today's terminology—international trade in intellectual property.

The movement of know-how—not goods—between the Andes and Mexico is perplexing in light of how other world regions experienced globalization. The movement of goods along a new pathway almost always preceded the movement of the crafts specialists who made them.

Yet the transfer of Andean know-how rather than objects makes sense when you take into account that Andean societies limited the use of certain metals to specific social groups. People at the top of the society—rulers, their relatives, high priests—possessed objects made of gold, silver, copper, and combinations of the three, whereas the poorest members of society did not own any metal items at all. Itinerant metalworkers could carry the knowledge of how to work metal with them, but they didn't possess high-quality goods made from gold and silver. Only royalty could have sent such gifts north, and it seems that they didn't know about the Maya.

Despite the lack of direct contact with their distant neighbors in Mexico, the Andeans traded extensively within their home region. The inhabitants of North Peru experimented with a combination of copper and arsenic to make the first bronzes, and the first regular use of bronze came around 850 or 900. This was when Andean peoples learned how to extract different metals from ore. Draft furnaces heated fuel and ore together to produce a slag with the main ingredient of copper that could be mixed with gold, silver, tin, and arsenic to make different types of bronzes. Of varying hues, these bronze alloys had different tastes and smells, as Spanish observers reported in the 1500s.

Around the year 1000 several different archeological cultures coexisted in the Andean region of modern Peru, Bolivia, northern Chile, and Argentina. The regular use of arsenic bronze distinguished Andean society from other metal-using societies all around the world. Arsenic bronze has certain advantages over the usual bronze made with copper and tin: it breaks less easily, it's harder, and it rusts more slowly. When the arsenic is being worked, it gives off poisonous fumes, but once the metal assumes its final shape, it poses no danger. (Almost no one uses arsenic bronze today because of the dangers of arsenic vapors.)

One distinctive local product some Andean peoples made from arsenic bronze was symbolic money. Sometimes they exchanged brand-new real-world axes; sometimes they cut axe-shaped pieces from sheet bronze and tied them into bundles. Similar axe-moneys, also made of arsenic bronze and tied together in bundles, have been found in western Mexico from around 1200. One type of axe-money circulated in the Andes, another in Mexico. The two were not a shared medium of exchange. Andean metalworkers must have transmitted the knowledge of how to make axe-money to the north.

Arsenic bronzes have also been found in central Peru, the core of the Wari archeological culture. The Wari controlled the largest territory in the Andes around the year 1000. Preceding the Inca, the Wari shared many practices with them. The Wari were the first people to use quipu records, wrapping colored threads around cords to show quantities or commodities; all remain undeciphered. The Andeans had no writing system; the only indigenous American writing systems arose in Mexico.

Both the Wari and Inca used an elaborate network of roads. Unlike the Maya white roads, these weren't ritual roads—they followed the contours of the land and connected major settlements, an especially important function given that people living at different elevations depended on each other for food.

Before the Spanish arrived, the Andean peoples had created an extensive trade network, importing turquoise and emeralds from Colombia, lapis lazuli from Chile, and gold nuggets from a tributary of the Amazon, the Marañón River. Although their metalworking techniques traveled north, they never traded directly with the Maya.

As was always the case, geography played a role. The dense jungle of Panama posed a major geographical obstacle for those going overland; it's the one place in Latin America uncrossed by major highways even today. Goods traveling from Panama to Colombia almost always go via container ships. In the Andes, llama caravans carried many commodities through the highlands where the llamas had ample supplies of fresh grass. Llamas could go up and down mountains and as far as the Peruvian coast, but because of the lack of grasslands at sea level, they couldn't travel along the coast for long. The only way to move along the coast was by boat.

But the sea journey north wasn't easy either. One computer simulation found that it would have taken two months to sail north from Ecuador to western Mexico but five months for the return leg, which required going deep into the ocean—out of sight from the coast—for an entire month because of ocean currents. Ocean currents also posed genuine challenges for those traveling in a dugout canoe without a sail, the only type of boat in certain use before contact with the Europeans.

As canoes traveled north along the Pacific coast, they also went up and down the Caribbean coast near Chichén Itzá. The coastal port of Isla Cerritos lies 56 miles (90 km) from Chichén Itzá on the north coast of the Yucatan Peninsula. Coming into use around 900, the port is a miniature Chichén Itzá, complete with a plaza, ball court, colonnade, and temple buildings. Archeologists have unearthed finds of obsidian, ceramic vessels with a metallic sheen, turquoise, jade, copper, and gold ornaments, which all came by boat. Isla Cerritos connected Chichén Itzá with northern and western Mexico, the southwestern U.S., and Panama and Costa Rica. Its size shows the importance of maritime trade to the Maya residents of the Yucatan.

★　★　★

The city of Chichén Itzá began to decline around 1100, the last year that any major monuments were built, and the city was abandoned sometime after 1200. As is so often the case, archeologists aren't certain why but suspect drought as the cause. Worship at the Sacred Cenote continued. A group called the Itza moved from the west coast of the Yucatan to Chichén Itzá in the 1220s, and gave their name to the city, which means "mouth of the well of the Itza."

After leaving Chichén Itzá, the Itza moved to the city of Mayapán in the late 1200s and killed all the Mayapán rulers except for a prince who was away on a trading expedition in western Honduras. This information, again from the Spaniard Bishop Landa, indicates the importance of trade. Royal princes joined trading expeditions and didn't delegate trade only to merchants. Recall, too, that the Maya worshipped the mysterious Merchant God L, a sign of their respect for commerce.

Mayapán was no Chichén Itzá. With neither a ball court nor any streets, the city was home to perhaps 15,000 people packed into an area of 2.5 square miles (6.5 sq km). Its one advantage was that cenotes provided a reliable supply of water to the residents of the walled city even when under siege.

After 1325, a new power, the Aztecs, appeared in northern Mexico, and the political center of Mexico shifted away from the Yucatan Peninsula to the Aztec capital of Tenochtitlan, directly under downtown Mexico City. The system of pathways across Mexico reoriented to serve this new center. Because the Aztecs had unified Mexico in the 1400s, much of their domain—but not the Yucatan Peninsula—fell into the Spaniards' laps after their capital was conquered and Montezuma was killed.

In the 1500s, when the Spanish arrived on the Yucatan Peninsula, they encountered twelve or thirteen warring groups, whom the Spanish had to defeat before they could claim sovereignty over the entire Maya region. The conquest took centuries. Even under Spanish rule, the Maya continued to live in the Yucatan and the tropical lowlands, still their homeland today, and to speak multiple languages descended from classical Mayan. One of the key breakthroughs in the deciphering of Mayan came in the 1970s when linguists realized that the vocabulary and syntax of these spoken Mayan dialects could help them to understand the inscriptions on monuments.

The sea remained important to the Maya in the centuries after they left Chichén Itzá. In 1502 Christopher Columbus, his son Ferdinand, and his men encountered a Maya dugout canoe near the island of Guanaja, 43 miles (70 km) north of Honduras. In his biography of his father, Ferdinand describes what his father saw: "Made of a single tree trunk like the other Indian canoes," the canoe was propelled by twenty-five paddlers and was as long as a "Venetian galley," probably around 65 feet (20 m). The Maya hollowed out the trunks of giant elephant ear trees (guanacaste) to make their dugout canoes. In addition to the crew, the canoe carried women, children, their possessions, different goods, and foods including roots, grains, and corn alcohol. Ferdinand didn't record the destination of the Maya canoe, but it could have been traveling along the coast or on its way to Cuba or another Caribbean island.

Columbus grasped the significance of the giant canoe: It revealed "in a single moment . . . all the products of that country." He confiscated "the costliest and handsomest things": embroidered and painted cotton clothing, wooden swords, "flint" (probably obsidian) knives "that cut like steel," and copper bells.

The Spaniards didn't understand everything they saw. Some of the crew mistook copper for gold. Columbus didn't recognize cacao beans—he called them almonds—but he did notice how carefully the crew handled them: "when they were brought aboard with the other goods, and some fell to the floor, all the Indians squatted down to pick them up as if they had lost something of great value." Columbus was an astute observer: each cacao bean was precious.

Among the goods in the canoe, Columbus listed "small hatchets similar to those made out of stone other Indians use, though these were made out of good-quality copper." This was Mexican axe-money, which was still circulating in Columbus's day.

Ferdinand's remarkable account reminds us of an important point we often forget: the resident peoples of the Americas had constructed a sophisticated network of pathways long before the Spanish came. In the year 1000 that network centered on Chichén Itzá, extended north to Chaco Canyon and to Cahokia, and reached to Colombia in the south. This network was flexible. When new cities arose, as Chichén Itzá did after 1000 or Cahokia after 1050, the locals opened new pathways or found seaways that connected to the new centers.

In 1492, when Columbus arrived, Chichén Itzá was no longer at the center of the American trade network; the Aztec capital of Tenochtitlan had displaced it. Columbus did not create a new Pan-American highway system. He simply connected the pathways in the Americas to those in Europe by adding a new transatlantic link. When the Norse traveled into Eastern Europe from their Scandinavian homeland, they created an entirely new system of pathways, as the next chapter will explain.

CHAPTER FOUR

European Slaves

Leif Erikson and the others who went to the Americas weren't the only Norse to leave one region and proceed to another. Around the year 1000, other Scandinavians sailed east instead, across the Baltic Sea, and opened up new pathways in Eastern Europe with far greater long-term consequences. We know these people today as the Rus, the wanderers who gave their name to Russia. Mostly male, they intermarried with local women, established permanent settlements, learned to speak Slavic languages, and eventually were completely absorbed into local society. Finding a steady supply of furs and slaves in Eastern Europe, the Rus positioned themselves as middlemen and profited hugely by selling to both Byzantine and Muslim consumers in Central Asia.

Although the silver and gold the Rus shipped back transformed the economy of their Scandinavian homeland, their impact on Eastern Europe was even greater. Over the course of the 900s, the Rus formed a trading confederation that gained control over a large area lightly populated by various tribes. The decision in 988 or 989 of the head of that confederation, the Rus ruler Prince Vladimir, to convert to Byzantine Orthodoxy redrew the map of the Christian world to include Eastern Europe and Russia. (The two major branches of Christianity at that time were Byzantine Orthodoxy and Roman Catholicism; Protestantism took shape after the Reformation in the 1520s.) When Vladimir converted, the Christian world wasn't yet fully formed: Rome replaced Constantinople as its center only in 1204 after the Fourth Crusade. A key development in globalization, the movement of ideas and the subsequent creation of new religious regions profoundly affected everyone, even those who stayed home.

The first Scandinavian migrants to Eastern Europe worshipped the same traditional deities as the Norse who went to the Americas did: Thor, the powerful deity of thunder, his father, Odin, the god of war, and Freya, the goddess of fertility. Contemporaries called these travelers "Rus," a word derived from the Finnish word for Sweden, which means "to row" or "the men who row." Although earlier Scandinavian scholars portrayed the Rus as purely Scandinavian, and pre-1989 Soviet scholars painted them as equally Slavic, the Rus weren't a single ethnicity. An amalgam of various northern peoples such as the Norse, the Anglo-Saxons, the Franks, and the Slavs, they joined together to form warbands and disbanded just as quickly.

Like the Norse who voyaged west to the Americas, the Rus chieftains who went east in search of plunder possessed—and sometimes exploited—a modest organizational superiority over the indigenous population. The peoples living in the forests of Eastern Europe fished, trapped animals, and traveled to seek out certain plants, including those that they planted in the spring and returned to in the fall to harvest. They traveled in small groups and lived very simply. Some small groups of Rus, particularly along the reaches of the northern Volga River basin, mixed with the locals and traded with them peacefully for furs. In other localities, the Rus obtained fur and slaves by force. Larger groups of Rus who regularly defeated the locals when they skirmished eventually began to charge "tribute," a euphemism for protection money. Typically, the locals paid furs and slaves to their Rus overlords once or twice a year.

The arrival of the Rus in the river valleys of Eastern Europe resembles the settlement of North America by European colonists in the 1600s and 1700s, although the American colonists enjoyed a far greater technological advantage. The two encounters had different outcomes: ultimately the American colonists created a society that disenfranchised the Amerindians, while the Rus intermarried with the indigenous peoples and adopted their languages and customs.

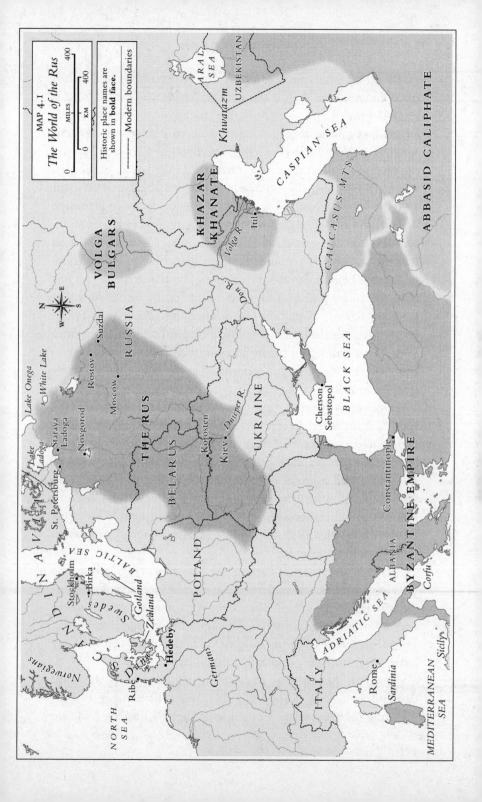

MAP 4.1
The World of the Rus

Historic place names are
shown in **bold face.**

------ Modern boundaries

0   400
MILES
0   400
KM

NORTH SEA

Norwegians

SCANDINAVIA

Danes

Ribe

Hedeby

Swedes

Stockholm

Birka

Gotland

Zealand

BALTIC SEA

Germans

POLAND

ITALY

Rome

Sardinia

Sicily

MEDITERRANEAN SEA

ADRIATIC SEA

ALBANIA

Corfu

BYZANTINE EMPIRE

Constantinople

BLACK SEA

Cherson
Sebastopol

UKRAINE

Kiev

Korosten

BELARUS

Dnieper R.

Don R.

THE RUS

RUSSIA

Moscow

Rostov

Suzdal

Novgorod

Staraya
Ladoga

St. Petersburg

Lake Ladoga

Lake Onega

White Lake

VOLGA BULGARS

KHAZAR KHANATE

Itil

Volga R.

CASPIAN SEA

CAUCASUS MTS.

ABBASID CALIPHATE

ARAL SEA

Khwarazm

UZBEKISTAN

N
W   E
S

By the late 700s and early 800s, the Rus warband leaders had made enough from the fur and slave trade that they started to send their earnings back to Scandinavia. Planned towns, built by chieftains who profited from the trade in Eastern Europe, sprang up in Sweden, Norway, and Denmark. The first cities arose to support the trade with Eastern Europe: Hedeby (on the border of modern Denmark and Germany) was the largest with a population between 1,000 and 1,500. Not as big, Ribe on the west coast of Denmark survives to this day, making it the oldest city in Scandinavia.

Birka, on the east coast of Sweden, some 20 miles (36 km) west of Stockholm, became the main launching point for those going into Eastern Europe. From there, the Rus traveled east just over 100 miles (160 km) to Staraya Ladoga, a city on the Lovat River in Russia. Its population included different groups: Finns, Balts, Slavs, and Scandinavians. Archeological finds of bones from squirrels, martins, and beaver alongside agricultural fields reveal that the early Rus engaged in farming at the same time that they trapped animals for their fur.

Bone and deer antler combs have confirmed the presence of the Rus. Muslim observers report that the Rus rarely bathed, yet both men and women combed their hair frequently. The combs found in Staraya Ladoga and its neighboring towns are nearly identical, suggesting that a group of Scandinavian craftsmen moved from settlement to settlement, carving combs for the Rus inhabitants. Like Andean metalworkers, these Scandinavians moved to a new region to practice their trade after hearing about opportunities outside their homelands.

In the initial phases of trading, the Rus didn't try to take over a certain region. At one settlement near the White Lake, for example, the Rus built a small settlement with only six to ten houses and no fortifications. Individual groups of Rus went into Eastern Europe in search of profits on their own, not at the behest of any ruler. Over time they gradually formed larger units.

The Rus moved into Eastern Europe because of the great demand for furs in Europe and the Middle East. Adam of Bremen, the historian who recorded what the Danish king told him about Vinland in 1076, bemoaned the desire among the Germans for "strange furs": the "odor of which has inoculated our world with the deadly poison of pride. . . . For right or wrong we hanker after a martenskin robe as much as for supreme happiness." Even in warmer climates, rulers accumulated thousands of fur robes, noted one tenth-century observer based in Baghdad.

The demand for slaves was also high, especially in the two biggest cities in Europe and the Middle East at the time—Constantinople, the capital of the Byzantine empire, and Baghdad, the capital of the Abbasid caliphate, in present-day Iraq. The residents of Constantinople and Baghdad used their wealth to purchase slaves, almost always people captured in raids on neighboring societies.

In the early 900s, a Muslim observer named Ibn Rusta noted that the Rus "treat their slaves well and dress them beautifully, because for them they are an article of trade." Adam of Bremen commented on the gold stored on the island of Zealand in Denmark, which Scandinavian pirates had accumulated from trading slaves. The Vikings, Adam said, "have no faith in one another, and as soon as one of them catches another, he mercilessly sells him into slavery." So many slaves came from Eastern Europe that the meaning of the Greek word for "Slav" (*sklabos*) shifted sometime in the 1000s from its original meaning, "Slav," to take on the broader meaning of "slave," whether of Slavic or another origin.

Profiting from the slave and fur trade, the Rus warband leaders acquired ever-larger followings whom they fed, clothed, and rewarded with a share of the loot from raiding. New territory offered ambitious men a chance to rise. If they made fortunes, they could attract their own retinues and become chieftains.

The Rus came into Eastern Europe traveling mainly in small dugout canoes equipped with oars, which were light enough to carry from one river to the next. No high mountains blocked them. The rivers of Eastern Europe all traversed relatively flat terrain, making it possible to portage boats overland where the rivers gave out or where the rapids were too rough.

The Dnieper was the only continuous waterway, but it had

dangerous rapids. One of the most dangerous stretches lay near Kiev, which the Rus had to pass to get to the Black Sea. There the river drops 108 feet (33 m) over the course of 38.5 miles (62 km). In a particularly difficult stretch, a Byzantine observer noted, the Rus had to walk overland for six miles leading their "slaves in their chains" before resuming boat travel.

The earliest written description of the Rus comes from Ibn Khurradadhbih (820–911), a Persian official who identified the Rus as one of the fair-haired peoples living in the lands of the Saqaliba, the Arabic catchall term for the peoples from Northern and Eastern Europe. ("Saqaliba" is also the origin of one of the many words for "slave" in Arabic.) "They carry beaver hides, black fox pelts, and swords from the farthest reaches of the Saqaliba to the Sea of Rum," or the Black Sea. Beaver and fox pelts commanded the highest prices because of the density of their fur.

Ibn Khurradadhbih didn't mention slaves, but he did remark on how advanced the Rus swords were. They were essential to the Rus ability to capture slaves and to exact furs from the residents of Eastern Europe, and they also commanded high prices at markets.

Rus swords excavated by archeologists fall into two groups; those smelted from locally worked iron containing many impurities, and those made from ingots of steel produced in crucibles, or small airtight molds. Several sources in Arabic describe the complex technology of making steel from iron. They reveal that the world-famous Damascus steel was not actually made in Syria. The Rus imported the crucible steel they used from other places, including Afghanistan.

Some of the highest-quality swords, with the greatest percentage of carbon, bear the name Ulfberht, likely the name of the smith who made them, with a plus sign before the *u*, after the final *t*, and between the *h* and the *t*, a practice that no one has yet explained successfully. About 100 Ulfberht swords survive today, but their quality is uneven; some contain a high percentage of carbon and have very sharp edges, while others with a lower percentage are much duller. After 1000, swordmakers continued to produce swords that still combined the letters of Ulfberht and plus signs but with a higher number of misspellings, a clear sign that the valuable Ulfberht brand was being ripped off.

Armed with steel swords and daggers, the Rus followed the different rivers of Eastern Europe south until they reached the Black Sea. From there they opened up new overland routes to today's Sevastopol, then called Cherson. The trip down the Dnieper took some twenty days.

Cherson was a major Byzantine outpost in the 900s with gridded streets and an imposing city wall. Herders and shepherds living in the grasslands to the north led their horses and sheep to the same city markets where Byzantine traders proffered silks, glassware, glazed pottery, metalware, wine, and olive oil while fishermen sold the day's catch. Forest dwellers sold furs, honey, and beeswax. Candles made from beeswax offered the highest-quality lighting in the medieval world; oils were cheaper but gave off an unpleasant smell, as did tallow candles.

Such markets were the perfect place to sell furs and slaves, and Cherson lay directly on the Rus route to Constantinople, a voyage across the Black Sea that took six days. The Rus traveling onward to Baghdad chose between two routes: overland from the Black Sea through the territory of the Khazars to the Caspian Sea, or south along the Volga to the important trading center of Itil.

There, Ibn Khurradadhbih explains in his *Book of Routes and Realms*, the Rus posed as Christians because Abbasid law allowed peoples of the book, Christians and Jews, to pay lower taxes than other non-Muslims. This shows that at least some Rus knew of Christianity but hadn't yet converted.

An eyewitness account from 922 contains more information about the traditional religious practices of the Rus than any other source. Ibn Fadlan was sent by the Abbasid caliph in response to the Bulgar ruler's request for a visit from someone knowledgeable about Islam. Justly famous, Ibn Fadlan's grisly, gripping portrait details the group sex and human sacrifice that occurred during the Rus funeral for "one of their great men." At one town in the middle Volga, Ibn Fadlan came upon a party of Rus traders cremating their chieftain along with his "slave girl" companion.

The family of the deceased leader asked for volunteers to be buried with him, and one slave girl agreed. (Ibn Fadlan doesn't explain why.) When the time for the funeral came, the slave girl drank a cup of alcohol. Then "six men entered the yurt. They all had intercourse with the slave girl." Ibn Fadlan doesn't judge. He reports what he saw dispassionately. Perhaps he didn't realize that he was observing a religious fertility rite, in which devotees of the Norse god of war, Odin, and the goddess of fertility, Freya, engaged in sex.

Then a "gloomy and corpulent but neither young nor old" priestess helped to prepare the burial ship for burning. Calling her the "Angel of Death," Ibn Fadlan summarizes her duties: "It is her responsibility to sew the chieftain's garments and prepare him properly, and it is she who kills the female slaves." Four men positioned the girl next to the deceased and held her down. The Angel of Death "placed a rope around her neck with the ends crossing one another and handed it to two of the men to pull on it. She advanced with a broad-bladed dagger and began to thrust it in and out between her ribs, here and there, while the two men throttled her with the rope until she died."

The deceased's closest kin then set fire to the funeral pyre on which they'd placed the boat and the bodies of the chieftain and the slave girl. Scandinavian funerary practices varied; in this instance, the Rus burned a ship laden with offerings for the dead, but archeologists have also found ships with their grave goods buried intact.

Rus merchants requested the assistance of their deities in conducting business. Ibn Fadlan reports that, when a trader arrived at the trading post of Itil, close to where the Volga River entered the Caspian Sea, he made a donation. He then prostrated himself before a large wooden statue of a deity surrounded by many smaller figurines, and prayed: "Lord, I have come from a distant land, with such and such a number of female slaves and such and such a number of sable pelts."

The merchant then requested of the deity, "I want you to bless me with a rich merchant with many dinars and dirhams who will buy from me whatever I wish and not haggle over any price I set." Dinars were coins of gold; dirhams, of silver. Both could be melted down to make bands for the arms and neck. Ibn Fadlan reports that the Rus chieftains gave their wives a silver neckband for each 10,000 silver dirham coins they had amassed.

Coins can reveal a great deal about the past, especially in societies with few written records such as Eastern Europe and Scandinavia at this time. If it weren't for coins, we would have no sense at all of the massive transfer of wealth to the Rus from Constantinople and the Islamic world that paid for the imported furs and slaves. Hundreds of hoards, some with over 10,000 coins, have surfaced in Northern and Eastern Europe. The Rus used containers of pottery, glass, metal, or birchbark to bury silver in the ground as temporary safety deposit boxes but, for whatever reason, they left many of these deposits in the ground until archeologists excavated them.

The largest stockpile of coins ever found in Scandinavia was buried sometime after 870 on the Swedish island of Gotland, some 125 miles (200 km) south of Stockholm in the Baltic Sea. Archeologists working in 1999 located a hoard that contained 14,295 coins, dating from 539 to 871, and 486 armbands, made from melted-down coins. Chieftains rewarded their followers with both coins and armbands. Altogether the silver artifacts weighed 147 pounds (67 kg). Some of the coins were intact while others had been cut into pieces.

Once the silver had been melted down and was no longer shaped like a coin, the only way to determine the value of a given item was to weigh it. To do so, the Rus adopted a new tool from the Islamic world: balance scales. These have surfaced all over Scandinavia and Eastern Europe—certain evidence of an early technology transfer. The new scales didn't displace any workers; no one in Scandinavia had weighed silver before. They proved immensely popular because they provided a new, much-needed service, just as cell phones do today.

Over time the Rus gradually stopped melting down coins to make armbands. A later hoard from the same island of Gotland, buried just after 991, reflects the growing trust in coins. With no armbands, it contained 1,911 silver coins: 1,298 with legends in Arabic, 591 from Germany, 11 from the Volga Bulgars, 6 from England, 3 from Byzantium, and 2 from Bohemia. These coins offer a valuable snapshot of the main trading partners of the Rus, information not available from documents. The Islamic world was much more important to the Rus than Western Europe. Around 950, the Samanid empire, a breakaway state in Central Asia, replaced the Abbasids as the makers of the purest silver coins.

How great was the transfer of wealth from the Islamic world to Scandinavia and the Rus territories? Consider first the astonishing quantity of excavated silver dirham coins minted between 670 and 1090: 80,000 in Sweden, 37,000 in Poland, and 207,000 for Russia, Belarus, and Ukraine. A recent survey puts the total number of Islamic silver coins found from the ninth and tenth centuries at 400,000. Of course, these are only the coins archeologists have recovered; the original number of buried coins must have been many times higher—say one million—because so many coins have since been melted down or lost.

How many slaves could one million coins buy? One hundred thousand over the course of the eleventh century, or roughly one thousand per year.

In the late 900s, the Islamic world began to suffer a region-wide shortage of silver. As a result, the amount of silver coming into Scandinavia from the Rus sale of furs and slaves tapered off. A few smaller hoards contain silver coins minted in the late 900s or early 1000s, but none dated after 1013.

The coins unearthed in Scandinavia also contained English coins, an important reminder that the Norse continued to raid the British Isles for centuries after their initial attack in 793. Sticking to their usual playbook, once the Norse had subjugated a different place in the British Isles, they demanded protection money. Taking control of large chunks of central England, the Norse implemented the laws of Denmark across an area known as the Danelaw.

For two centuries, from the 850s to the 1060s, neither the Norse nor the English side gained lasting control, but the Norse king Cnut the Great came closest to unifying Denmark, Norway, and England. In 1016, he defeated the English and in 1018 exacted 82,500 pounds of silver from his English subjects so that he could reward his followers. (The pound then weighed less than a modern pound, so this was just over 30,000 kg.) In 1028, Cnut took the title "king of all England, Denmark and Norway, and part of Sweden." But after his death in 1035, the throne of England reverted to Edward the Confessor, and England was governed separately from Denmark and Norway.

One hoard from the Swedish island of Gotland has produced twenty-four coins from Spain, confirmation of Viking activities in the Mediterranean, which was as far south as they went in Europe. Archeologists have interpreted with great ingenuity the slim evidence of the Norse in the south. For example, a site on the Atlantic island of Madeira has produced mouse bones dating to between 900 and 1036. Since the DNA of those mice is closer to that of Scandinavian and German mice, archeologists have concluded that the Scandinavians arrived on Madeira before the Portuguese did in the 1400s.

Written records also document the voyages of the Norse to Sicily, where they arrived around 900. After expelling the reigning monarchs, their descendant Roger II (reigned 1130–1154), ruled as the Norman king of the island in the 1100s and was famous for providing financial support to Christian and Muslim artists and scholars alike. Roger's court is where al-Idrisi produced his round silver map of Afro-Eurasia that measured 2 yards (2 m) in diameter.

At the height of the coin exports, some of the Rus traveling south ended up in Constantinople as mercenaries. They were the "Varangians," an old Norse term that began to appear in 950 and meant "men of the pledge," and by extension, Scandinavians. The Byzantine emperor had a separate division of Varangian guards, who were famed for their ferocity. Two of these Varangian guards may have scratched graffiti written in Old Norse runes onto a balcony in the Hagia Sophia cathedral (some experts doubt their authenticity).

Other Scandinavians were simply adventurers and seekers of fortune.

One, a typical warband leader called Ingvar the Far Traveler, is the hero of his own saga, a narrative that recounts multiple battles with dragons and giants. Ingvar and his companions sailed down the Dnieper River, crossed the Black Sea, traversed the Caucasus Mountains, and finally reached the Caspian Sea. Aspiring to be king of his own realm, he is all of twenty in the saga, an indication of how the young could rise in the rough-and-tumble of warband society.

Eventually Ingvar falls ill, as do half of his men, and dies at the age of twenty-five, somewhere in Central Asia, most likely the Khwarazm region of modern Uzbekistan. This was the farthest point to the east that the Norse reached. Before dying, Ingvar asks his followers "to take my body back to Sweden," a request that explains the presence of twenty-six runestone graves of his followers in central Sweden.

The world of plundering chieftains slowly gave way to tax-collecting monarchies around the year 1000. Kings rewarded their followers with land, not loot. An early example was William the Conqueror, whose ancestors had come to France in the early 900s as pirates, collected protection money, and eventually became the Norman kings of England, events depicted in the world-famous Bayeux Tapestry.

The 1066 invasion of England marked the end of the Viking Age. Indeed, William's administration in England implemented the same changes taking place in multiple Scandinavian lands, in which rulers rewarded their followers with specific lands, and the farming revenue made it possible for the new landowners to pay taxes on their holdings.

When Prince Vladimir, the leader who chose Christianity for the Rus, came to power, a comparable shift occurred in the Rus domain. The multiple warbands of earlier times gave way to a new kind of ruling structure, shared leadership by multiple members of a charismatic clan. Here we do not have to tease out what happened from coins because we can consult a detailed source, the *Russian Primary Chronicle*, which provides a year-by-year history of the Rus princes. It was written down sometime between 1050 and 1113.

The entry for 860–862 explains how the first Rus princes came to power. The Scandinavians living in Eastern Europe "went overseas to the Varangian Rus" and invited three brothers to come and govern them. The brothers founded the Rurikid dynasty. Note that the *Primary Chronicle* explicitly identifies the new overlords from across the sea as foreign. The arrival of the Rurikids didn't bring an end to the era of warbands. Succession from one ruler to the next was just as chaotic and contested as before. A free-for-all broke out each time a Rurikid ruler died until a victor emerged.

The Rus formed a formidable navy by 941, we learn from Liudprand of Cremona (920–972), an acerbic Italian envoy. Sent by the Ottonian kings of Germany to Constantinople, Liudprand wasn't in the city in 941, when the Rus attacked, but his stepfather told him about the 1,000-ship fleet led by Prince Igor, the leader of the Rus who had come to power in 912.

To defend the capital, the Byzantine emperor retrofitted fifteen warships so that they could shoot Greek fire, the most powerful of the Byzantine weapons. The Byzantines kept the ingredients secret for centuries: Greek fire contained petroleum, and like modern napalm, it continued to burn even after it came into contact with water. With the Byzantine vessels spewing Greek fire, the Rus survived only by jumping ship and swimming to shore.

Constantinople impressed Liudprand of Cremona as the most advanced city of his day (he never visited Baghdad). The city's wonders included mechanical birds and lions placed around the throne of Emperor Constantine VII (reigned 913–959). The varying species of birds sang different melodies, and gold-plated lions "seemed to guard him [Constantine], and, striking the ground with their tails, they emitted a roar with mouths open and tongues flickering." Liudprand was especially fascinated with the king's throne, which rose to the ceiling by means of a hidden device (probably a pulley).

In 945, the Rus signed a treaty with the Byzantines. The Rus leader Igor still had to consult with his relatives, a sign that he had not yet become a full-fledged monarch. Because Rus leaders shared power with others, historians call them "prince" rather than "king." The treaty also reveals that some of the Rus had been baptized as Christians and were no longer posing as Christians simply to obtain a tax break.

Igor's realm differed from agrarian monarchies of the time, such as France, in that the Rus princes had only enough officials to tax commerce, but not agriculture. Taxing commerce involved posting officials at all transport nodes, a relatively straightforward task, whereas taxing agriculture required a larger, more established bureaucracy.

Despite their defeat at Constantinople, the Rurikids were generally successful in their raids against Byzantium, but they didn't control the Dnieper Valley. In 945, the Derevlians, a people based to the east of Kiev, rose up against the Rus, refused to pay tribute, and killed Igor. To avenge her husband, Igor's widow, Olga, led a successful military campaign against them, enslaved or killed all the survivors, and destroyed their capital, as excavations at modern-day Korosten in western Ukraine have confirmed.

Olga also changed the way that the Rus collected tribute. Rather than having the Rus officials visit individual tribes to collect a share of different products each winter, she ordered the Rus subjects to proceed to local trading posts. There they paid furs and other forest products directly to her officials, which was a major step in strengthening the Rus monarchy because it regularized the princes' income stream.

Olga was one of the first Rurikids to convert to Christianity. While serving as regent for Igor's son Sviatoslav between 945 and 961, when he was too young to rule on his own, she chose to be baptized at Constantinople. The *Primary Chronicle* reports that the Byzantine emperor Constantine proposed to her. Her refusal was clever: "How can you marry me, after yourself baptizing me and calling me your daughter? For among Christians that is unlawful, as you yourself must know." Constantine apparently took no offense since he quickly admitted defeat: "Olga, you have outwitted me." The two players may not have spoken these exact words, but Olga certainly converted to the Byzantine form of Christianity, and she definitely never married Constantine.

When Olga requested that Constantine dispatch missionaries to the Rus to teach them about Christianity, he refused. She then asked the German king Otto I, who also took no action. This sequence shows that the Rus looked first to the Byzantines and then to the Ottonians for help. Some of Olga's subjects in Kiev were already Christian, as mid-tenth-century graves of women who were buried with crosses around their necks indicate. When her son Sviatoslav I succeeded to the throne in 963, Olga stepped down as regent, and Sviatoslav I refused to convert.

The two cities of Novgorod and Kiev became the most important cities in Sviatoslav's realm. Novgorod, in the north, was easy to defend; the first citadel, or kremlin, was built on its walls around 1000. To the south, situated on a high bank on the western side of the Dnieper, Kiev took off as the key point for the north–south trade. By 1000 several thousand people lived there.

Like many warband leaders before him, Sviatoslav left instructions regarding which son should succeed him as ruler after his death. He specified that Vladimir, the child of a slave girl, should rule in Novgorod and that Vladimir's half-brother Iaropolk should take over in Kiev. Still, as was so often the case, the peaceful succession he planned didn't occur. A vicious power struggle broke out among his sons. In 980, after eight years of fighting, Vladimir and an army of Scandinavian mercenaries invaded Kiev, killed his half-brother, and gained control of the city.

Only then did Vladimir's precarious position prompt him to consider converting to Christianity, a religion he knew from his grandmother Olga. As the child of an unfree housekeeper, he desired legitimacy, and he needed to overcome the blow to his reputation that came from murdering his brother. Vladimir had other problems as well. His accession to power coincided with a financial crisis: the Europe-wide silver shortage after 1000. Vladimir faced declining revenues from the slave trade, which had been a major income stream for the Rus.

In his quest to gain support, Vladimir put up statues to six traditional Rus deities, including Perun, the god of lightning. Yet Vladimir realized that, because his subjects had no belief system in common, they lacked a shared identity, which weakened his hold over them. A political rival could easily challenge Vladimir's rule by rallying his supporters around a competing deity.

Vladimir began to look for a major religion that could command the loyalty of all his subjects. Once he selected the right religion and required his subjects to convert to it, he could ban the worship of other deities and head off any challenges to his government.

Vladimir wasn't alone. Other monarchs were sending envoys to learn about the religious practices of their neighbors. When they chose a religion for their realms, these monarchs knew little of a given church's teachings, perhaps just what a single missionary had told them. Still, the rulers devoted considerable thought to the question of which religion to adopt for themselves and their subjects.

They had much to gain by the right choice. In addition to the benefits of worshipping a more powerful divinity and joining a larger church, they also hoped to ally with other rulers who supported the same faith. Increased contacts led to the clustering of conversions around the year 1000 and to the formation of large religious blocs surprisingly similar to those that exist for trade and defense even today.

In 986, according to the *Primary Chronicle*, Vladimir received envoys from four neighbors: the Jewish Khazars, the Muslim Bulgars, the Roman Christian Ottonian rulers of Germany, and the Byzantine Christians in Constantinople.

Vladimir knew something about Judaism, as he revealed in his response to the envoys from the Khazars, who'd converted to Judaism perhaps a hundred years earlier. The Khazars controlled a wide swath of land between the upper reaches of the Don and the lower reaches of the Volga. Apparently Judaism offered the Khazars a middle ground between the Christianity of the Byzantine empire and the Islam of the Abbasid caliphate because both Christian and Islamic teachings acknowledged Judaism as a legitimate religion. Still, Judaism was a strange choice. There were no powerful Jewish allies nearby (although some earlier rulers in northern Iraq, Yemen, and North Africa had converted to Judaism). In fact, there were no other Jewish states anywhere in Eurasia.

The Khazars had a dual monarchy. One king, called the beg, was in charge of the day-to-day workings of the government while a second ruler, called the kaghan, was the ceremonial head. It is possible that the king of the Khazars—but not the kaghan—converted to Judaism sometime between 800 and 810, but the conversion didn't affect his subjects.

In 837–838, when it seems likely that an individual kaghan converted, the Khazar mints issued three new types of coins. The Moses dirhams are the most famous of these coins even though only seven survive today. Made of silver and inscribed in Arabic, they are nearly identical copies of the dirham coins issued by the Abbasids. The only difference is that they say, "Moses is the Messenger of God"—not "Muhammad is the Messenger of God."

The process of conversion among the Khazars to Judaism was gradual and only partial; the Persian geographer Ibn al-Faqih, writing in 902 or 903, noted, "all of the Khazars are Jews, but they have been Judaicized recently." Archeologists have searched in vain for evidence of Judaism among ordinary people. Going through thousands of mud bricks with various graffiti and drawings on them, they've found no menorahs or other Jewish symbols.

Historians sometimes face this type of situation when the written record says one thing, but the archeological record produces little to substantiate it. If the written record is correct, the Khazars formed the largest Jewish state in existence between the destruction of the Temple of ancient Israel in AD 70 and the founding of modern Israel in 1948.

The Khazars were sufficiently observant that the authors of the *Russian Primary Chronicle* report that a group of Khazars tried to convert Vladimir to Judaism around 986 with these talking points: Judaism's teachings included "circumcision, not eating pork or hare, and observing the Sabbath." The taboo on hare meat is a typical Jewish dietary observance, and it's plausible that the Khazars didn't eat rabbit. Archeologists have found many fertility amulets made from hare's feet, suggesting that the Khazars venerated hares.

The Khazar envoys explained that as Jews they didn't live in their native land of Jerusalem because "God was angry at our forefathers, and scattered us among the gentiles on account of our sins." At this, Vladimir summarily rejected their overture: "If God loved you and your faith, you wouldn't be thus dispersed in foreign lands. Do you expect us to accept that fate also?" Vladimir's response shows that he knew that Jerusalem wasn't governed by Jews (the Fatimid dynasty of Egypt who controlled the city at the time were Shi'ite Muslims).

Vladimir didn't want to convert to the religion of any power whose strength was declining. He was seeking an ally more powerful than himself. In the following year, when he sent representatives to the various countries whose emissaries had urged him to take their religion as his own, he didn't even bother to send a representative to the Khazars.

The next candidate, the Volga Bulgars, were much more powerful. In 986, the Bulgar emissaries explained to Vladimir that Muhammad "instructed them to practice circumcision, to eat no pork, to drink no wine." After death, the Bulgar envoys continued, Muhammad promised to give each male believer "seventy fair women. He may choose one fair one, and upon that woman will Muhammad confer the charms of them all, and she shall be his wife. Muhammad promises that one may then satisfy every desire." The Arabic word translated here as "fair woman" literally means the bright whiteness of the eye in contrast to an exceptionally black pupil, a quality believed to be possessed by only the most beautiful virgins.

The pro-Christian author of the *Primary Chronicle* intended the description of heaven's sexual pleasures as a slur. He adds that the Volga Bulgars "also spoke other false things which out of modesty may not be written down." When the Bulgar envoys urged Vladimir to convert to Islam, the Rus prince summarily refused, explaining that "drinking is the joy of the Rus. We cannot exist without that pleasure."

The takeaway from the *Primary Chronicle* is clear: neither the

Jewish Khazars nor the Muslim Bulgars were strong enough to offer Vladimir any real benefits if he converted to their religions.

A third delegation came from the Roman Christian Ottonian kings of Germany. They controlled parts of Italy, including Rome, and appointed the pope. The Germans relayed the pope's view: "Your country is like our country, but your faith is not as ours." This truncated conversation must have been inserted into the *Primary Chronicle* at a later date because it suggests a rift between the church in Rome and the church in Constantinople. In fact, in 986, the two branches of the Christian church in Rome and Constantinople were still unified.

The *Primary Chronicle* doesn't present an accurate description of events as they actually unfolded. It's obvious that the account of Vladimir's conversion has been cut apart and awkwardly joined to the different years of the annals. The inclusion of the Roman Christians in Germany is most likely to be a later interpolation, and the too neat tripartite scheme of Orthodoxy, Islam, and Judaism also raises suspicions.

But even if the entire account is an invented story written to explain what happened—whose religion could Vladimir accept if not that of his immediate neighbor, the Byzantines?—it still shows the types of information about religion circulating soon after 1000, when the *Primary Chronicle* took shape. And we do have outside confirmation—from an Islamic account—that a Rus ruler named "Vladimir" sent four kinsmen to the ruler of Khwarazm asking for information about Islam. This external source shows that Vladimir actively sought information about the various belief systems of his neighbors as he wrestled with the decision of which one to convert to.

The *Primary Chronicle* devotes much more space to the teachings of the Byzantine church, as related by a scholar who gives a full account of creation, Jesus's crucifixion, and the Day of Judgment. Known as the Philosopher's Speech, this was clearly added to the text later by the editors. Still, it underlines an important reality: as long as Christian texts hadn't been translated into Slavonic, all new religious teachings had to be conveyed orally. After listening to the speech and asking a few questions, Vladimir responded, "I shall wait yet a little longer," again postponing the choice of a religion for his realm.

In 987, after consulting with his nobles, and city elders, Vladimir dispatched a team of ten advisors first to the Volga Bulgars, then to Germany, and finally to Constantinople. They rejected the Islam of the Volga Bulgars and the Roman Christianity of the Germans.

Constantinople, in contrast, overwhelmed them. After their visit to the cathedral of Hagia Sophia, they reported: "We knew not whether we were in heaven or on earth. For on earth there is no such splendor or such beauty, and we are at a loss how to describe it. We only know that God dwells there among men, and their service is fairer than the ceremonies of other nations. For we cannot forget that beauty." Despite their unanimous counsel to choose the Christianity of the Byzantines, Vladimir still hesitated.

The *Primary Chronicle* presents Vladimir's decision to convert to Byzantine Christianity as a sequence of four events. First, at Cherson his armies defeat the forces of Bardas Phokas, a claimant to the Byzantine throne. Second, he loses his sight. Third, he is baptized and his sight returns. Fourth and finally, he marries Anna, the sister of the Byzantine ruler Basil II.

No contemporary observer in either Byzantium or Germany viewed Vladimir's conversion to Christianity as a major event; to them, it was a minor local matter between the Byzantines and the Rus.

From our vantage point today, though, Vladimir's conversion marked a key step in the formation of the Christian world. Vladimir's realm had five million people living in an area of more than 400,000 square miles (1,000,000 sq km), twice the size of France. With Vladimir's switch to Christianity, Eastern Europe turned to face Byzantium—not Jerusalem, Rome, or Mecca. The Rus maintained intensive economic and cultural ties with Western Europe, but they had only one sacral center, and it was in Byzantium.

Each time a ruler such as Vladimir made a decision to convert to a new religion, the borders of the different religious blocs shifted. The chart below lists some of the rulers who chose a religion for their realm around the year 1000. In almost every instance the rulers chose to associate with one or several of their neighbors; the peoples with whom they shared the new faith became their military allies as well as primary trade partners. Although they continued to have contact with rulers of other faiths, they had closer ties to their coreligionists, and they often conceived of the world as divided into religious blocs.

People no longer had a single identity as coming from one locality. They (and this included everyone who stayed at home) began to think of their native regions as part of religious blocs, and so they started to identify with much larger groups of people, a key step in globalization.

CONVERSIONS AROUND THE YEAR 1000

Year	People	Ruler	Converted to
early 900s	Khazars	(name not known)	Judaism
early 900s	Volga Bulgars	(name not known)	Islam
955	Karakhanids	Satuq Bugra Khan	Islam
ca. 960	Danes	Harald Bluetooth	Roman Christianity
985	Seljuks	Seljuk ibn Duqaq	Islam
988–89	Rus	Vladimir	Byzantine Orthodoxy
990s	Norwegians	Olav Tryggvason Olav Haraldsson	Roman Christianity
991	Polish	Mieszko I	Roman Christianity
999–1000	Icelanders	Althing Assembly	Roman Christianity
after 1000	Ghanaians	(name not known)	Islam

Sources: Anders Winroth, *Conversion of Scandinavia*, 112–18, 162–63; Andreas Kaplony, "The Conversion of the Turks," in *Islamisation de l'Asie Centrale*, 319–38; Barbara H. Rosenwein, *A Short History of the Middle Ages*, 86; Peter B. Golden, "The Karakhanids and Early Islam," in *The Cambridge History of Early Inner Asia*, 362.

These conversions weren't all to Christianity. To the east of Vladimir's realm was the territory of the Turkic Oghuz tribe near the Aral Sea. When Ibn Fadlan crossed through their lands in 921–922, he noticed that the Oghuz recognized Tengri as the Heavenly Supreme Power and frequently consulted shamans. He also observed that the weather was unusually cold, a sign that the regional climate was cooling just as Europe was entering the Medieval Warming Period. By the late 900s many of the Oghuz had settled just east of the Aral Sea, where their leader, Seljuk ibn Duqaq, converted to Islam. One source reports that Seljuk explained the conversion saying, "If we don't enter the faith of the people of the country in which we desire [to live] and make a pact with them (or conform to their customs) . . . we shall be a small and solitary people."

Seljuk's followers adopted his name as the name of their tribe and came to be known as the Seljuks. Although few sources about the early history of this people exist, Seljuk ibn Duqaq seems to have converted to Islam because, just like Vladimir, he wanted to become more powerful. At the time of his conversion around 1000, his people were just one tribe among many in Central Asia, but in the mid-1000s, under the leadership of his grandsons, the Seljuk dynasty became one of the world's major Islamic powers.

Several Scandinavian rulers converted to Christianity at this time. Like Vladimir, the Danish king Harald Bluetooth (910–985) was raised as a non-Christian. In the 960s he united Denmark and gained temporary control of Norway. Recognizing the power of Christian monotheism as a unifying force for his new kingdom, he made the decision to convert. (Intel and Ericsson engineers chose to call their new technology "Bluetooth" because it brought computers and mobile phones together just as Harald had unified Denmark and Norway.)

Once a ruler converted to a major religion, he gained access to clerics who could assist him in governing. Because they could read, write, and do math, the clergy helped monarchs such as Vladimir gain greater control. Those skills became increasingly

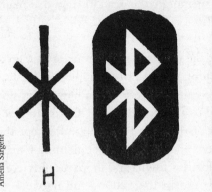

Amelia Sargent

Swedish telecom engineers created the Bluetooth logo by combining the runes for the two initials, H and B, of King Harald Bluetooth.

important around 1000, especially as rulers needed literate officials to help them draft documents and numerate staff to count the taxes they collected.

Sometime after Vladimir was baptized in 988 or 989, his subjects received mass baptism in the Dnieper. For the first century after Vladimir's conversion, only the imperial family and nobles were regularly married within the church. In the Rus areas beyond the bishops' seats, ordinary people accepted the teachings of the new religion more slowly. They had contact with government officials only once or twice a year, when they submitted fur tribute. Because those who were baptized en masse received no religious instruction, they continued their worship of traditional deities.

Vladimir appointed bishops to the different parts of his realm. Kiev became the equivalent of an archdiocese, under the patriarch of Constantinople. The mid-Dnieper region was the core area for the new religion, which was most active within a 150-mile (250 km) area around Kiev.

Some Christian practices had great appeal. Vladimir exhumed the bodies of his two brothers Oleg and Iaropolk, his rivals for the throne, so that he could baptize their remains. This wasn't standard Christian worship—in fact, the church forbade such a practice.

But Vladimir chose to commemorate the dead in ways that made sense to him and his subjects.

Vladimir's baptism was just the first step in the process of Christianization, which usually took centuries to complete. This was true in each country whose ruler converted to a new belief system. Vladimir's subjects had to abandon their pre-Christian practices, absorb the teachings of the new religion, and accept the religious leadership of bishops and clergy to become fully Christian. In the 1100s, smaller fortress towns and more recently conquered localities converted, and in the 1200s a full network of parishes took shape. Byzantine craftsmen came in large numbers to build new churches all over the Rus realm, and eventually the entire populace accepted the teachings of Christianity. This was globalization at work in the year 1000: once a ruler converted, even his subjects who remained on their farms had to adopt the religious practices of a church whose center was located far from their homes.

When Vladimir converted, the Byzantine church was much more powerful than the Vatican in Rome. But in just two centuries the Roman church replaced Byzantium as the most powerful in the Christian world, and the pope became far more influential than the patriarch of the Byzantine church in Constantinople. Between 1000 and 1200 Western Europe experienced a massive surge of growth just as the Byzantine empire was losing territory. These changes transformed the relationship between the Vatican and Constantinople. And once Rome became the center of the Christian church, it never lost that position.

In the fourth century, after receiving recognition from the Roman emperor, the Christian church had centers in five cities: Antioch, Alexandria, Jerusalem, Constantinople, and Rome. The top-ranking clerics in the first four cities all had the same title of patriarch; the bishop of Rome was known as pope. As the four patriarchs and the pope in Rome had the same rank, no individual served as the head of the Christian church.

After Alexandria, Antioch, and Jerusalem came under Muslim

rule in the 630s and 640s, their patriarchs continued to guide the Christians in their flocks. Yet because the pope in Rome and the patriarch in Constantinople presided over Christian churches in non-Muslim areas, they became the two most powerful Christian clerics. When Vladimir converted to Orthodoxy, certain practices of the Roman and Byzantine churches differed. The Eastern liturgy was read in Greek; the Roman, in Latin. Eastern clergy were accustomed to having beards; Western clergy were not. Eastern congregants ate bread leavened with yeast at Communion; Western congregants, unleavened bread.

In 1053, the Norman rulers of southern Italy, whose ancestors were Norse, attacked the Byzantine lands nearby, and the pope, sensing an opportunity to increase his standing, counterattacked and ended up being taken prisoner. One might think that sharing a common enemy—the Normans—would bring Rome and Byzantium together, but the opposite occurred.

After his release, in 1054, the pope sent two letters (one 17,000 words long) to the patriarch in Constantinople. Rejecting the view that Rome and Constantinople were equal, the pope maintained that the Roman church was actually the mother church to her daughters, the churches of Jerusalem, Antioch, Alexandria, and Constantinople. As the war of words escalated between hardliners on both sides, the pope excommunicated the Eastern patriarch, and the patriarch retaliated by excommunicating the papal envoy. Yet, for all the acrimony, contemporary observers didn't see the breach of 1054 as permanent.

The conflict between the two churches came just as the Byzantine empire was hemorrhaging territory. In 1071, the Seljuks defeated Byzantium in the Battle of Manzikert in eastern Turkey and went on to conquer much of the breadbasket of the Byzantine empire in Anatolia. Equally devastating, and in the same year, was the Norman victory at the city of Bari on the east coast of Italy, which led to the loss of all Byzantine territory in southern Italy.

Even so, at this point, the Eastern church in Constantinople was still the focus of the Christian world. The church in Rome was mired in conflict: the German king Henry IV so strongly objected to Pope Gregory VII's attempts to increase his own authority that the king invaded Rome in 1084 and replaced the existing pope with a new pope, whom historians call the antipope.

It took 120 years (between 1084 and 1204) for the center of the Christian world to move from Constantinople to Rome. The shift came at a time when the Rus leaders didn't involve themselves in Western Europe. The events are so complicated, and the players so many, that it's better to focus on two key developments to get a sense of what happened. First we'll look at the city of Constantinople and learn what made the city's residents so angry at the expatriate Italians living there. Then we'll shift to a broader canvas and see how the Crusades contributed to the strengthening of Rome and the near-destruction of Constantinople.

The history of the Italian community in Constantinople illustrates another aspect of globalization: a sizable group of foreigners came to a city to do business, established households (often with local women), and thoroughly antagonized everyone around them. The trouble all began in 1081, a decade after the defeat at Manzikert, when the Byzantine emperor asked the Venetian merchants in Constantinople for help fighting the Normans in Albania.

At this time, several Italian republics were extremely prosperous and commanded powerful armies, and the Venetians were the wealthiest of all. In exchange for their assistance, the Byzantine emperor granted Venetian merchants the right to trade almost everywhere in the empire. In addition, he completely exempted the Venetians from all commercial taxes.

Later Byzantine emperors realized that they'd given too much to the Venetians, but whenever they tried to scale back these privileges, the Venetians attacked, forcing the emperors to back down. Hoping to empower rivals to the Venetians, the emperor offered merchants from Pisa and Genoa their own residential districts in Constantinople, just next to that of the Venetians. He also granted them tax breaks, but none as generous as those the Venetians enjoyed.

The Venetian merchants behaved no differently than modern businesspeople who cling to preferential tax treatment in free trade zones. They formed trading enterprises far larger than any run by Byzantines. As the population of Venetian expatriates in Constantinople neared 10,000, the Byzantine Emperor Manuel granted them an even larger district in the city in 1148.

Soon frequent street fights broke out between the privileged Venetians and the resentful locals. In one incident in 1149 on the island of Corfu, a marketplace skirmish escalated into a major battle. When the Byzantine navy managed to drive the Venetians away, the Venetians proceeded to a port on a neighboring island where they seized the emperor's prize warship. Once on board, they staged a mock coronation ceremony with an Ethiopian playing the role of the emperor. The skit had clear racial implications: the Byzantine emperor Manuel was known for his dark complexion.

The situation continued to worsen, with tensions arising among the Pisans, Genoese, and Venetians. In 1171 the Venetians went on a rampage in the Genoese quarter. The Byzantine emperor retaliated by arresting all the Venetians in the city (women and children, too) and confiscating their property.

Tensions continued to simmer and ten years later, they exploded. At this time there were about 60,000 Italians, mostly from Pisa and Genoa (the Venetians had either fled ten years earlier or were in prison). During the struggle between the emperor and a rival to the throne, one group of local residents rioted and killed thousands of Italians in what came to be called the Massacre of the Latins.

Even though the city's residents and the expats were all Christian, the clergy of the Orthodox church encouraged their followers to target the Italian-speaking Catholic clerics. After the crowds cut off the head of the pope's representative in Constantinople, they attached it to the tail of a dog who dragged it through the streets. The Byzantines sold 4,000 of the surviving Italians as slaves to the Seljuk Turks. The Massacre of the Latins marked a new low in the relations between the residents of Constantinople and the foreign merchants and also between the Byzantine and Roman churches.

These events show how quickly the forces of early globalization changed people's lives, creating prosperity but also profound resentment. In the space of only a century, the Italian communities in Constantinople had mushroomed to 60,000. The Italian merchants had taken advantage of tax breaks to amass far greater fortunes than any Byzantine merchant. Their arrogant behavior so alienated the residents of Constantinople that the enraged locals ending up murdering them—despite their being fellow Christians. The Massacre of the Latins stands as a classic example of the have-nots attacking the haves—we might even call them the one percenters.

What really destroyed Constantinople, though, were external events: the Crusades were occurring at the same time as the incidents leading up to the Massacre of the Latins. The Roman and Byzantine churches had been at loggerheads since 1054, but when a new pope named Urban II came into power in 1088, he reached out to the Byzantine emperor to see if he could broker a compromise. He hoped to strengthen his position vis-à-vis the antipope. The Byzantine emperor Alexios I was sympathetic, and he appointed a council of clergy from the two churches to discuss their differences.

So when, seven years later in 1095, the Byzantine emperor asked Pope Urban II for help against Muslim enemies, Urban said yes. The pope traveled to Clermont, France, to urge a group of church leaders to send armies to restore Jerusalem, then under the rule of the Muslim Seljuks, to Christian rule.

Those who responded to his call didn't form a powerful or unified army. One contigent, the People's Crusade, consisted of ordinary men and women who traveled overland all the way to Constantinople. On their journey through the Rhine Valley of Germany, they targeted Jews living in Mainz, Cologne, Speyer, and Worms in an anti-Semitic spree of mass murder and forced conversions.

Of the 50,000 who departed from Europe on the First Crusade, only 10,000 arrived in Jerusalem, and of that 10,000, only 1,500, many aristocrats, possessed a knight's full armor and were

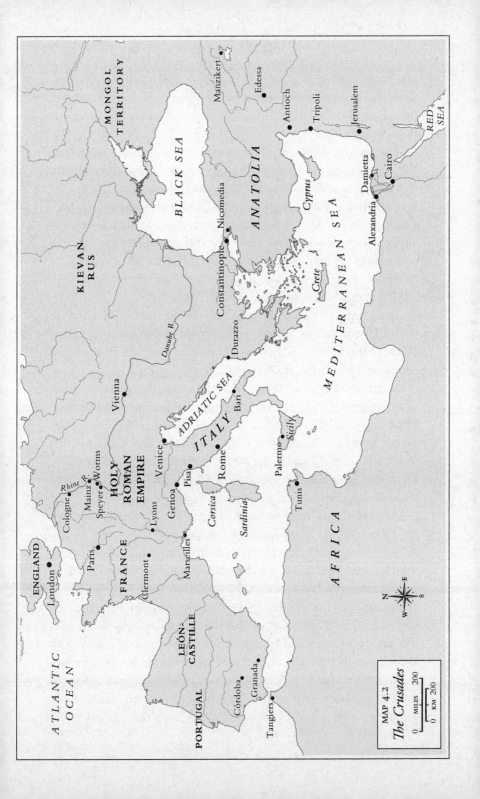

MAP 4.2
The Crusades

MONGOL TERRITORY

KIEVAN RUS

ENGLAND
London

ATLANTIC OCEAN

Paris
FRANCE
Clermont

Cologne
Rhine R.
Mainz
Speyer
Worms
HOLY ROMAN EMPIRE
Lyons
Vienna
Danube R.

Genoa
Pisa
Corsica
Rome
ITALY
Sardinia
Marseilles

PORTUGAL
LEÓN-CASTILLE
Córdoba
Granada
Tangiers

Palermo
Sicily
Bari
ADRIATIC SEA
Venice
Durazzo

Tunis

AFRICA

BLACK SEA

ANATOLIA
Manzikert
Edessa
Nicomedia
Constantinople

Antioch
Tripoli
Jerusalem

Cyprus
Crete
MEDITERRANEAN SEA
Damietta
Cairo
Alexandria

RED SEA

N
E
W
S

0   MILES   200
0   KM   200

able to engage in warfare. Despite their disadvantages, they triumphed. With the conquest of Jerusalem, the Western European powers, and Pope Urban II in particular, won an important symbolic victory.

During the eighty-eight years of Christian rule in Jerusalem, the European forces struggled to retain control of the region around the city. When a regional Muslim power conquered Edessa, the area northeast of the Holy Land, the Europeans launched the Second Crusade in 1147. They failed to recover any of the lost territory. The Crusaders also proved unable to counter the rise of a remarkable general, Saladin, who overthrew the Fatimid dynasty of Egypt, founded a new dynasty, and allied with the Seljuks. In 1187, Saladin's armies reconquered Jerusalem.

In response to the fall of Jerusalem, the Europeans launched the Third Crusade. The French and English contingents, including Richard the Lionheart, bypassed Constantinople on their way to Jerusalem, which they failed to take back.

Relations between Western Europe and the Byzantines hit rock bottom during the Fourth Crusade, which was launched by Pope Innocent III in 1201. The trouble began when the leaders of the Fourth Crusade took out a loan from the Venetians that they couldn't repay and so decided to ransack Constantinople. The Crusaders smashed the altar at the Hagia Sophia cathedral and divided the gems and precious metals among the troops.

After looting Constantinople in 1204, the Crusaders didn't go on to Jerusalem. They replaced the Byzantine emperor with a Westerner and imposed a new government called the Latin Empire, which lasted until 1261. The Byzantine empire never regained its former strength. By the early 1400s, it controlled only the city of Constantinople, which fell in 1453 to the Muslim armies of the Ottoman Turks. The fall of Constantinople redrew the border between Christian and Islamic lands to where it is today, with lands controlled by Christian rulers primarily occupying the area north of the Mediterranean, and lands ruled by Muslims located on the southern coast of the Mediterranean as well as the Holy Land.

The division of today's Europe into Eastern Orthodox and Roman Christian sectors is largely due to Vladimir's decision to convert to Byzantine Christianity and the rise of the Roman church in the following centuries. These same centuries between 1000 and 1200 saw the expansion of the Islamic world, as we'll see in the next chapter.

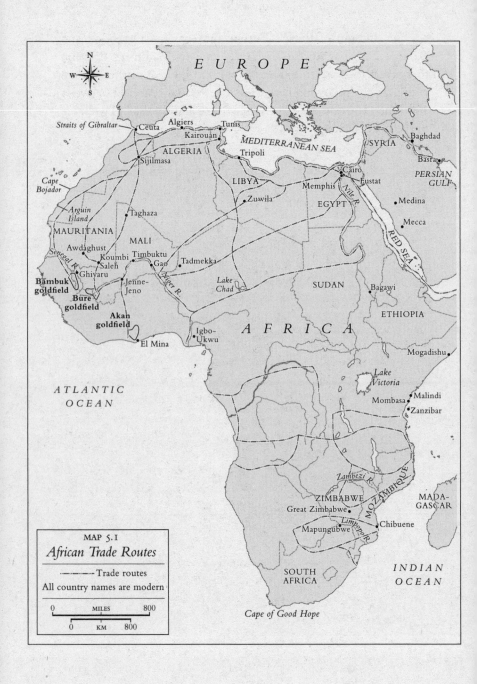

EUROPE

N
W E
S

Straits of Gibraltar — Ceuta
Algiers   Tunis
Kairouan
MEDITERRANEAN SEA   **SYRIA**   Baghdad
Tripoli   Basra
ALGERIA   Cairo   **PERSIAN**
Sijilmasa   Fustat   **GULF**
Cape   **LIBYA**   Memphis
Bojador   Zuwila   Medina
Arguin   Taghaza   **EGYPT**   Mecca
Island   **MAURITANIA**
Awdaghust   **MALI**
Koumbi   Timbuktu   Tadmekka   **RED SEA**
Saleh   Gao
Senegal R.   Ghiyaru
Bambuk   Jenne-   **SUDAN**   Bagawi
goldfield   Jeno
Bure   Lake   **ETHIOPIA**
goldfield   Chad
Akan   Niger R.
goldfield   Igbo-
El Mina   Ukwu   **A F R I C A**   Mogadishu

ATLANTIC   Lake
OCEAN   Victoria   Malindi
Mombasa
Zanzibar

Zambezi R.
ZIMBABWE   **MOZAMBIQUE**   **MADA-**
Great Zimbabwe   **GASCAR**
Limpopo R.   Chibuene
Mapungubwe

MAP 5.1
African Trade Routes

----- Trade routes
All country names are modern

0   MILES   800
0   KM   800

SOUTH   **INDIAN**
AFRICA   **OCEAN**

Cape of Good Hope

CHAPTER FIVE

The World's Richest Man

In the year 1000, as today, having a rich and powerful neighbor nearby offered business opportunities for those smart enough to recognize them. Like the Rus in Eastern Europe, rulers and merchants in East and West Africa perceived the commercial advantages of marketing to consumers living in Baghdad and the other major cities of the Islamic world who purchased slaves and gold in vast quantities. With their profits, Africans imported glass beads, Chinese and Iranian ceramics, and silk and cotton textiles.

The new connections with regions outside of Africa also brought far-reaching religious change. As African rulers, merchants, and ordinary people adopted Islam, the new religion spread south along the East African coast and to the valleys of the Senegal and Niger Rivers in West Africa. This Islamicization wasn't simply the product of Muslim outsiders settling in Africa. It occurred because Africans, often traders, chose to associate themselves with the larger Islamic world, and their decisions exposed local inhabitants to the forces of globalization.

Consider the earliest written document found in West Africa, from the trading town of Tadmekka and dated to 1011. Written in Arabic and incised with a pointed metal tool onto a boulder, it reads: "Muhammadin son of al-Hasan wrote this, and he professes that there is no god but God, and that Muhammad is His servant and His messenger." As the standard profession of faith, this is the first tenet of Islam.

Another inscription is located near a cliff that opens onto the town. It explains that Tadmekka is named after Mecca: "There will remain to the town of Tadmekka a market rising to the level of Mecca." Tadmekka is unusual in having many inscriptions in Arabic, some on boulders, some on gravestones. The shape of the Arabic letters points to authorship by local residents, not expats. This type of inscription marks the expansion of Islam into vast new territories in West and East Africa just around 1000. The locals identified themselves with Islam at precisely the same moment people all over Afro-Eurasia were converting to one of the universal religions.

The inscriptions from Tadmekka provide a powerful reminder of the crucial role Africans played in the trade that linked them to other continents—even if many of the surviving sources were written by outsiders. Although an earlier generation of historians credited Arabs with bringing commerce and progress to Africa, modern historians emphatically reject this view because it overlooks African initiative.

Africans played a key role in the growing trade between the Islamic world and Africa. Some two thirds of the gold entering Europe and Asia before 1492 came from West Africa. And the number of slaves who left Africa for the Islamic world between 800 and 1800 was so great that it rivaled the total number of slaves shipped across the Atlantic.

Although the African slave trade began early—certainly by Roman times—only in the mid-900s do we gain a clear picture of how it worked. That information appears in a collection of sailor's tales attributed to a Persian named Buzurg and set in the Persian Gulf. One tale recounts a series of events so implausible that they must be fictional. Yet because the backdrop is true-to-life, we learn much about the pricing of slaves, the location of markets, and conversion to Islam.

The story opens when a ship from the port of Oman is blown off course to Sofala, an East African port in central Mozambique. As the tale unfolds, the narrator explains, "when I saw the place, I knew that we had reached the land of the man-eating Zanj [residents of East Africa]. Indeed, we arrived at this place most certain of our death." But contrary to expectation, the local king welcomes the foreign merchants warmly and gives them permission to buy and sell their goods without paying any duties. After they've completed their trading, the captain rewards the king for his role in facilitating the slave trade with lavish gifts.

But then the story takes an unexpected turn. When the king comes on board the ship to say goodbye, the narrator thinks to himself, "In the Oman auction this king would fetch 30 dinars, and his seven companions 160 dinars. On their back are clothes worth 20 dinars." (A modern study puts the average cost of a slave between 800 and 1100 at 20–30 gold dinars, exactly the price range given in the story.) The captain orders the crew to set sail immediately so that he can sell the king and his companions at the slave market in Oman.

The captain's assessment of the resale value of the king and his entourage chills the modern reader: he might as well be estimating the value of a load of elephant tusks or gold, the other common exports from East Africa. The captain has no guilt about selling his fellow human beings or betraying the ruler who facilitated his purchase of slaves.

Yes, in retrospect, it is tempting to condemn those—here the Omani ship captain and the African king prior to his abduction—who profited from the slave trade. But we must realize that, in the preindustrial world, the constant demand for labor meant that the slave trade existed almost everywhere. The first abolitionist critics of slavery spoke up only in the 1750s. For much of human history, slavery was a big business.

When the ship arrives in Oman, and the captain sells the former king at the slave market, the two men part ways, seemingly for good.

A few years later, the captain's ship lands at the same East African port, where locals in canoes once again lead the ship's crew to the ruler. The captain fears that he'll be punished for abducting the king, but when he arrives at court, he's stunned to see the very king he'd sold in the Oman slave market. To the captain's astonishment, the king treats the captain and his crew kindly and allows them to trade freely.

Before the ship departs, the king explains what happened. When the ship landed in Oman, he was sold and taken to Basra, the port closest to Baghdad, where his owner permitted him to study Islamic teachings. After he was sold a second time, he moved to Baghdad. There he mastered spoken Arabic, completed his studies of the Quran, and escaped to join a group of Central Asian pilgrims on their way to Mecca. From Mecca he went to Cairo, and from there, he followed the Nile south back to his kingdom. Once home, he learned that, despite his long absence, no one had replaced him, and he was able to resume his position as king. (Yes, this is definitely a fable!)

Forgiving the captain, the king urges him to return to trade and to bring Muslim traders with him when he comes back. The king does, though, opt to say his goodbyes on land, uttering a final ironic comment, "as for accompanying you to your ship, there's no way for me to do it."

The unstated moral of the story? It's okay to participate in the slave trade, but you should treat other participants in the trade honestly, especially if they happen to be Muslims.

As a slave from Africa, the king was able to study the Quran, learn to speak Arabic, and participate in the hajj pilgrimage to Mecca. Here fiction matched real life. African brokers actually did bring slaves from the interior of sub-Saharan Africa to coastal ports on the East Africa coast and sell them to foreign slavers who transported them to the Middle East. One rare description of a slave market 80 miles (125 km) north of Baghdad reports the existence of an open square with roads branching out where "the houses contained upper stories and rooms as well as shops for slaves."

The fictional king's home port of Sofala marks the southernmost point on the East African coast that monsoon winds reach. South of that, goods had to travel either overland or in small boats rowed along the coast, which is why fewer trading towns are located there.

Starting in 900, several settlements arose on the Limpopo River in Zimbabwe, directly west of the Sofala port and just across the border with South Africa. Each town was larger than its predecessor; Mapungubwe had a population of 5,000 people. The inhabitants made their living by tending cattle and by farming. Those with means used copper and gold ornaments and iron tools, while the poorest people had access to only stone and bone tools.

These areas prospered because the locals traveled along the Limpopo River to the coastal port of Chibuene, some 400 miles (640 km) to the east, and connected to the Indian Ocean trade. There they exchanged slaves, gold, ivory, and animal skins for different imported goods, including small glass beads brought from Cairo, which they used as a currency and melted down to make larger beads. Initially, this import and export trade may have affected just a few people, but over time, as the trade expanded, local workers began to supply gold to distant consumers and felt the effects of globalization.

The largest gold-producing site on the East African coast was Great Zimbabwe, just inland from Sofala, and south of the Zambezi River. The modern site of Great Zimbabwe contains multiple buildings constructed with cut granite blocks between 1000 and 1300. One building, the Elliptical Building, forms an oval 292 feet (89 m) in diameter. Its walls measure 17 feet (5 m) thick and 32 feet (almost 10 m) tall. The biggest stone structure built before 1500 in all of sub-Saharan Africa, it testifies to the wealth resulting from the gold trade. Eight stone statues with the bodies of eagles and human lips and toes were found on the site; perhaps the statues portrayed messengers who flew between the dead and the living.

Great Zimbabwe would eventually produce one ton of gold per annum. It became a bustling city of 10,000 people that was a primary center for the coastal trade, as demonstrated by the presence of broken pieces of Chinese green celadon vessels and Iranian plates with script on them. Tens of thousands of beads have also been found at the site, an indication that African demand for imports—not simply the external desire for gold and slaves—drove that trade.

As the sailor's tale about the slave king suggests, Muslims welcomed all converts and treated all men, including slaves, as equal in the eyes of God, if not socially. Male slaves in the Islamic world carried goods and rowed boats, but they also managed stores and even tended the personal libraries of their owners. Although the Quran forbade the practice, slave dealers castrated young boys because eunuch slaves were in high demand as supervisors of women's quarters. Male slaves, particularly those from Central Asia, also served in the armies of different military powers.

Large numbers of male slaves also worked in nonmilitary positions in southern Iraq near Basra, where between 600 and 900 they labored to drain marshes and to remove the surface crust of nitrates and saltpeter so that the soil underneath could be cultivated. Two short-lived uprisings occurred there in the 690s, and one in the 870s lasted more than a decade. The rebels posed a significant challenge to Abbasid rule, partially because of their numbers and partially because of the difficulties of sending troops to the malarial terrain they occupied.

The 870s rebellion, known as the Zanj Rebellion, involved tens of thousands of slaves, mostly from East Africa. (The Arabic word *zanj* referred to both the region of East Africa and its residents.) The slaves' leader was a well-educated scholar from Iran. Rising up to protest their brutal working conditions, the slaves enjoyed about fifteen years of self-rule before the central government—with great difficulty—suppressed the rebellion. After 900 no further slave rebellions occurred, possibly because owners stopped assigning such onerous tasks to such large numbers of unsupervised slaves.

We can learn much about slavery in the Islamic world from a manual for slave buyers written by a Christian doctor named Ibn Butlan. An expert in hygiene and macrobiotics, Ibn Butlan was able to read Syriac, Greek, and his native Arabic. A resident of Baghdad, he even penned a satire spoofing untrained quacks. Writing in the 1050s, his goal was to use his knowledge of world geography and human anatomy to help readers purchase the best slaves they could. His readers were able to inspect prospective slaves closely and find out where they had been born.

Ibn Butlan subscribed to the Islamic view (inherited from the ancient Greeks) that environment profoundly affects the functioning of the human body. The best slaves, in his opinion, were from the east (India, Afghanistan, and Pakistan): rarely falling ill, they had good physiques and even temperaments. Slaves from the west (Syria, Egypt, and North Africa) were in poor health because their climate wasn't as good and their nourishment poor. Male slaves from the north—this includes the Rus and other Slavs—were strong and lived a long time, but northern females couldn't give birth because they didn't menstruate, he believed. Slaves from the south differed from their northern counterparts: they had short lifespans because they were malnourished as children and suffered constantly from diarrhea.

This kind of thinking tends to generate stereotypes, and Ibn Butlan's book doesn't disappoint. At one point he quoted a proverb, "Were a Zanj slave to fall from the sky to earth, the one quality he'd possess would be rhythm."

Unlike the legal systems of either ancient Rome or the American South, Islamic law offered slaves multiple routes to emancipation. Muslim jurists agreed on the basic principles but differed on many details. Muslims were permitted to own both non-Muslims and already enslaved Muslims, but they weren't allowed to enslave free Muslims (though they sometimes did all the same).

Although slavery was commonplace, Muslim leaders since the time of Muhammad had encouraged the freeing of slaves. Islamic law permitted owners to have sex with their female slaves but required them to recognize any resulting offspring as their legitimate children. When he died, the owner had to free the mother of his children, if he hadn't done so already. The overall effect of these measures encouraging emancipation of slaves was that the slave population needed constant replenishing. This is why the Islamic world continued to import slaves in such large quantities and for so long.

The three main sources of slaves for the Islamic world were Africa, Eastern Europe, and Central Asia. Clearly the men, women, and children who were taken from their homes and sold in Middle Eastern slave markets suffered most directly from the globalized slave trade. But the people who remained in their homes were also affected by the departure of their compatriots. Many who came into contact with Muslim slave traders converted to Islam, which contributed to the spread of Islam into West and East Africa.

In Baghdad, and throughout the Islamic world, female slaves outnumbered male slaves, and Ibn Butlan devoted much more space to female slaves than to males. He generalized about their physical appearance, odor, and ability to procreate. He noted, too, which groups were suitable for temporary marriage contracts. This was a legal workaround that allowed men to marry prostitutes for the time they spent together, even just a few hours, and divorce them when done. This elaborate fiction was necessary because Islamic law prescribed that sexual relations could only occur between married people or a master and his female slaves.

In his discussion of the women from the Bagawi border region between modern Sudan and Ethiopia, Ibn Butlan included a startling detail. They made good temporary marriage slaves provided that "they are imported when young and no one has hurt them yet, because in that country they practice excision. Using a razor, they completely remove external skin located on top of the vulva until the bone appears." Describing female genital mutilation that occurred in the slaves' homeland, Ibn Butlan also claimed that slave dealers also performed deeply invasive surgery on male slaves, removing their kneecaps so that they wouldn't run away.

Ibn Butlan praised certain groups for their pleasant personalities, their willingness to serve their masters, and their ability to be good parents. But he closed his treatise with a warning, "To wrap up the matter: the Armenian slaves are the worst of the whites just as the Zanj are the worst of the blacks." Ibn Butlan reminds us that globalization often led to the greater circulation of information, but not all of the information that moved was accurate. Disinformation could travel long distances, too.

Ibn Butlan's book provides an unparalleled view of the geographic origins of the slaves coming into Baghdad, the primary distribution point for slaves throughout the Islamic world in the year 1000. He lists such African origin points as the Lake Chad region, northeastern Ethiopia, central Ethiopia, Nubia in modern Sudan, North Africa, and East Africa. Slaves came from other places outside Africa as well: India, Pakistan, Afghanistan, Central Asia, the Caspian Sea, modern Turkey, Armenia, and the Arabian Peninsula. Almost all of the sources of slaves were in non-Muslim lands located near the borders of the Abbasid empire, which makes perfect sense. Once slave traders had obtained slaves, they brought them the shortest possible distance and sold them.

The volume of the trans-Saharan slave trade before 1500 was massive, but it's hard to pin down exact figures because there are no sources like those documenting the transatlantic slave trade. Because the ships that brought slaves to the Americas listed them on manifests, or passenger lists, historians have been able to calculate that 12.5 million slaves crossed the Atlantic between the start of the slave trade in the early 1500s and its abolition throughout the British empire in 1833.

It is extremely difficult to estimate the number of slaves who moved on foot across the Sahara. The most heavily used trans-Saharan slave routes in 1000 ran from West Africa to the Mediterranean. The earliest road connected Zuwila, a town in modern Libya on the northern edge of the Sahara, to the Lake Chad region. Until sometime around AD 300, North Africans used wheeled vehicles including chariots to cross the Sahara. Between 300 and 600, the camel was domesticated. With the introduction of camel transport, caravans could shift to multiple pathways through the desert because camels didn't require roads.

Few sources give the number of slaves moving across the Sahara. Occasionally an eyewitness provides a single number. For example, in 1353, on his way home to Morocco, the famous traveler Ibn Battuta counted 600 female slaves in a caravan crossing the Sahara. Traveling in such a large group heightened the risks. Because slave traders allowed for only minimal rations of food and drink, the slightest mishap could cause multiple deaths. One fifth of all the slaves crossing the desert may have died in transit.

University of Chicago professor Ralph A. Austen wove scraps of information like this together to estimate that between 650 and

1600 some 5,500 slaves crossed the Sahara each year on their way to North Africa and the Middle East. The number may have reached 8,700 per year between 900 and 1100, the peak of the Islamic slave trade. Working with Austen's research, one recent estimate puts the total number of slaves taken from sub-Saharan Africa between 650 and 1900 at 11.75 million, slightly less than the estimated 12.5 million slaves who crossed the Atlantic between 1500 and 1850.

The conquest of North Africa by the caliphate's armies in the seventh century regularized and increased the number of slaves sold to purchasers outside Africa. An early Arabic source reports that slaves sold at Zuwila were "bought for short pieces of red cloth." Red cloth may seem utterly ordinary to us now, but it had enormous appeal to those unfamiliar with colored fabrics, whether in North Africa or North America (recall how eagerly the Skraelings traded for red cloth from the Norse).

Routes across West Africa were the primary conduit for slaves traveling to North Africa and Cairo. In the 800s, caravans pioneered a new route across the Sahara that connected the town of Sijilmasa, on the northern edge of the Sahara in modern Morocco, with the Niger River Valley. Arabic geographers report that Sijilmasa, located on "a bare plain," originated as a small meeting place for traders who met only at certain times of the year. In due course, "it became a town," as its rulers profited from the taxes they levied on traders. Thanks to globalization, small settlements became bigger towns and eventually cities.

With the opening of the road from Sijilmasa, Arabic-speaking merchants and missionaries crossed the Sahara into sub-Saharan Africa with increasing frequency. As a result, many local rulers converted to Islam.

One Arabic geographer describes the circumstances that led to the conversion of the king of Malal in the Upper Senegal River Valley. During a long drought the king sacrificed cattle until all were dead, yet no rain came. When the king bemoaned the situation, a Muslim visitor replied, "O King, if you believed in the prophetic mission of Muhammad (God bless him and give him peace), and if you accepted all the religious laws of Islam, I would wish for your deliverance from your plight and that God's mercy would envelop all the people of your country." Hearing that, the king "accepted Islam and became a sincere Muslim," and the visitor "made him recite from the Koran some easy passages and taught him religious obligations and practices."

The Muslim requested that the king wait until the following Friday, the Islamic Sabbath. The two men prayed until dawn when "God caused abundant rain to descend upon them." At that the king then ordered the destruction of all images in his kingdom and expelled all the "sorcerers." The king came to be known as "the Muslim," and his descendants and the nobles in the kingdom also converted, but "the common people of his kingdom remained polytheists"—a revealing detail given that this narrative showcases the power of Islam.

This, the most informative account about Islam in early West Africa, comes from a Muslim scholar who never visited Africa. Based in Córdoba, Spain, al-Bakri collected the testimony of travelers and merchants returning from Africa. He also quotes information from a now-lost source written in 955 by al-Warraq. Al-Bakri's information was surprisingly current for its time. He includes the name of a king who ascended to the throne of Ghana in 1063, just five years before he completed his book.

Al-Bakri's book provides an excellent example of "routes and realms" writings that described the people and places—and especially the new commercial pathways—coming into use in the year 1000. He followed the model of Ibn Khurradadhbih, a native speaker of Persian who wrote in Arabic. Ibn Khurradadhbih served as the master of post and information in the Jabal district in Iran in the ninth century. (He may have later moved to the Abbasid capital of Baghdad as the head of the ministry of communications.)

Living two centuries before al-Bakri, Ibn Khurradadhbih witnessed the height of the Abbasid caliphate. Extending all the way from North Africa to Central Asia, the Abbasid realm was so large that officials didn't always know the most direct route to each locality. And if, as was common, an emergency or uprising occurred, they had to act quickly to send troops. Ibn Khurradadhbih's goal was to provide the caliph and his officials with the most up-to-date geographical information available.

Ibn Khurradadhbih organized his findings to provide "an outline that would elucidate the routes and realms of the earth, and their description, along with how distant and how near they are, with information concerning the parts of the earth cultivated, versus those that are wasteland, and the distances between such areas, including the way stations that lead to the remote ends of the world." Understanding the need for itineraries with accurate distances from one point to another, his "routes" provide the travel time from one town to the next. "Realms" refers to the description he gave of each place: local products, inhabitants, and their customs and beliefs.

The "routes and realms" writings describe peoples living in different parts of the world and consistently say more about the peoples of Afro-Eurasia than any other source from the year 1000. This is why I so often quote Arab observers. They provide key information about the Rus to supplement the *Primary Chronicle*, and their observations of Africans are even more important because so few sources describe sub-Saharan Africa before the late 1400s.

In Ibn Khurradadhbih's day, Baghdad was one of the great intellectual centers in the world; its only possible rival, the Tang dynasty capital of Chang'an, also had schools, libraries, and an educated elite, but Chinese scholars focused almost entirely on the Chinese-language tradition, which stretched back for more than 1,000 years. Arabic, in contrast, was a relatively new language, with few texts written down before Muhammad's death in 632.

Deeply interested in the learning of other societies, the second Abbasid caliph, Mansur, who reigned from 754 to 775, financed the translation from Greek, Latin, Sanskrit, and Persian into Arabic of books about geography, medicine, math, physics, and logic. Sometime after 800, factories in Baghdad began to produce paper in large quantities using Chinese manufacturing techniques, another early example of technological transfer. The scholars of Baghdad didn't simply translate; they annotated so intensively that they superseded the findings of the Greeks. Their efforts preserved the learning of the classical world for all time. Translators in Renaissance Italy were able to recover certain ancient Greek texts only because they survived in Arabic.

Thanks to the translation movement, al-Bakri could assume an educated readership who wanted to learn about the entire world. The routes and realms genre offered him an excellent template to organize his information. Like Ibn Khurradadhbih, al-Bakri made no claim to have visited the places he wrote about.

Al-Bakri explained that, after converting to Islam because the drought ended, the king of Malal was able to continue as the ruler of his kingdom. In earlier periods, when the Islamic world was unified under a single ruler, any king who converted would have had to accept the reigning caliph as his spiritual and political leader. The word "caliph" means "successor" and it refers to all leaders of the Islamic community after Muhammad.

When Muhammad died in 632, no one knew who should succeed him because none of Muhammad's sons lived to adulthood. Only his daughter Fatima survived him, and as a woman she couldn't lead the new community. The Sunnis felt that the Muslim community should collectively choose the new leader from Muhammad's tribe, the Quraysh, while the Shi'ites believed that Muhammad's cousin Ali, who was married to Fatima, and his descendants had a special claim to rule.

A third, smaller group called the Kharijites broke away from the Muslim community in the 650s and 660s. Believing that the leader of the Muslim community should be chosen only on the basis of his pious conduct, they accepted the claim of Muhammad and the first two caliphs to rule, but not that of the third caliph or of Ali, who became the fourth caliph.

A subgroup of the Kharijites were the Ibadis, who were more willing to compromise with other Muslims than were the Kharijites. The visitor who persuaded the king of Malal to convert was probably an Ibadi. Successful merchants, the Ibadis were the first missionaries to travel south of Tripoli as they established trade networks and actively tried to convert Africans.

In the early years after Muhammad's death, the caliph's armies conquered vast swaths of territory across the Middle East and North Africa. Many people today think that the armies forced the conquered peoples to convert—this is the stereotype of conversion by the sword—but that's actually not historically accurate. Because Muslims paid lower taxes than non-Muslims, most rulers didn't want the residents of newly conquered lands to convert. They needed the higher taxes paid by non-Muslims. In Iran, for example, it took centuries before a majority of the population converted to Islam. During the first two centuries of Muslim rule, from 622 to 822, 40 percent did, and by the year 1000, some 80 percent had. After 1000 Islam spread far beyond Iran to both Africa and Central Asia.

Rewarding their troops with a share of the plunder, Islamic armies were extremely successful in conquering new lands, but the caliphs didn't succeed in creating lasting structures that successfully extracted revenue from their subjects. Naming governors to rule large provinces, the Abbasid rulers sometimes gave them de facto independence by granting them extensive stretches of territory. In such an arrangement, the governor gained the right to collect taxes in his own territory in any way he pleased as long as he sent an annual share of the revenue to the caliph. But if he failed to do so, the caliph had little recourse except to send troops. This wasn't always possible, especially if the caliph needed his troops to fight a rival claimant to the throne. Many times when a caliph died, his sons—and sometimes his brothers—engaged in a free-for-all until someone defeated all his enemies.

One of the first governors to break away from the Abbasids was the free son of a Turkish slave soldier, named Ahmad ibn Tulun. Unable to attract enough volunteers to their army, the Abbasids recruited thousands of Turkic soldiers from Central Asia, some as paid mercenaries, some as purchased military slaves. After entering the army, both groups earned salaries, and both could rise to high positions.

As a paid recruit, Ibn Tulun grew up in Iraq and was stationed in Egypt as a junior officer. Eventually he rose to become governor of Fustat, a predecessor city to Cairo, and took over collecting taxes for all of Egypt. The mosque he built is still one of the most popular tourist attractions in Cairo because of its imposing court-yard and unusual minaret. Ibn Tulun never forwarded tax reve-nues on a regular basis (modern Cairo residents delight in telling stories about how he tricked the caliph over 1,000 years ago), but the caliph was powerless to take action against him.

A key source of Ibn Tulun's power was the army, which was loyal to him—and not the caliph—because he'd recruited it. In addition to 24,000 military slaves from Turkic Central Asia, the army also had 42,000 slaves and free men from the southern reaches of the Nile and West Africa. "Greeks," a blanket term for anyone living in Byzantine territories, also served in his army. Ibn Tulun ruled until his death in 884, when his son succeeded him. In 905, the Abbasids temporarily reestablished control in Egypt.

In 945, though, the Abbasid caliphs lost control of their entire empire. Three brothers from the Buyid tribe who'd built up their own powerful armies took over the administration of the most important cities in the Abbasid heartland, including Baghdad. The caliph named one of the brothers the "commander of command-ers," ceding all of his military authority to him, and the Buyid ruler imprisoned the caliph in his Baghdad palace.

In 1055 the Seljuks conquered Baghdad and replaced the Buy-ids as the caliph's captors. This arrangement allowed the Abbasid ruler to continue as titular caliph until 1258, when the Mongols invaded Baghdad and killed the last Abbasid caliph, but the caliphs had no armies of their own and no actual power. Whoever held the caliph captive became the de facto ruler of Baghdad. In the various regions previously under Abbasid rule, independent rulers took power.

These post-Abbasid rulers included the Buyids, the Seljuks, and still other dynasties. All but one of the breakaway challengers to the Abbasid caliph were Muslim. That one exception tried to revive the ancient Iranian religion of Zoroastrianism but failed.

The term "Muslim commonwealth"—coined by the eminent British historian of Islam Hugh Kennedy—sums up the political and religious situation of the Abbasid caliphate after 945. Similar to the British monarch today, the caliph had no political or military authority, but he did remain the symbolic figurehead of the Muslim community, and prayer leaders all over the Islamic world mentioned him in their Friday prayers. His position as the head of the commonwealth allowed him to intervene in disputes between Sunni and Shi'ite Muslims.

Even though politically divided, everyone living in the different parts of the Muslim commonwealth believed in Islam, accepted the authority of Muhammad, read the Quran in Arabic, and performed the hajj pilgrimage to Mecca when possible. Baghdad continued to be the most important city of learning.

By this time, Cairo was rising as a major city, marking a turning point in North African history. The Nile Delta, with its strategic location, may seem a natural choice for the capital of Egypt. But with the exception of Memphis, the capitals of the past were located far to the south of Cairo. The spread of Islam and establishment of new trade routes across Africa contributed to Cairo's prosperity. The trade routes, whether by land or sea, converged where the Nile met the Mediterranean. Caravans and boats laden with West African goods traveled along the Mediterranean coast while goods shipped north along the East African coast were carried from the Persian Gulf ports overland to Cairo.

Cairo's official founding came in 969, when the Fatimids, a Shi'ite dynasty named for Muhammad's daughter Fatima, relocated to Fustat from their original base in modern Algeria. There they built an entirely new city named al-Qahira, "the Victorious," the source of the English word Cairo. Parts of the original Fatimid wall survive even today, and Fustat is the name of a district on the Nile River that faces Giza.

Visitors to Cairo can walk along a street that connects two gates on opposite sides of the wall. Along the way you can see a mosque built in the year 1000 by the reigning Fatimid caliph, al-Hakim, who was infamous for issuing eccentric orders, such as banning several popular vegetables and forbidding shoemakers to make footwear for women, so that they had to stay inside. Many

hold him responsible for destroying the Church of the Holy Sep-
ulcher in Jerusalem, but a Muslim observer who visited forty years
later described minimal damage. Because the 400th anniversary
of Muhammad's 622 journey (the start of the Islamic calendar)
fell during al-Hakim's reign, he issued a high number of edicts
in preparation for a possible Day of Judgment, a day that Muslims welcomed because it would free the dead from their wait-
ing and suffering. In 1021, al-Hakim set off into the desert but
didn't return, and his body was never found. His sister took over
as regent for her nephew, and Fatimid rule continued.

That same Cairo street contains a single building, or *wikala*, that
houses a hostel, mosque, warehouse, and multi-floor workshop
and market used by traders, which could easily have functioned
as a slave market. Unlike earlier dynasties who had accepted the
nominal leadership of the Abbasid caliphs, the Fatimids claimed
the title of caliph for themselves, asserting their right to lead the
entire Islamic community. The Fatimids controlled Egypt.

Cairo, when governed by the Shi'ite Fatimids, had large Christian and Jewish populations. One synagogue, Ben Ezra, close to
the Coptic Museum in modern Cairo, preserved every piece of
paper with Hebrew letters on it (Hebrew was thought to be the
language of God) in a repository called a geniza, from which over
200,000 fragments survive.

The geniza materials show that Jews also kept slaves, but some
of their practices differed from those of Muslims. Where Islamic
law allowed male owners to cohabit with their female slaves, Jewish law forbade male owners to live in the same house as a female
slave unless a female relative lived there, too. The randomly preserved materials from the geniza offer a glimpse of daily life as
it actually happened, not as legal regulations said that it should.
Friends congratulated each other on the purchase of a male slave,
just as they did when a son was born, and they wrote condolence
notes to the owners when their slave girls died.

Cairo thrived under Fatimid rule. It became the biggest city in
Africa in the year 1000, with a population around 500,000.

From Alexandria, the Egyptian port nearest to Cairo, one

could cross the Mediterranean to Sicily and Italy, and a large group of merchants from the Amalfi coast of Italy (near Naples) took up residence in the new capital. One of the main goods they traded in was ivory, which they sourced in both East and West Africa. Many beautifully carved ivory boxes and objects survive from the 1000s and 1100s.

Like the Venetians in Constantinople during the Crusades, merchants from the Italian republic of Amalfi lived in their own district in Fatimid-ruled Cairo. Several spontaneous outbreaks of violence against Christians occurred in the 960s when the news of Byzantine victories against the Muslim rulers of Cyprus and Crete reached Cairo. The city's Muslim residents identified with non-Fatimid Muslim states simply because of their shared religious identity, a sign that, thanks to globalization, formerly local identities had expanded to become regional.

In 996 the residents of Cairo rioted against the Amalfi merchants. The immediate cause was a fire on May 5 that destroyed sixteen newly built ships in the Fatimid navy. The locals blamed the Amalfi merchants for the damage, torched their houses and storehouses, and killed more than 100 Italians. Occurring exactly one century before the First Crusades began in 1096, this outbreak demonstrates that the Muslim residents of Cairo resented the wealth of the foreign merchants just as intensely as the Christian residents of Constantinople did.

In the year 1000 the export goods from Africa—apart from slaves—that passed through Cairo included ivory, copper, bronze, and most alluring of all, gold. A major mystery of the era was identifying the origin of the gold—learning not just where the mines were located but identifying who controlled the mines and who sold the gold they produced. Because this knowledge could allow the bearer to challenge the middlemen who ran the gold trade, the middlemen did everything in their power to prevent outsiders from learning how they operated. They kept their secrets for centuries.

One king in Ghana had so much gold that al-Bakri devoted considerable space to his holdings. The king sports a hat decorated with gold, and his ten pages wield gold shields and swords. The young nobles at his court braid their hair with gold. His horses wear gold-embroidered cloths, and around the necks of the king's guard dogs are "collars of gold and silver studded with a number of balls of the same metals." Implausible perhaps, but al-Bakri's fixation with gold is genuine. The king monopolizes gold production, he reports: while his subjects are permitted to collect only gold dust, he is entitled to all nuggets, and he owns one "as large as a big stone."

The king's realm in Ghana, al-Bakri said, "consists of two towns situated on a plain. One of these is inhabited by Muslims. It is large and possesses twelve mosques, in one of which they assemble for the Friday prayers." This town's residents included those who issued the call to prayer, legal experts, and scholars. Even though some of his subjects and many of his ministers accepted Islam, the king did not. The king's army had 200,000 soldiers. Ruling a large territory, the king needed literate Muslims to staff his bureaucracy just as Vladimir and other new European monarchs needed literate Christian clergy to staff theirs.

The other town, some 7.5 miles (12 km) away, was the king's town, where the "sorcerers of these people, men in charge of the religious cult," were influential. (It had a single mosque for visitors.) Believers in the local religion disposed of the dead differently than those who believed in Islam. Where Muslims placed the dead in the ground with no grave goods, practitioners of the local religion buried the king with his bed, carpets, cushions, weapons, plates and cups loaded with food and drink, and even with the corpses of "the men who used to serve his meals." As unlikely as al-Bakri's report may seem, archeologists have found graves of kings buried with their attendants in the region of the Niger River.

But where precisely was the king's capital located? Most likely, it was the city of Koumbi Saleh in Mauritania. There, excavators in the early twentieth century unearthed Arabic inscriptions and sections of a mosque, indicating occupation by Muslims, as well as common trade goods of the day, especially beads and glass weights. This might have been the Muslims' town described by al-Bakri, and archeologists suggest that the kingdom probably had multiple capitals, which the king visited seasonally, a common phenomenon in Africa.

Al-Bakri identifies the source of the Ghana king's gold as Ghiyaru, a trading post on the opposite bank of the Senegal River from the gold fields of Bambuk. But he says nothing about who mines the gold or controls the gold trade. Al-Bakri reports that the trading post lay 15 miles (24 km) "distant from the Nile River and contains many Muslims."

The Nile, of course, flowed nowhere near West Africa. But since Ptolemy believed that the Nile River connected all the settlements in Africa, al-Bakri follows the Greek geographer and calls multiple rivers the Nile. Although he doesn't name the Senegal or Niger Rivers, al-Bakri knows something of their courses; he correctly describes the major bend in the Niger River near Gao.

The king of Ghana had a tax policy so unusual that al-Bakri made a note of it: "On every donkey-load of salt when it is brought into the country their king levies one gold dinar [coin], and two dinars when it is sent out." This policy encouraged traders from the town of Taghaza, on the southern edge of the Sahara, to bring camel caravans carrying large blocks of salt to Ghana (it had no supply of its own) and to sell it there. We might wonder why, if the king wanted to encourage salt imports, he taxed them at all, but he must have needed the revenue.

The Ghana king's innovative tax collection made it possible for him to benefit from the movement of goods, a key source of income for West African rulers. As long as rulers controlled the gates to their cities, and hired a few market supervisors, they could profit by taxing trade.

The taxes on goods coming into the kingdom also varied: although most goods were taxed at 10 percent, copper was charged only 5 percent to encourage imports. Ghana didn't produce copper, but the people living at the nearby site of Igbo-Ukwu, in eastern Nigeria, did. They made two types of bronze by adding tin—or lead and tin—to copper.

The Igbo-Ukwu bronzes, dating to around 1000, depict human figures, insects, birds, and snakes. They are stunning examples of the lost-wax manufacturing process although their makers probably used latex, which grows on a local shrub, instead of wax to make the molds into which they poured molten bronze. Some of the most intriguing bronze vessels from Igbo-Ukwu are decorated with small glass beads from Cairo—just like those in use in Mapungubwe on the East African coast—showing that West and East African buyers alike purchased large quantities of imported beads.

The Igbo-Ukwu site had two major deposits of artifacts. A royal burial contained three elephant tusks, copper anklets, and other items, and some iron goods. A separate storehouse of regalia held over 100,000 imported glass and carnelian beads, most likely from India, and multiple bronze vessels of different shapes and sizes. The raw materials for these objects—including copper, tin, and lead—came from all over the Niger Valley and testify to the new trade routes crisscrossing West Africa.

The movement of goods across the region benefited the local people as well as their rulers. The size of the archeological site of Jenne-jeno, 2 miles (3 km) southeast of the modern city of Jenne indicates the wealth of the entire stretch of the Niger River between the two cities of Jenne and Timbuktu. A major gold entrepôt, Jenne-jeno had multiple deposits of discarded pottery. One was 26 feet (8 m) deep and contained 1.5 million pottery fragments dating from 300 BC to AD 1400. Only a large population could have produced it. Around 1000, Jenne's population reached 20,000 at the times of year when the rains were heavy and it was difficult to travel or herd animals. We know that the city's residents came from many different places because they buried their dead in forty different ways. As at Chaco Canyon, different types of burial point to diverse populations living together, another sign of early globalization.

A roof tile with Arabic script on it surfaced in the level dating to around the year 900. (The locals still put similar tiles with the identical Arabic phrase on their roofs today.) The pottery fragments continue well below that level, showing that outsiders didn't initiate trade in West Africa; it predated their arrival by more than 1,000 years.

The goods that moved across Africa and other parts of the Islamic world also included crops, as al-Bakri explains in describing Awdaghust, now Tegdaoust in Mauritania, another important gold-trading town south of the Sahara. There the locals grew wheat, sorghum, and cucumbers, as well as "dates and raisins," which they imported "from the domains of Islam despite the great distance." Dates originated in southern Iraq near the Persian Gulf and entered Africa from there, while sorghum moved in the opposite direction from West Africa to the Islamic heartland. After the Indians mastered the processing of cane sugar into sugar crystals, sugar traveled into Iraq and from there to Egypt, where it became a popular crop. Sugar spread throughout Europe in the 1000s. Expensive, it was generally used in small quantities as a spice, not as a sweetener. New foodstuffs from distant lands affected everyone, not just those directly involved in trade.

Major commercial and agricultural centers like Awdaghust continued to thrive after the Almoravids conquered West Africa in 1054. The founder of the Almoravids was a member of a Berber tribe living north of the Sahara Desert. Returning from a hajj pilgrimage to Mecca, he was determined to raise the level of compliance with Islamic law in his home society, and so he recruited a spiritual advisor who'd studied law in Morocco. The founder began by leading his tribesmen on raids. Any defeated neighboring peoples had to submit one third of their property, a valuable source of revenue for a growing movement.

The Almoravid state succeeded in uniting the peoples living along the West African coast as well as in southern Spain. Much of the gold exported from West Africa ended up in Spain as Almoravid coins. The Almoravids ruled for more than a century until they were defeated by the Almohads, a reforming dynasty who championed the essential unity of God. Almoravid rule had an important lasting effect: it permanently reduced the influence of the Kharijite Muslims, whose missionaries had been active since the 900s in West Africa and had converted the king of Malal.

Under the Almoravids, a triangle trade arose with three points on it. Europeans brought manufactured goods, such as beads and textiles, to the ports of North Africa. From there the European goods moved inland to trading towns such as Sijilmasa, where they were placed on trans-Saharan caravans going to Taghaza and other towns in the south. At Taghaza, the locals traded salt for beads and textiles and the caravans loaded up with blocks of salt. When they reached their destinations in the Niger River Valley, which had no salt, they traded the salt for gold and slaves. Reversing direction, they carried the gold and slaves to the north, where the cycle resumed when the caravans exchanged gold and slaves for yet more beads and textiles.

The residents of Taghaza didn't simply provide salt for caravans going south. They devised a new product made from gold that caravans could carry on their way north: blank gold coins. These were called "bald dinars," as al-Bakri explained, "because they are of pure gold without any stamp." Kings bought these blank coins, stamped them with inscriptions, and allowed them to circulate in their realms. Their governments profited from the difference between the higher face value of the coins and the actual value of the metal, called seigniorage. The molds used to cast such gold coins have been found in the town of Tadmekka, southeast of Taghaza and the location of the earliest Arabic-language inscriptions in Africa.

Archeologists haven't yet uncovered any shipments of gold abandoned by caravans, but one site located on the Mali-Mauritania border was an abandoned caravan shipment with one ton (.9 metric ton) of brass rods and nine pounds (4 kg) of cowrie shells. The owners abandoned these goods in the desert perhaps because their camels ran away or died. Originating in the Maldives, the shells were used as currency. They testify to the West African demand for goods from the Indian Ocean trade.

Al-Bakri describes a truly unusual good from West Africa whose path into Eurasia vividly illustrates the expansion of trade routes after 1000: a cloth woven from threads that could pass through flames without ever catching on fire. "A trustworthy person" tells al-Bakri of a "merchant" who brought a "handkerchief made of this substance" to Ferdinand, a monarch ruling in northwest Spain in the 1060s and 1070s. Believing that the asbestos handkerchief had "belonged to one of the Apostles," Ferdinand presented it as a gift to the Byzantine emperor in Constantinople. Others, al-Bakri explains, reported that a different asbestos handkerchief had been seen in Baghdad, another example of African goods traveling on new pathways. (No asbestos handkerchiefs from the time survive today, but legend has it that Charlemagne wowed his guests by throwing a dirty asbestos tablecloth into the fire and pulling out a spotlessly white one.)

Al-Bakri writes about such rare trade goods—as is standard for routes and realms writing—but acknowledges the greater importance of gold, saying "The gold of Awdaghust is better and purer than that of any other people on earth." Al-Bakri also mentions a man named Yarisna, a merchant who exports gold to other countries, but doesn't say much, because the details of where the gold was mined and how it was sold remained secret.

Other writers offer their own explanations for how the gold trade worked. Some describe a silent trade in which buyers and sellers never met one another. The earliest historian to do so was Herodotus, an ancient Greek historian writing in the fifth century BC. The Carthaginians, Herodotus reports, left the goods they wanted to trade on a beach and lit fires to alert those who had gold of their arrival. The locals then placed gold next to the goods they wanted to purchase and retreated to a distant place to see what happened. If the price was acceptable, the Carthaginians accepted the gold payments and left their goods behind. "There is perfect honesty on both sides," claims Herodotus. This statement alone provides good reason to doubt his explanation! Silent trading presumes not just an honest world but also an utterly safe one in which bars of gold left unattended all night long will still be there in the morning.

The Arabic writer al-Masudi, who wrote in the 900s, recounts that merchants brought goods from Sijilmasa, the trading center north of the Sahara where many caravans began their trips, to "the land of gold." His description repeats Herodotus's claim of silent trade with the curious addition that if the sellers from Sijilmasa weren't happy with the original amount of gold and "desired an increase," they could leave the gold next to the goods being offered and try to get a better offer.

Writers who hadn't seen the actual trade were most likely to invoke the myth of the silent trade. The truth was that the gold trade involved a sophisticated trading network including brokers who negotiated the price of gold directly with mine owners, all the while keeping their important role secret. Even in the 1300s an observer tells the story of northern merchants who visited Ghana for a few days so that they could recruit locals to take them to meet gold miners. This observer goes on to repeat the same old myth about the silent trade, showing that he, too, failed to pull back the middlemen's shroud of secrecy.

The kingdom of Ghana declined in the 1000s. Several Arabic sources report that the Almoravids conquered Ghana in 1076, but the excavations at the capital of Koumbi Saleh produced evidence of the city's continued prosperity for another century after that date. It's also possible that the region was experiencing climate change at this time.

The evidence from lake cores indicates that the climate of West Africa south of the Sahara in the Sahel zone experienced a period of increased rainfall starting in 1050 that continued until sometime between 1300 and 1400. The rainfall contributed to plentiful supplies of fodder, which sustained a growing number of horses who had come to the region from Europe between 500 and 800. The horses altered the nature of warfare. Before 1050, the armed warriors of the Ghana kings and the Almoravids rode on camels, as many as 100,000, according to al-Bakri. But after 1200, rulers shifted to fighting with horses.

A major political change occurred around this time in Cairo, when a group of purchased military slaves called the Mamluks (the word is one of several in Arabic meaning "slave") overthrew the last ruler of the Ayyubid dynasty in 1250 and took power for themselves. Reaping considerable profits from the gold and slave trade, the Mamluks ruled for several centuries.

The trans-Saharan trade in gold peaked in the mid-fourteenth century because the demand for gold in Europe was so great. Quantities are difficult to estimate, but it's likely that 3 or 4 tons of gold (2.7–3.6 metric tons, worth around $150 million at today's prices) traveled north across the Sahara each year around 1000 and continued into later centuries.

One man in particular rode the gold bonanza to the top— Mansa Musa, the king of Mali for about twenty-five years in the early 1300s. His caravan of 100 camel loads of gold dazzled the residents of Cairo when he passed through the city in 1324 on his way to Mecca. *Mansa* means "supreme ruler," and Musa was the Arabic pronunciation of Moses, so his name meant King Moses. The extent of the king's wealth stunned everyone. He and his entourage spent so generously that he single-handedly caused the price of gold in Cairo to fall. Contemporaries estimated that Mansa Musa carried between 13 and 18 tons (12–15 metric tons) of gold on his journey, making him the richest man in the world in his day.

Mansa Musa talked to two of the city's residents about the gold trade. These observers began to piece together the gold trade's where, what, and how.

One of the men Mansa Musa spoke to in Cairo, al-Dukkali, who'd lived in Mali, observed that the peoples who brought gold dust to Mansa Musa weren't Muslims. "If the sultan Mansa Musa wished, he could extend his authority over them, but the kings of this kingdom have learned by experience that as soon as one of them conquers one of the gold towns and Islam spreads and the muezzin calls to prayer there the gold there begins to decrease and then disappears, while it increases in the neighboring non-believer countries." Because of this peculiar pattern, the kings of Mali chose to leave the gold-producing regions "under the control of the non-believing peoples." Al-Dukkali's explanation for why Mansa Musa's gold mines lay outside the realm of Islam is so contorted that it doesn't make sense.

The second informant, a legal specialist named al-Zawawi who'd also spoken personally with Mansa Musa, understood the kingdom's relationship with the gold miners differently. In his telling, the non-Muslim peoples who worked in the gold mines lived inside Mansa Musa's kingdom. To obtain the gold, al-Zawawi explained, "holes are dug in the gold mines to the depth of about a man's height and the gold is found in the sides of the pits or sometimes collected at the bottom of them." The miners paid a share of the gold they mined to Mansa Musa.

According to al-Zawawi, Mansa Musa also imported gold by exchanging copper produced within his kingdom for it. The tax on copper was the only one Mansa Musa's government collected (unlike the earlier kings of Ghana, he didn't tax salt). The king's agents exported the copper to an unspecified land of "unbeliever blacks" who traded gold for copper, paying 66.66 units of gold for 100 units of copper. Al-Zawawi's explanation makes much more sense. Whatever the precise details, it's clear that Mansa Musa reached an accommodation with non-Muslim miners, both inside and outside his realm, so that he could obtain the gold he needed.

With the Black Death of 1347–48, which reduced Europe's population from 75 to 55 million, the demand for gold dropped off. But Mansa Musa's reputation as one of the wealthiest monarchs of his day persisted. In 1375 Abraham Cresques, a Jewish cartographer based in Majorca, chose Mansa Musa's portrait to illustrate the map of West Africa. His Catalan Atlas was the most up-to-date set of maps covering Afro-Eurasia made before the Portuguese explorations at the end of the 1400s, by which time the European demand for gold had recovered.

The Portuguese were the first Europeans to sail along the west coast of Africa, an effort led by Prince Henry the Navigator. The Portuguese didn't have to create a new trading system because one already existed. It was complete with entrepôts, middlemen, sources of market information (though poorly understood in the case of gold), logistics (towns and villages that served the camel caravans), and of course, products—some in high demand in Europe, others in high demand within Africa. In the mid-1400s, the Portuguese tapped a preexisting trade network in gold and slaves. They didn't start globalization; it was already in full force.

At first Prince Henry the Navigator sent ships to the North African coast, hoping to recover Mediterranean towns such as Ceuta from their Islamic rulers. He didn't want his mariners to sail too far south down the West African coast because he feared the Torrid Zone. Described by the geographers of ancient Rome, this region was supposedly so hot that no one could survive the trip across it.

But when a Portuguese ship sailed past Cape Bojador in modern Mauritania and returned unscathed in 1434, Prince Henry realized that the Torrid Zone didn't exist. He dispatched ships south to bring African slaves to Portugal. In 1444 he hosted an elaborate procession in Lisbon to display the captured Africans to his subjects, and his ships continued to travel south along the West African coast, trading European horses for slaves. Over the course of Henry's life (he died in 1460), he was responsible for bringing between 15,000 and 20,000 slaves from Africa to Portugal.

The Portuguese quickly located the gold mines of West Africa. The gold trade entered a new phase in 1482 when the Portuguese established a trading fort at El Mina ("The Mine") in modern-day western Ghana, then the major center of gold mining. In the early 1500s, the Portuguese shipped some 1,500 pounds (700 kg) of gold per year from Africa to Lisbon. Europe's annual production at the time was about 4 tons (3.6 metric tons), and Portugal had no gold mines at all. All the gold in Europe could fit into a block a little over 2 yards (2 m) on each side; this small quantity meant that gold was extremely susceptible to price fluctuations.

A Portuguese trader named João Rodrigues solved the mystery of who actually controlled the African gold trade. Living between the coastal town of Arguin and the Senegal River between 1493 and 1495, Rodrigues studied the indigenous gold trade closely. He identified the different towns involved in the caravan trade, explained how salt traveled south across the Sahara to Timbuktu, and observed boats laden with North African goods being pulled up river from Timbuktu for two weeks to Jenne (a larger town near Jenne-jeno), where they met the merchants who dealt in gold. "These traders belong to a particular race called the Wangaras, who are red or brown. In fact, no one else is allowed to approach these mines save those of this race, to the exclusion of others, because they are regarded as very worthy of confidence." The name Wangara had already been in use for several centuries, and their group identity tightened over time. By the end of the fifteenth century they formed a kind of mercantile caste, whose members Rodrigues described as having skin of a reddish and brownish hue.

Identifying the Wangara allowed Rodrigues to put an end to the myth of the silent trade. "It is said that the merchants who bring the salt do not see others, but put their heaps to be taken by the Blacks who put down the gold. But this is not so." Rodrigues realized the silent trade was simply a cover to protect the Wangara monopoly.

Rodrigues also noticed the important role of slaves in the gold trade: "When the Wangara arrive in Jenne, each merchant consigns a hundred or two hundred black slaves, or more, to carry the salt on their heads from Jenne to the gold mines, and from there to bring back the gold. They carry everything on their heads, which in consequence are bald and bare." The Wangara profited from the slaves' misery: some traded as much as 10,000 ounces of gold in a single year.

Between 1450 and 1500 the total number of African slaves leaving Africa for Portugal was 80,000; between 1500 and 1600 it mushroomed to 337,000. Before 1600 the slave trade from the Sahara Desert, the Red Sea, and the Indian Ocean was greater than that across the Atlantic. After 1600 the Atlantic slave trade displaced the trade to North Africa and the Middle East.

As Rodrigues observed, by the time that the Portuguese sailed along the West African coast, a sophisticated system of pathways traversed Africa and connected North and East Africa to the outside world. Gold and asbestos handkerchiefs traveled across the Strait of Gibraltar to Spain; ivory and gold to Italy; ivory and slaves up the East African coast to Oman, Basra, and the rest of the Islamic world. Trade routes brought goods into West Africa, too, particularly beads and cloth from both the Mediterranean and the Indian Ocean. The heaviest traffic was carried by the triangle trade caravans taking beads and cloth south across the Sahara, picking up salt on the way, and returning to the Mediterranean ports with slaves and gold.

The existence of these sophisticated commercial arteries casts the Portuguese voyages along the west coast of Africa in a new light. The Europeans didn't introduce trade to the kings and merchants they encountered in the coastal ports. They did their best to circumvent the African middlemen who played such a crucial role in the thriving slave and gold trade. As great as the number of African slaves was, slave buyers still sought out slaves from Central Asia, and the next chapter will explain why.

CHAPTER SIX

Central Asia Splits in Two

In the world of 1000, Central Asia had only one resource that mattered: mounted warriors more skilled than any in Europe or Asia. When horsemen attacked in formation, the showers of arrows from their bows were the most destructive weapon in existence, something like today's low-flying gunships that spew bullets at enemy infantry. Only after 1500 could gunpowder weapons such as the cannon defeat the nomads' arrow power.

Ambitious leaders used different ways to tap the force of these ferocious warriors. A chieftain on the rise might form an army of his own tribesmen and award them a share of plunder. He could also recruit soldiers from other tribes and build larger confederations of multiple tribes. Or he might form an army staffed entirely by purchased warrior slaves. He could try raiding nearby agricultural societies—China and India were the prime targets. The most successful leaders didn't conduct raids at all; they received regular payments of protection money from sedentary rulers.

Mounted warriors covered overland distances at a faster rate than any other mode of transport at that time. Individual couriers could sometimes travel 300 miles (nearly 500 km) in a day, while soldiers participating in a rapid military campaign might average 60 miles (100 km) each day. Because of the logistical difficulties of moving thousands of men, even on horseback, the usual pace for large armies was slower, around 15 miles (24 km) per day, comparable to armies in other parts of the world.

The enormous belt of grassland that stretched from Hungary to the area north of China served as a natural pathway over

4,000 miles (7,000 km) long. Whenever horses needed to graze, they could stop and feed before moving on. Those same grasslands formed the heart of what would become the Mongol empire, which, after 1200, conquered and unified all the preexisting powers of Central Asia and East Asia.

Leading up to the year 1000, Central Asian warriors opened up pathways stretching across all of Eurasia. Traders used these new routes to transport commodities that were small and light. The most sought-after items? The warriors themselves and their horses, whether they moved of their own volition or as purchased slaves. Next came textiles (perfect for hanging on tent walls), furs (warm and ideal as a gift for retainers), and gems (light and easy to carry). State-of-the-art expertise in science, mathematics, and calendar science—the most prized knowledge of all—moved along these routes as well, as scholars traveled from the court of one leader to another in search of a good patron.

As always, the political context influenced the formation of pathways and the movement of goods and ideas across the region.

Once the Abbasids lost control of Central Asia, a bewildering array of Islamic dynasties arose and fell. The most important for our story are the Samanids, the Ghaznavids, the Karakhanids, and the Seljuks. These hard-to-pronounce (and remember) Muslim dynasties introduced Islam to the Central Asian residents of Afghanistan, present-day Uzbekistan, North India, and northwestern China—a truly massive slice of the globe that still remains Muslim—which is why these dynasties deserve our attention.

The globalization of 1000 caused the major world religions to expand into new areas. Christianity came to Eastern and Northern Europe at precisely the same time that Islam moved into West Africa and Central Asia.

As Islam spread, local rulers faced exactly the same choices about religion as did their counterparts in other places: which universal religion best served their interests and could bring the most powerful allies? Some tribal leaders opted for Islam, the religion of the Abbasid caliphs and Samanid rulers, whose capitals lay nearby at Baghdad and Bukhara. Surprisingly, given the appeal of Islam to

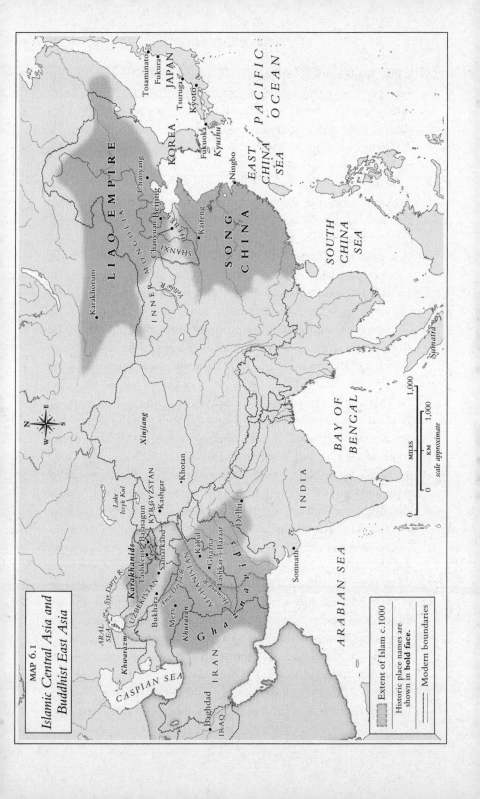

MAP 6.1
*Islamic Central Asia and
Buddhist East Asia*

PACIFIC

OCEAN

EAST
CHINA
SEA

JAPAN
Tosaminato
Fukura
Tsuruga
Kyoto
Fukuoka
Kyushu

KOREA

LIAO EMPIRE

Chaoyang
Chanyuan
Beijing
HEBEI
SHANXI
Karakhorum
INNER MONGOLIA
MONGOLIA
Yellow R.

SONG
CHINA
Kaifeng
Ningbo

SOUTH
CHINA
SEA

Sumatra

BAY OF
BENGAL

INDIA

Xinjiang

Lake
Issyk Kul
KYRGYZSTAN
Kashgar
Khotan

Delhi

Somnath

ARABIAN
SEA

Karakhanids
UZBEKISTAN
Tashkent
Balasagun
Samarkand
Bukhara
Merv
Khurasan
AFGHANISTAN
Kabul
Ghazna
Lashkar-i Bazaar
Ghaznavids
Helmand R.
Amu Darya R.
Syr Darya R.

ARAL
SEA
Khwarizm
IRAN
Baghdad
IRAQ

CASPIAN SEA

N
E
W
S

0   1,000
MILES
0   1,000
KM
scale approximate

Extent of Islam c.1000

Historic place names are
shown in **bold face.**

Modern boundaries

tribal peoples, some leaders chose Buddhism. The result? The line between the two religious blocs ran down the middle of Central Asia, close to where it is today in the Xinjiang region of modern China. The ongoing tensions between the Muslim majority in Xinjiang and the non-Muslim government of China have a lot to do with this fault line.

The first independent Islamic rulers in today's Uzbekistan broke off from the Abbasids by doing precisely what Ibn Tulun, the ambitious governor of Egypt, had done: they simply stopped forwarding revenue to Baghdad. The Samanids, the descendants of a powerful Central Asian family whose surname was Saman, converted to Islam soon after the caliphate armies conquered the lands held by the Sasanian empire of Iran. Members of the Samanid family quickly gained positions in the Abbasid bureaucracy.

Their responsibilities were precisely those of all officials within the Abbasid empire—collecting taxes and providing troops whenever the ruler needed them. In 819 four brothers from the Saman family were named as governors of different cities, including Bukhara, their capital, and Samarkand, a major center of learning. As their armies increased in size and the ability of the Abbasids to send troops dwindled, the Samanid governors withheld more and more of the revenues owed to Baghdad.

In 875, the Abbasids formally recognized the Samanids as their representatives in Central Asia. The Samanids paid lip service to the Abbasid caliphs in the usual ways: mentioning their names as the leaders of the Islamic community in Friday prayers and sending reports and gifts at regular intervals, but they never again paid regular taxes to Baghdad. The Samanids' realm occupied much of modern Uzbekistan. Even after their empire broke apart, subsequent Muslim rulers in Central Asia aspired to reunify the territory once under Samanid rule. These different successor states supported Islam, a change that affected everyone in the region.

Because the Samanids controlled the routes connecting the grasslands to the Abbasid and Fatimid empires, where Baghdad, Cairo, and other major slave markets were located, they were able to raise revenues by selling war captives as slaves. Consider a single example: in one campaign a Samanid prince defeated some Turkic tribes living in the Khwarazm region between the Aral and Caspian Seas. Capturing some 2,000 prisoners, he sold them for a handsome profit of 600,000 silver coins. Multiplying that several times gives a sense of the magnitude of the Central Asian slave trade and the considerable revenues it could produce.

Along with Eastern Europe and Africa, Central Asia was the third major source of slaves entering the Islamic world. The sale of Central Asian slaves caused a major forced migration in the world of 1000.

Once they realized that skilled slave soldiers commanded a higher price than unskilled slaves, the Samanids established a school to train military slaves. The revenues from the slave trade made the Samanids so rich that they continued to mint silver coins with a high degree of purity until the continent-wide silver shortage cut off their silver supplies sometime after 1000.

At the time of Samanid rule, Persian became the second most important language of learning in the Islamic world. Written in 982, a major geographic work entitled *The Limits of the World* synthesized multiple geographic traditions about the lands of both Muslim believers and non-Muslims. Its composition in Persian—and not Arabic—demonstrated the growing popularity of the language in Central Asia as opposed to the area around Baghdad, where Arabic remained the main language.

Some of the most brilliant Islamic scholars lived at the time of the Samanids. One of the most talented was al-Biruni, who studied the movements of celestial bodies, the existence of continents on the opposite side of the earth from Eurasia, and swordmaking with Damascus steel. Conversant in both Persian and Arabic, he usually wrote in Arabic, the language of science during his lifetime. He was one of history's most accomplished Muslim scientists; even a metro station in Tashkent, Uzbekistan, bears his name.

Traveling from court to court in the rapidly shifting political situation of the 990s, al-Biruni gathered material for a comprehensive study of calendars in different societies. Sometime after

1000, he returned to his home region of Khwarazm on the southern coast of the Aral Sea to continue his research. Al-Biruni combined rigorous textual study—in the pre-printing era he collected as many handwritten manuscripts as he could—with interviews with experts. He is remarkably free of prejudice against believers in non-Islamic religions. He reports when he thinks information is inaccurate, and he refuses to write about unfamiliar topics, such as the calendar used by Syriac Christians in India, because he couldn't interview anyone sufficiently knowledgeable on the subject.

In the year 1000, when he was only twenty-seven, he completed a sophisticated, pioneering book on the various calendars in use among Muslims and their neighbors, including Jews, Christians, and Zoroastrians, as well as peoples of the distant past such as the Egyptians and Romans. Two significant gaps in coverage were China and India, countries that fascinated him and he learned about only later in his life, after new pathways to South and East Asia opened up.

In the era of iPhones, many of us take the movements of the moon, planets, and sun for granted—if we notice them at all. But people living in the past had to know when to expect the start of spring so that they could stretch out their food supplies and decide when to plant seeds. All societies faced this challenge, made much more difficult because the movements of the moon, the planets, and the sun don't coincide within a single year.

In the opening paragraph of his book, *The Chronology of Ancient Nations*, al-Biruni explains that a single night and a single day form one unit (the solar day), which begins at sundown because that is when Muslims start each new month (the Jews also define the day as beginning at sunset). His prose is dense but methodical; he defines his terms with great care.

The length of the day wasn't the most pressing problem: calculating the exact length of the year was more important and much more difficult. We know today that the solar year measures around 365.24219 days long, and calendars had to take that extra quarter day into account or they would fall behind. If they did, it would be impossible to calculate the planting season correctly.

As was standard practice throughout the Islamic world, the cartographer al-Idrisi put the south at the top when he made his atlas in 1154. With the source of the Nile shown as three dots connected to a mountain, Africa appears above the Mediterranean. If you turn the map upside down, you can make out Europe on the left and Asia on the right. Islamic geographers knew more about the world in 1000 than anyone else.

The discovery of this cloak-fastening pin proved that the Vikings—
and not the indigenous peoples of northeastern Canada—arrived at the
site of L'Anse aux Meadows in 1000. They stayed for only ten years.

Found in Maine, this silver penny is an authentic Viking
coin that shows the crowned Norwegian king Olaf III.
Minted between 1065 and 1080, it suggests that the Vikings
returned to the Americas to obtain lumber even after they
abandoned their settlement at L'Anse aux Meadows.

Two years after a wedding occurred in this chapel, the Norse withdrew from Greenland. One of many non-European peoples opening new pathways in the year 1000, the Thule ancestors of the Inuit were able to displace the Vikings because of their superior seal-hunting technology.

The Lewis chessmen, one of the most popular items in the British Museum, were carved in 1150 from walrus ivory. At a time when most of the higher-quality African elephant ivory went straight to richer customers in Asia, European consumers had to make do with rougher walrus ivory.

Ann Axtell Morris

In this typical battle scene from the Temple of the Warriors, Maya artists use different colors to distinguish the gray attackers from their opponents, who have horizontal black stripes on their skin. Above, the two sides fight to take over a village; in the lower frame, two victorious gray warriors walk behind their captives.

Ann Axtell Morris

Captive Vikings? One prisoner is in the water with his arms bound, while a captor grabs the hair of another. Both men have blond hair, light eyes, and pale skin. These portraits from the Temple of the Warriors provide compelling evidence that some Norse ships were blown off course as far as the Yucatan Peninsula just around the year 1000.

Ann Axtell Morris

We know exactly what Viking ships looked like and how they were made because the Norse buried the dead in intact boats such as this example found at Gokstad.

This Maya mural from the Las Monjas building at Chichén Itzá shows a ship with distinct wooden planks just like those in the Gokstad Viking boat.

The flat stomach of this chacmool statue at Chichén Itzá may have served as a platform for offerings such as eviscerated hearts of sacrificial victims. Such statues are a sign of the new international architectural style that appeared at the site after 950.

When archeologists tested residues in these storage vessels from Chaco Canyon, New Mexico, they found evidence of long-distance chocolate trade with the Maya. Traces of theobromine, the chemical signature of cacao beans, demonstrated that the Ancestral Puebloans imported chocolate from some 2,500 miles (4,000 km) away.

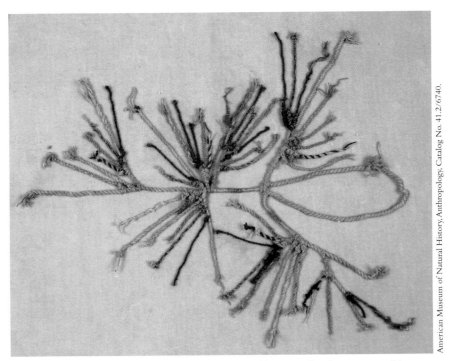

The rulers of the Wari empire in today's Peru used knots and strings wrapped in color threads to record varying quantities of commodities, most likely tax payments. Five hundred years later, the Inca used similar quipu records to administer their complex economy.

Buried in hoards all over Scandinavia and Eastern Europe, some 400,000 silver coins, many with Arabic inscriptions, constitute hard evidence that Middle Easterners bought Slavic and Scandinavian slaves from warband leaders in Europe. The leaders shared with their followers a portion of the payments they received either in the form of coins or armbands made from melted-down coins.

In 988 or 989, Prince Vladimir chose Eastern Orthodoxy as the religion for the Rus kingdom, a key step in the rise of global religions around 1000. More than a thousand years later, in 2016, Vladimir Putin gave a speech in Moscow next to a brand-new 56-foot (17 m) tall statue of his namesake Prince Vladimir.

In 1011, the inhabitants carved these Arabic inscriptions in a Mali trading town. One reads "There is no god but God," and another explains why the local town is named after Mecca. In the year 1000 people all over Afro-Eurasia gave up local deities for Islam, Christianity, Buddhism, or Hinduism.

The chance find of this golden rhinoceros, some 6 inches (15 cm) long, in Mapungubwe, on the border of modern Zimbabwe and South Africa, led to the discovery of a major gold-exporting society. In 1000 and the succeeding centuries, Africans managed the mining, long-distance shipment, and sale of gold.

When the king of Mali passed through Cairo on his way to Mecca, he brought 100 camel loads of gold worth some $800 million today. News of his wealth spread to Spain, where a mapmaker made the only image we have of King Mansa Musa.

A beautiful arch frames the Ghaznavid winter palace in Bost, Afghanistan. In 1027 Mahmud received an envoy from the Buddhist Liao dynasty in North China. But in rebuffing the diplomatic overture, Mahmud drew the boundary between the Buddhist and Muslim worlds.

Through conquests and astute alliances, the ruler Mahmud of Ghazna strengthened Islam in Central Asia. Here, he stands on his throne wearing a robe bestowed by the Abbasid caliph, who in 999 named him "trustworthy supporter of the faith."

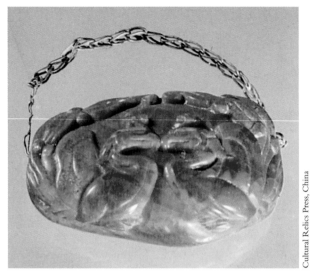

A Liao dynasty princess was buried in 1018 clenching
this amber handgrip, which shows two facing phoenixes.
Imperial craftsmen often carved amber originating in the
Baltic region of Scandinavia 4,000 miles (6,400 km) away.

This Chinese painting captures the ferocity of a Central Asian mounted warrior just
about to reload an arrow. Central Asia became one of the main suppliers of military
slaves in the year 1000 because so many rulers purchased the ultimate weapon of
their day—thousands of skilled archers.

Located in today's Indonesia, Borobudur, the world's largest Buddhist temple, attracted visitors from all over Southeast Asia, many traveling to the site by boat. Pilgrims climbed nine levels and walked 3 miles (4.8 km) before reaching the top where seventy-two statues stood.

This Borobudur bas-relief of a double-masted ship with an outrigger shows a vessel in use after 800. Unusually, Southeast Asian boatwrights did not use nails. They tied planks together with dowels and cord. Such vessels could carry up to 600,000 ceramic dishes.

By observing the waves, birds, and stars, traditional Polynesian mariners navigated their way across the Pacific using no instruments at all. They made their vessels by lashing two canoes to a wooden frame and attaching a sail.

These two vessels, both made around 1000, come from the same Persian city. The smooth white surface of the Chinese-made vessel on the left represents the cutting-edge technology of the day, which Persian potters copied so that they could retain market share. They were able to replicate the spout but not the glossy shine.

In this artist's rendering of a scene from *The Tale of Genji*, Prince Genji sits with his half-brother and reads a letter submitted with the entry of two jars to an incense-making contest. The use of imported fragrant woods by Japanese and Chinese courtiers contributed to aromatics becoming a widely available consumer good.

Geoff Steven; Our Place World Heritage Collection

Korea was a major international publishing center where Chinese, Japanese, and Kitan buyers came to find hard-to-locate texts, which were printed by pressing sheets of paper on top of inked woodblocks. Here a monk in the Haeinsa Monastery examines one block from a set of 81,000 made in the 1200s.

Alamy

Knowing the world was going to end in 1052, the regent of Japan, who governed on behalf of the boy emperor, prepared for the apocalypse by turning his home in Uji, near Kyoto, into a Buddhist temple—now so admired that it's on the ten-yen coin.

Modern calendars handle the leftover fraction of the day by adding an extra day every four years. Because the Muslim calendar was entirely lunar, the religious year began in a different month each year, so Muslims used a solar calendar to determine when to plant and when to collect agricultural taxes. Jews added seven months over the course of every nineteen years so that their solar calendar would stay in step with the lunar calendar. Al-Biruni delights in explaining such matters because he derives so much pleasure from analyzing large amounts of disparate material in different languages. He also revels in the complex mathematical calculations required to predict the movement of the sun, moon, and planets.

Al-Biruni lived at the start of what today is called the period of Sunni Internationalism, a term coined by the late University of Chicago scholar Marshall G. S. Hodgson. Although not politically unified after the breakup of the Abbasid empire, the Middle East was still culturally unified. Beginning in the 1000s, scholars studying Arabic or Persian could travel along new pathways to study with teachers almost anywhere in the Islamic world. This, in turn, led to a second development: the rise of a new kind of school, called a madrasa.

Madrasas differed from earlier schools because they had endowments, and so they could offer students a place to live, not simply to study. Most law students studied with a single teacher for long periods, usually four years followed by an apprenticeship, and their goal was to obtain a license so that they could instruct others in law and write legal opinions. Because being able to live where they studied made a lot of sense for such students, madrasas became particularly popular among law students. Once established, madrasas became so widespread that in Cairo, along a single street, seventy-three different madrasas offered instruction in the four major legal schools of the Sunnis.

Women couldn't stay in madrasas—they had no separate rooms for female students—but some women, particularly from prominent scholarly families, pursued their studies and managed to achieve a high level of scholarly attainment. Thirty-seven biographical dictionaries listing prominent scholars and interpreters of the Quran preserve the names of hundreds of female scholars. Twenty-three percent of the scholars listed in one dictionary written in 1201 turned out to be female. Multiple female scholars attained sufficient scholarly eminence that men, including those who weren't their relatives, traveled to study with them. Because information about teachers and students moved along the same pathways as did commercial goods, even the people who stayed home were exposed to new ways of thought and novel products.

Scholars and students moved freely among Islamic countries, if conflict allowed. In the waning years of Samanid rule, though, Bukhara suffered great turmoil. The Samanid rulers' military slaves had become increasingly agitated. Over the course of the tenth century, the Samanids found it more and more difficult to recruit sons of landholding families to positions in government and the army so they filled empty staff positions with purchased Turkic slaves.

The dangers of outsourcing governance to slave soldiers became apparent almost immediately. In 914 the Turkic troops murdered the Samanid ruler, and in 943 they forced his successor to abdicate. From this point on, Samanid rule was a fiction; the military slaves were fully in charge with the members of the Saman family as merely their puppets, just as the imprisoned Abbasid caliphs were the puppets of the Buyids after 945.

In 961, when two factions of military slaves couldn't agree on a new ruler, one army commander, himself a former slave named Alptegin, left Samanid territory. Alptegin led his armies to a remote outpost in the town of Ghazna (now Ghazni), Afghanistan. Nominally subordinate to the Samanid dynasty but actually fully independent, Alptegin created a new power, financed by raids on Delhi and North India. After Alptegin died in 963, his soldiers chose various men, some from a slave background, some not, who ruled for brief periods of time. And in 998 they selected Mahmud, the son of a military slave, as their leader. At the age of twenty-seven, he became the head of one of the most important powers in Central Asia, the Ghaznavids, who supported Islam in Afghanistan, a Buddhist region in earlier centuries.

Mahmud claimed to be the defender of the imprisoned Abbasid caliphs, who, though held captive, continued as the spiritual leaders of the Muslim world. The caliph named Mahmud the governor of Khurasan, the region on the southeastern corner of the Caspian Sea. In 999, the caliph bestowed two titles on Mahmud, "right hand of the dynasty," and "trustworthy supporter of the faith." He gave him a robe as well, which was an intensely personal gift because clothing retained the personal odor of the giver.

Mahmud was the first ruler from a military slave background to receive the caliph's endorsement. His contemporaries began to refer to him as sultan, "the authority," a title that suggests just how powerful he was. After founding the Ghaznavid dynasty, Mahmud retained power for a full thirty-two years until his death in 1030 at the age of fifty-nine.

Up until this point, the founders of all Islamic dynasties had been native speakers of Arabic or Persian, but Mahmud, a native of Central Asia, spoke a Turkic language as his mother tongue. Even so, as ruler, Mahmud championed the use of Persian, which contributed to its rise as a language of learning second to Arabic. (The founder of the Seljuk dynasty, active at this time in Iraq and Anatolia, also spoke a Turkic language and encouraged the use of Persian.) Mahmud's dynasty was important because it was the first Islamic empire to rule Iran, Afghanistan, Pakistan, and North India.

The Ghaznavids and the Seljuks both recruited ghazi warriors, or "volunteer fighters for the faith." Such warriors moved from one army to the next so that they could participate in campaigns against non-Muslim peoples. Their fighting had a religious purpose—defeating the infidel—but they also fought for their share of the plunder.

The core of Mahmud's large army was 4,000 cavalry, all originally purchased military slaves, but at times the army attracted an additional 50,000 men. Within striking distance of North India from his base in Afghanistan, Mahmud ordered his armies to attack in the winter when the weather wasn't as hot.

The Ghaznavids' main target was the bullion stored in Hindu palaces and temples. Mahmud used Muslim fighters to plunder

Hindu temples—permissible because Hindus didn't qualify as *dhimmi*, or protected peoples. The Hindus' status as unbelievers meant that any Muslim who destroyed Hindu shrines was performing a religious duty, a belief that rallied Mahmud's forces and contributed to the spread of Islam throughout Central Asia.

Mahmud also developed ingenious work-arounds for when Islamic law got in the way of his raiding. Because Muslims were not permitted to kill or to enslave other Muslims, Mahmud sometimes enlisted Hindu captives into his war machine so that they could loot cities with Muslim populations. The families of his Hindu soldiers lived in a district in Ghazna. When it suited his purposes, he formed alliances with several different Hindu kings in North India, just as King Mansa Musa of Mali obtained gold from non-Muslims.

Under Mahmud's rule, Afghanistan became increasingly Muslim, but North India didn't convert because Mahmud didn't encourage conversion. (North India became predominantly Muslim only in the 1200s under the rule of a later dynasty.) Mahmud's preferred method of raising revenue was to raid.

His most infamous attack? The 1025–1026 plundering of the shrine to Shiva at Somnath, an important port on the northwest coast of India. As even a cursory Google search will indicate, this remains among the most controversial sackings of a Hindu temple ever done by Muslims. Al-Biruni included a detailed description of Mahmud's campaign in Somnath in his masterwork, *On India*, a study that represented al-Biruni's efforts to explain all the complexities of Indian religion and society to a non-Indian audience.

Such studies were also part of globalization: books appeared that explained the customs of other peoples to their readers. *On India* offered a much longer, more in-depth study of India than did any routes and realms writing.

Mahmud, then in his mid-fifties, entered the temple at Somnath, where he destroyed the main image of Shiva, which was in the form of a lingam, or phallus, to which Hindu priests made ritual offerings. Embodying the reproductive power of humans, the lingam represented all the creative forces of the universe. As al-Biruni related, Mahmud "ordered the upper part to be broken and the remainder to be transported to his residence, Ghazna, with all its coverings and trappings of gold, jewels, and embroidered garments." Mahmud buried another part of the damaged lingam in front of the mosque in Ghazna, where Muslims showed their disdain by wiping their feet on it. Mahmud may have had Hindu soldiers in his army, and he may have formed alliances with Hindu rulers, but he understood that attacking non-Muslims was an effective way to motivate his warriors.

Mahmud used the proceeds from the Somnath and other raids to pay his army and to build a new capital at Lashkar-i Bazaar, located on the Helmand River, some 400 miles (600 km) southwest of Kabul. He also constructed new mosques at Ghazna.

Mahmud's next target was a Muslim power to the north: the nomadic confederation, the Karakhanids, who didn't make use of purchased slaves. Instead, the Karakhanid leaders recruited soldiers by using the time-honored method of attacking neighboring tribes and inviting the defeated leader's followers to join their confederation.

Sometime around 950, the Karakhanid leader Satuq Bughra Khan had converted to Islam after meeting a Muslim jurist. This encounter began the Islamicization of the Xinjiang region in northwestern China today. The Karakhanids had two leaders: the Western Khan, based in Samarkand, was subordinate to the Eastern Khan, based in Balasagun in modern Kyrgyzstan and Kashgar on the western edge of China. In 999, the Eastern Karakhanids conquered the Samanid capital of Bukhara.

The year 999 marks the official end of the Samanid dynasty, and the start of a twenty-year contest between the Ghaznavids and Karakhanids to gain control over the former Samanid lands. The Ghaznavids intensified the hold of Islam in Afghanistan, while the Karakhanids brought Islam to western Xinjiang.

Sometime before 1006, the Karakhanids conquered Khotan, a major Buddhist oasis 350 miles (500 km) southeast of Kashgar. A prominent poet based in Kashgar later wrote about the fall of the oasis city from the point of view of the invading forces:

We came down on them like a flood,
We went out among their cities,
We tore down the idol-temples,
We shat on the Buddha's head!

The poem voices the Karakhanids' desire for plunder, which they justified as a righteous attack on Buddhist infidels.

Intent on expanding their empires and gaining control of all the former Samanid territory, the Karakhanids and the Ghaznavids often battled each other. Contributing further to the instability, the Karakhanid princes continued to vie for power with each other even after a new leader had been chosen. Mahmud directly interfered in the Karakhanid succession disputes, supporting one candidate until he became too strong, and then abruptly switching his support to a rival.

Another nearby kingdom that attracted Mahmud's attention was Khwarazm, which lay south of the Aral Sea and bordered the territory of both the Karakhanids and the Ghaznavids. Khwarazm was the farthest east that the Rus had come; Ingvar the Far Traveler died there. It was also where al-Biruni was born. The Khwarazm ruler managed to stay independent for a full fifteen years, but in 1017 Mahmud engineered a mutiny by the local armies. When his troops set the palace on fire, the ruler died in the flames. Mahmud then conquered the city.

Al-Biruni moved to Ghazna at this time. So did the Persian poet Firdawsi, who in 1010 completed the most important literary work ever written in Persian, the *Shahnameh*, or Book of Kings. This was a history of the ancient kings of Iran up to 651, when the caliphate armies defeated the last Sasanian emperor. It portrays a centuries-long struggle between the forces of civilization in Iran and their nomadic enemies in Turan, the lands beyond Iran.

Of the many heroes whose brave deeds the book recounts, the most famous was Rostam, a physically imposing man with an unusually talented horse Rakhsh who is capable of both bearing Rostam's weight and killing lions and dragons. Frequent physical contests between Rostam and his opponents propel the narrative forward. One of the most moving moments comes when Rostam kills a boy he has fathered because he doesn't recognize him.

Firdawsi chose to write about the ancient enemies of the rulers of Iran rather than about Mahmud and his contemporaries. Still, the book takes place in a world like that of 1000, in which the Chinese and the Byzantine empires are both key players. Although set in the distant past, the book presents a model of kingship that Firdawsi believed should apply to the present. Kings (and sometimes queens) needed enormous physical prowess, and they had to be able to rule justly, too.

Firdawsi requested financial support from Mahmud, but he never received it, and at the end of his life he wrote a satire deeply critical of Mahmud. Other scholars in Khwarazm, including the medical expert and philosopher Avicenna, chose not to go to Mahmud's palace. Instead they moved west to the courts of different Iranian rulers, showing that scholars could still move through the various countries of the no-longer-united Islamic world.

In 1019–1020 the Karakhanids and the Ghaznavids stopped their fighting when Mahmud threw his support behind an aspiring Karakhanid leader named Kadir Khan Yusuf, who in 1024 became the undisputed ruler of the Karakhanids. As a sign of their close ties, Mahmud married his daughter to Kadir Khan's son in 1025.

At war since 999, the two main Islamic powers in Central Asia were finally at peace. Exchanges among the different Islamic powers in the western grasslands intensified as a result. As scholars, books, and trade goods circulated along new pathways, the knowledge of Arabic and Persian spread, and the practice of Islam deepened.

The Karakhanids responded to the new era of peace by reaching out to a new power to their east, the Kitan peoples, who ruled a swath of the Eurasian grasslands across the modern north Chinese provinces of Liaoning, Inner Mongolia, Hebei, and Shanxi. Kadir Khan asked the Kitans to send a princess to marry his son.

Claiming descent from the Turkic rulers of the Northern Wei

dynasty (386–536), the Kitan ruling house supported Buddhism. Whenever non-Chinese peoples defeated the Chinese in battle and took over part of the empire, they had to select which Chinese religion to support from among Confucianism, Daoism, and Buddhism. Otherwise their Chinese subjects would not accept their rule. Few conquering dynasties chose Confucianism or Daoism with their daunting textual traditions.

Buddhism, a belief system that originated in India and became popular in China, appealed to foreign rulers because of its teachings about ideal monarchs, called chakravartin rulers. Such rulers didn't have to live in monasteries or take vows of sexual abstinence as monks did. Continuing to rule in the secular world, they contributed land, money, and other gifts to the Buddhists and so fulfilled the traditional chakravartin ideal. By ruling in accordance with Buddhist tenets and encouraging their subjects to follow Buddhism, they accrued Buddhist merit.

A Kitan leader named Abaoji had unified the different tribes living in the North Asian grasslands in the early 900s. He was particularly skilled at tapping the wealth of the powers to his south, whether by raiding their border districts or by capturing Chinese craftsmen and forcing them to move north. As he built up his empire, Abaoji benefited from political developments in the neighboring Tang dynasty, which had all but collapsed in 885, when the emperor was placed under house arrest by a powerful regional commander, and came to a formal end in 907 when the last boy-emperor was killed. Consciously positioning himself as the successor to the Tang, Abaoji backdated the start of his reign to 907 (it actually began a few years later). His dynasty became the most important nomadic power in the eastern grasslands of Central Asia, but, unlike the Muslim Karakhanids and the Ghaznavids, the Kitans were committed to Buddhism.

The tribes in the Kitan confederation had much in common with other Turkic tribes like the Karakhanids and the Ghaznavids, and historians use the word "tanistry" for their governing system. The basic principle of tanistry was rule by the most qualified member of the chiefly house. This may sound democratic, but in practice it wasn't at all. The ruler established his qualifications to rule by defeating all his rivals, including brothers, sons, uncles, or nephews. Once the free-for-all was over, all the surviving men and some powerful women met together to ratify the victor as the new leader.

Himself a product of this system, Abaoji resisted it. He particularly objected to having to seek the approval of all the tribal leaders every three years as was the Kitan custom. In 916 he founded a Chinese-style dynasty later called the Liao and named himself emperor. Ending the triannual meetings, he asserted that he couldn't be replaced.

The Kitans, who numbered no more than one million, were a tiny fraction of the people living in their realm. Their dynasty ruled over a largely Chinese population that included different ethnic groups such as the Uighurs. These different groups came together in Liao society, whose members spoke Kitan, Chinese, and other languages and blended their respective cultural practices.

Abaoji realized how different his nomadic subjects were from agriculturalists. In a remarkable innovation, he created a form of government called dual administration, setting up a north-facing government for nomadic tribes and a south-facing one for sedentary subjects. The south-facing government was staffed by officials who kept records in Chinese and worked in offices. The north-facing government included a large multilingual entourage who traveled with the emperor wherever he went. Determined that his native Kitan language should be written down, Abaoji ordered the creation of two scripts. Indirectly related to Mongolian, Kitan has only been partially deciphered because so few original documents survive and there is no equivalent of the Rosetta Stone.

Abaoji's descendants, the Liao dynasty emperors, were constantly on the move with their nobles as they migrated from one imperial campsite to another in search of good hunting. In 938 the modern-day city of Beijing became one of five capitals from which the empire was administered; the Kitan were the first to name Beijing as a capital city. (Successive later dynasties retained the city as their capital, which is how it became China's capital today.)

Abaoji formed his empire after the former Tang dynasty holdings had broken apart, but after 960, when the Song dynasty was founded, his successors faced a powerful challenger to the south. The Song and Liao dynasties fought several major wars. In 1004 the Liao forces invaded the region south of Beijing in a powerful blitzkrieg maneuver, all the more rapid because they didn't lay siege to the cities on their way but kept moving toward Kaifeng, the Song capital. After less than a year of fighting, when the Kitan armies neared the town of Chanyuan on the Yellow River, just 100 miles (160 km) from Kaifeng, the Chinese sued for peace.

The Song and the Liao emperors signed the Treaty of Chanyuan in 1005. The Song agreed to send annual payments north—200,000 bolts of silk and 100,000 Chinese ounces of silver, which consisted of 2,000 ingots weighing around 4 pounds (1.9 kg).

Saving face, the Song officials who drafted the treaty didn't admit that the payments to the Kitan were "tribute," which they, the weaker power, paid to the stronger Liao. Instead they called the payments "military assistance." The Treaty of Chanyuan established an arrangement that suited both sides so well that it lasted for over a century. The quantities of silver and silk were high, but the Chinese could certainly afford them: they were equal to the central government's annual income from just one or two towns. The ongoing payments from the Song ensured the Liao had a steady income stream, which they didn't have to conduct raids to obtain. The Liao had discovered the most efficient way for steppe tribes to wrest revenue from wealthy sedentary powers, more efficient even than Mahmud's ongoing raids on North India.

When the Liao and the Song signed the Treaty of Chanyuan, they created a heavily patrolled border that restricted trade to certain specified market towns, prompting the Song to reorient south to face Southeast Asia, which became their primary overseas trading partner.

Most of the regional powers, including the Goryeo rulers of

Korea and the Heian monarchs of Japan, maintained relations with both the Song and the Liao. Recognizing the superior military power of the Liao, they often had to deal with the Kitan—but they respected the literary accomplishments of the Song and still continued to import books and other goods from China.

The Korean, Japanese, and Liao territories formed a North Asian Buddhist bloc comparable to the Islamic bloc of western Central Asia. In North Asia, almost everyone was Buddhist while in West Asia, Muslim. The use of different languages distinguished the two blocs: the Islamic bloc used Arabic and Persian, while the Buddhist bloc used Chinese characters. Experts consulted with each other on a wide variety of topics, scholars studied in neighboring countries, and books circulated within but not across the blocs.

Japan didn't maintain official trade relations with Song dynasty China, but merchants frequently traveled between the Chinese port of Ningbo and the port of Fukuoka (then called Hakata) on Kyushu Island, the only port in Japan where foreign merchants were allowed. Nearby—about an hour's train ride away today—was a local government office in charge of handling frontier relations that decided which visitors landing in Fukuoka could enter Japan and which could not.

The port of Fukuoka provided access to goods, books, and news from Song dynasty China, and it was also a conduit for commodities from and information about the Liao realm. The compilers of the dynastic histories of the Liao and the Song (as well as many other historians) record numerous exchanges of gifts among rulers, but no one knew what these items actually looked like until the 1980s and 1990s, when a stream of breathtaking archeological discoveries emerged from the Liao dynasty heartland.

The tomb of the Princess of Chen, a granddaughter of a Liao emperor who died and was buried in 1018, is unusually rich because it was never looted. The contents testify to the wide range of luxuries the Kitan royal family consumed, many of which were shipped thousands of miles. Glass vessels and brass pots came from Syria, Egypt, and Iran, while small items in rock crystal, which looked very similar to glass but had to be carefully carved so that it didn't shatter, originated in Sumatra and India. These items were most likely gifts to the Liao royal family from envoys who attended the funerals of rulers and their relatives.

Softer and easier to work than either agate or rock crystal, amber was clearly the Kitans' favorite material. The Kitan brought chunks of material such as amber, to their territory, where artisans (often Chinese) worked them into objects.

The largest number of items in the princess's tomb were made from amber: beads, pendants, containers shaped like animals, knife handles, and amulets that could be held in the hand. Adding to its allure, amber gave off a slight pinelike fragrance when placed against the body. One Arabic observer, a geographer named al-Marwazi, explained that the Chinese—a term that for him included the subjects of both the Liao and Song dynasties—preferred amber from the "Slavonic sea" to local amber because it was lighter in color. Archeological testing, specifically infrared spectroscopy, has shown that al-Marwazi was correct. Some chunks of amber originated in the Baltic region of Northern Europe (al-Marwazi's "Slavonic sea"), over 4,000 miles (6,500 km) away from the Liao court. The amber route was one of the longest overland pathways in the world of 1000.

The contents of the Princess of Chen's tomb vividly illustrate the prosperity of the Liao after they signed the Treaty of Chanyuan with the Song dynasty in 1005. Once they were at peace, they threw themselves into other campaigns. In 1010, the Kitan emperors launched an invasion of the Korean Peninsula, where they fought unsuccessfully until 1020. This put a temporary stop to commerce, but once the war ended, trade resumed, and the Liao emperors welcomed overtures from rulers to their west. That's precisely why, in 1021, they accepted the request for a Liao princess from the Karakhanid ruler Kadir Khan.

Three years later, the Liao dynasty issued its own invitation to the Ghaznavids. The Liao dynasty emperor Shengzong, who ruled for nearly fifty years from 982 to 1031, dispatched an envoy to Ghazna with a letter proposing that he and Mahmud establish diplomatic relations. The envoy's name was Qalitunka, we learn from a detailed account written by the geographer al-Marwazi.

Qalitunka traveled with a second envoy, who was from the Uighurs, another Central Asian power. Their trip of 2,500 miles, or 4,000 km, was arduous. It took the two envoys three years to cover a distance from Liao territory to the Ghaznavid realm that under ordinary circumstances should have taken only six months. Crossing from the Buddhist to the Islamic bloc, their diplomatic mission opened a new pathway through the grasslands that linked the two distant regions of North China and Afghanistan.

When the two envoys arrived at Mahmud's court in Ghazna in 1026, they met different people including the brilliant scholar al-Biruni. They discussed walrus ivory (the word for the material in Arabic was *khutu*, a rare loan word from the Kitan language). The envoys told al-Biruni about the key property of walrus tusk, which accounted for its popularity in both Song and Liao territory: when it was placed near poison, it purportedly perspired, or gave off liquid, a visible warning of danger. Al-Biruni also learned about tea, which became popular in the Islamic world centuries later.

Al-Marwazi provides the Arabic translation of the letters from the Uighur and Liao rulers and describes the reception of the envoys in Mahmud's court. The letters were probably originally written in Turkic or Uighur, closely related languages used in Central Asia. Al-Marwazi's clearheaded account discusses only this one set of letters, and their contents are entirely credible.

The Liao emperor Shengzong begins his letter by telling Mahmud that he knows "of his excellence in bravery and courage, of his prominence in might and majesty, of his supremacy over the emirs by fear," a direct reference showing that news of the Ghaznavid conquests had reached the Kitan court.

The envoy Qalitunka carried numerous and costly gifts for Mahmud, some from the Kitan territory, some regifted from other places. Twenty-one tunics were probably sewn from silk paid by the Song in accordance with the Treaty of Chanyuan.

The Liao envoy also presented musk, a rare medicine and costly and powerful aromatic, which was harvested from the glands of musk deer who lived on the Tibetan plains. In front of their penises, the male deer have a small ball-shaped gland about 1.6 inches (4 cm) across, which sprays an odorous secretion. If you kill the deer, dry the gland, and cut it open, you will obtain a substance that perfume and incense makers use to create more-fragrant and more-lasting blends. This ability to intensify fragrance made musk, like ambergris from whales, extremely valuable.

Some 200 sable skins and 1,000 gray squirrel skins were certainly from the territories controlled by the Kitan. The goods from the Liao emperor typify the gifts exchanged by the rulers of the Islamic and Buddhist blocs: furs, textiles, and aromatics.

Last was a gift from the Liao emperor expressing his desire to ally with Mahmud: a single bow with ten arrows. The Uighur envoy offered Mahmud only a slave and a single arrow "as a symbol," explaining lamely that the road was too dangerous to carry any gifts of value.

As the next step in establishing a relationship, the Liao emperor requested that the Ghaznavids send an envoy who is "chosen from among men of sound judgment, intelligence, and fortitude." The purpose of sending such an emissary? "So that we may inform him of how things stand with us, and communicate with him on how things stand with him, while establishing the custom of mutual donations, in friendship with him." This succinct statement explains why rulers all around the world in 1000 dispatched representatives to each other's courts: they desired both information about their neighbors and unusual commodities.

Mahmud was different. He refused the Liao emperor's offer point-blank: "Peace and truce exist only for ending war and battles. But there is no religion that brings us together and through which we are connected to each other. Distance and the area between us that needs to be traversed grant security for each of us from the deceit caused by the other party. I have no need of close relations with you until you accept Islam. Goodbye."

His brutally frank reply demonstrates that rulers knew about the conversions occurring around 1000, and that they—not just modern historians—divided the world into religious blocs. Mahmud turned Emperor Shengzong down because he wasn't a Muslim and because he lived at such a great distance. Mahmud conceived of a world in which his Muslim allies were on one side, and everyone else, including the Buddhist Liao emperor, was on the other.

Mahmud's reaction to the Liao emperor's overture occurred at the exact moment when bumper cars from two different cultures collided on newly opened pathways, a moment that our sources often miss. Such moments occurred elsewhere: think of the Crusades, the century-long conflict between Muslims and Christians to establish control of the Holy Land.

As a Turkic tribal confederacy, Kitan culture had much in common with that of the Ghaznavids and Karakhanids, and one might expect them to have converted to Islam. But the Liao rulers maintained their long tradition of supporting Buddhism even after Mahmud's refusal to ally with them.

One way the Liao rulers demonstrated their beliefs was by building pagodas. Buddhist devotees enclosed offerings to the Buddha in containers, which they placed in closed spaces located at the top or the bottom of pagodas. These often held fragments of cremated bone or pieces of glass or rock, believed to be relics of the Buddha.

One of the richest deposits was found in a hidden chamber at the top of the Northern Pagoda, which was built by the Liao imperial family in 1043 in Chaoyang city in Liaoning province. A stone box dated to May 19, 1043, in the Liao calendar, had an inscription that read, "with seven years remaining of Semblance Dharma followed by entry into the Final Dharma." These are Buddhist names of specific eras. This inscription raises complex calendrical problems: when did the current Semblance Dharma era begin? And when precisely would the Final Dharma era start? That was when Buddhists believed the world would come to an end.

The answer hinged on when to start the count. The calendar that the Liao ruling family used began with the death of the Buddha in 949 BC, which marked the end of the era of the True Dharma, when the Buddha's followers fully comprehended his teachings. After 1,000 years, in AD 51, that first idealized age gave way to a time when people had access only to a watered-down version of those teachings, the Semblance Dharma, which would end in 1051. In 1052, when the Final Dharma would begin, everything would be destroyed.

How could Buddhists best prepare for the end of the world?

They believed that they should provide the Buddha of the Future with whatever he would need to restart Buddhism after the apocalypse. That is why they placed different offerings in a repository at the top of the Northern Pagoda at Chaoyang.

The pagoda's contents, which fill an entire museum, testify to the broad trading contacts the Liao imperial family maintained with distant peoples. The most remarkable object is a house of jewels measuring just over one yard (1 m) tall, made by stringing together thousands of precious and semiprecious stones including pearls, coral, jade, rock crystal, agate, glass, and the Kitans' favorite amber. Multiple international suppliers sourced these from every corner of Afro-Eurasia.

The Liao ruling family provided Buddhist texts for the recovery from the apocalypse in a different Buddhist monastery located in the Fangshan district in southwestern Beijing. There, they financed the carving of a massive library of Buddhist texts on thousands of stone tablets, which functioned as printing blocks. Printers could ink the blocks, place sheets of paper on top of them, and make impressions of the texts. They buried these tablets in a huge underground storehouse that modern tourists can visit today.

Buddhists disagreed about the exact date when the world would end. No one in Song dynasty China expected the apocalypse to arrive in 1052 (they thought it would come five centuries earlier), but the Japanese dreaded 1052 as much as the Liao Buddhists. Various omens terrified the Japanese. Between 995 and 1030, the capital city of Kyoto suffered multiple outbreaks of different diseases including smallpox, measles, and flu, and in 1006 a supernova caused great consternation.

It certainly seemed as though the world was coming to an end, and the Japanese, like the Liao imperial family, thought it would do so in 1052. The shared belief in the same end date shows that Japanese and Liao Buddhists had close ties, a finding that upends the prevailing view that Japan and the Liao realm had minimal contact.

True, the official histories record very few tribute missions between the two countries. Although Fukuoka was the only Japanese port allowed to receive foreign goods, several unofficial ports on the west coast of Japan, such as Tsuruga, Fukura, and Tosaminato, saw considerable traffic with the Liao dynasty in the 990s, including the import of eagle's wings and furs, as Yale art historian Mimi Yiengpruksawan has persuasively demonstrated.

At this time real power in Japan lay in the hand of regents from the Fujiwara clan who ruled on behalf of child emperors. Each time the emperor reached adulthood, he would abdicate in favor of a young child, allowing the regents to continue in power. The regent named Fujiwara no Michinaga was the power behind the throne from 996 to 1017, when his son Fujiwara no Yorimichi took over and ruled until 1058.

Like the Liao imperial family, the Japanese regents also buried objects in the ground in preparation for the impending destruction of the world. In 1007 the regent Fujiwara no Michinaga interred fifteen Buddhist texts on a mountain outside Nara. Hundreds of such burials contain a variety of objects, some made in Japan, some in Song dynasty China, and some in Liao territory, all indicating the existence of an unofficial trading zone among the Buddhist countries of North Asia.

Books moved along these same pathways, too. When Fujiwara no Yorimichi heard about a Buddhist text circulating in Liao territory that he wanted to read (this was before he became regent), he asked a monk living in the Song capital of Kaifeng to find a copy for him. Although the Treaty of Chanyuan banned the export of Chinese books, it was not effective, and the monk was able to ship the book from Kaifeng to the Japanese port of Fukuoka.

As the apocalypse neared, the Japanese sought accurate calendrical information even more aggressively. Rulers valued the calendrical sciences because a knowledge of the skies could help them to maintain political control. They believed that abnormal events, such as a surprise eclipse that no one predicted, signaled the displeasure of the powers that controlled the cosmos, and the impending demise of the world required even closer observation than usual.

In 1040, when two astronomers at the imperial court in Kyoto disagreed about the timing of a coming eclipse, the regent Yorimichi tried to head off the dispute by checking the most up-to-date Chinese calendar. He sent agents to the Goryeo kingdom on Korea, a major printing center, to locate a copy. The belief in the 1052 end of the world was shared by the various powers in the Buddhist bloc—the Liao realm, Japan, and Korea—and books traveled along the pathways that linked them. Korean calendrical experts conferred with their counterparts in Japan and the Liao realm just as al-Biruni consulted with like-minded experts in the Islamic bloc.

When 1052 finally arrived, the regent Yorimichi converted a villa he owned in the Uji suburb of Kyoto into a Buddhist temple later called Phoenix Hall (Byodoin in Japanese), because of its resemblance to a bird with outstretched wings. The completed Byodoin temple is such an iconic symbol of Japanese culture that it's on the face of the ten-yen coin. Yet the Phoenix Hall displays multiple signs of Liao influence. In a large inner hall with no columns holding up the roof, the designers placed a large statue of the Buddha and decorated the hall with multiple mirrors and unusual metal ornamentation.

To everyone's surprise, the year 1052 came and went without any major catastrophe. Some believed that the era of the Final Dharma had arrived quietly, but others weren't so sure. After a few years, everything settled down again. No one proposed a new date for the Final Dharma, and life went on much as it had before.

Between 1000 and 1200, a bewildering set of dynastic changes occurred. Mahmud's son succeeded him in 1030 when Mahmud died at the age of fifty-nine, but then the Seljuks defeated the Ghaznavids in 1040. The Jurchen, one of the subject peoples of the Liao dynasty, overthrew them in 1125, and in the 1140s signed a treaty that required the Song to make even higher annual payments than those stipulated in the 1005 Treaty of Chanyuan. Even so, these events didn't budge the border between the Buddhist and Islamic blocs.

Surprisingly, despite all the infighting among different branches of the royal house, the Karakhanids retained power until 1211, when they, like every other power in Central Asia, surrendered to an almost unbeatable opponent, Chinggis Khan. (This is his Mongolian name; Genghis Khan is the Persian translation.) Chinggis formed an army of steppe peoples larger and more powerful than any earlier confederation. Every soldier had multiple mounts, each capable of different movements (such as being steady enough that a rider could swoop down to pick something up off the ground), and complex cavalry maneuvers that allowed the freshest warriors to ride at the head of the armies. Chinggis learned much from the peoples he conquered, including a branch of the Kitan who survived in western Xinjiang. He didn't purchase slave soldiers. Instead he gave a larger share of the plunder to those who fought hardest.

Chinggis added one important ingredient to the existing Central Asian model: terror. Whenever the Mongol forces reached a new place, they offered the ruler a chance to surrender, accept the Mongol khan's sovereignty, and submit regular high payments to his representative. If the ruler agreed, the Mongols appointed a governor to supervise the region, allowing the former ruler to stay in place and continue to rule provided he paid taxes. Although the Mongols continued to worship their own pantheon (the sky god Tengri was particularly important to them), they didn't force their beliefs on their Muslim and Buddhist subjects.

The outcome was very different when a ruler *didn't* surrender. Then, the Mongols carried out their threats of annihilation. In one city the Mongols conquered, they piled the skulls of the slain occupants in a huge mound outside the city wall—in another, just their severed ears. Their goal was always the same: to persuade all those in their way to capitulate rather than fight. Once a city had fallen, the Mongols divided the residents into different groups. Skilled weavers and metalworkers were sent to the capital. The Mongol armies absorbed those with any useful expertise, such as military engineers who could launch bundles of gunpowder that exploded on contact (a Chinese innovation) or use a ballista to cast giant stones through the air to destroy targets.

When a Franciscan missionary from Belgium named William of Rubruck visited the capital at Karakhorum, in modern Mongolia, he encountered European prisoners of war from as far away as France. One man was a skilled silversmith who made elaborate fountains. Captives like the silversmith were able to marry, form families, and live comfortably, but they couldn't return home. The movement of so many people across the grasslands resulted in unprecedented exchanges of information: Iranian and Chinese astronomers consulted with each other, and one Iranian historian wrote a history of the world that covered the Islamic world as well as China in considerable detail. Another result of the new connections was the rapid spread of the Black Death, or bubonic plague, which originated in western Central Asia and spread to the Middle East and Europe.

The Mongols succeeded in forming the largest contiguous land empire in history. It stretched across the Eurasian grasslands all the way from modern Hungary to China. The various sections of the empire pledged allegiance to the great khan, and they were required to provide mounts for both the members of his postal service and for envoys from other lands.

The Mongol empire held together during the lifetime of Chinggis and the son who succeeded him. Unusual for the leader of a tribe, Chinggis was able to name his successor; two years after his death, his warriors acclaimed his third son as his successor at a grand meeting, similar to those among the Kitan that Abaoji abolished. But when that son died, and Chinggis's grandsons had to choose the next leader, they didn't fight to see which brother would rule a unified empire. Instead, they divided their realm into four quadrants: Iran, the Volga Valley and parts of Siberia, Central Asia, and China and Mongolia.

Although Chinggis and his immediate descendants didn't convert to either Islam or Buddhism, the rulers of the various quadrants eventually did. By the 1330s, the rulers of the three western quadrants had all embraced Islam, while only the eastern quadrant, which consisted of China and Mongolia, remained Buddhist. There the Mongols founded a Chinese-style dynasty, whose emperors were particularly drawn to the teachings of Tibetan Buddhist teachers.

The last Mongol-style ruler of Central Asia was Tamerlane (Timur the Lame) who tapped the power of the steppe warriors to unify the three Muslim quadrants of the Mongol empire. Styling himself a traditional ruler like Chinggis (he married a descendant of Chinggis to buttress this dubious claim), he also explicitly identified as a Muslim. But when he died in 1405 while trying to invade China, the ideal of a land-based empire created by steppe warriors died with him. Other contemporary rulers also hoped to build large empires, but they focused on the sea, not land, and used ships rather than horsemen, as we'll see in the next chapter.

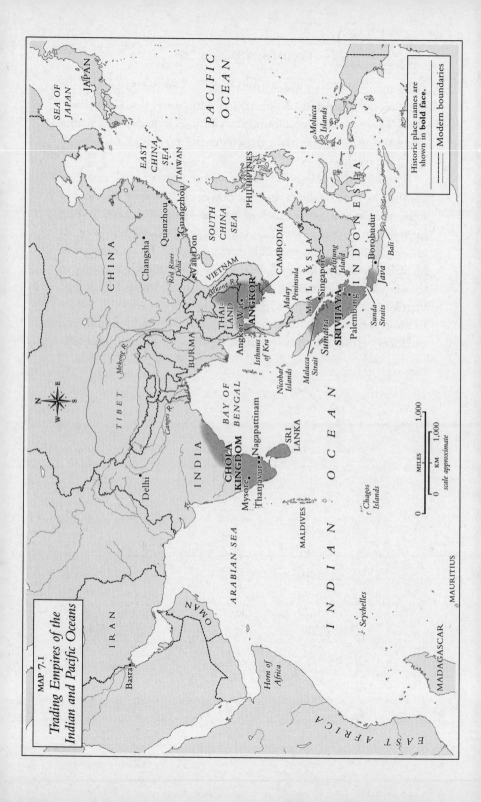

MAP 7.1
*Trading Empires of the
Indian and Pacific Oceans*

Historic place names are
shown in **bold face.**

- - - - - Modern boundaries

SEA OF
JAPAN

JAPAN

PACIFIC
OCEAN

EAST
CHINA
SEA

CHINA

Changsha

Quanzhou

Guangzhou

TAIWAN

Red River
Delta

Vân Don

SOUTH
CHINA
SEA

PHILIPPINES

VIETNAM

Mekong R.

CAMBODIA

Molucca
Islands

TIBET

Mekong R.

BURMA

THAI-
LAND

ANGKOR

Angkor Wat

Isthmus
of Kra

Malay
Peninsula

MALAYSIA

Singapore

Belitung
Island

INDONESIA

Borobudur

Ganges R.

INDIA

BAY OF
BENGAL

Nicobar
Islands

Malacca
Strait

Sumatra

SRIVIJAYA

Palembang

Sunda
Straits

Java

Bali

N
E
S
W

Delhi

CHOLA
KINGDOM

Mysore

Thanjavur

Nagapattinam

SRI
LANKA

INDIAN OCEAN

Chagos
Islands

IRAN

OMAN

Basra

ARABIAN
SEA

MALDIVES

Seychelles

MAURITIUS

Horn of
Africa

EAST AFRICA

MADAGASCAR

0   1,000
MILES
0   KM   1,000
scale approximate

CHAPTER SEVEN

Surprising Journeys

Mapmakers divide the waters between Africa and Japan into different seas—the Arabian Sea, the Indian Ocean, the Bay of Bengal, the South China Sea, the East China Sea, and the Pacific Ocean—but in actuality these formed one continuous waterway, which mariners traveled along by hugging the coastline.

Their early voyages took advantage of the monsoon winds to explore and to transport goods from the Arabian Peninsula to India and later to China. The winds determine the best times to travel in the Indian Ocean. In winter, the Eurasian landmass cools down, sending dry air over the oceans, and in summer, when Eurasia heats up, it creates a vacuum that sucks in water-laden air from over the oceans, causing the heavy rains so essential to agriculture. By 200 BC, sailors in the Bay of Bengal understood the annual rhythms of the monsoon well enough to ride its winds between India and Southeast Asia, and by AD 1000, they were certainly voyaging across the open ocean.

The main items traded in the region were locally grown fragrant woods, plants, and spices, all of which qualify as "aromatics," a convenient catchall term for these different products. The Spice Islands, or the Moluccas of modern Indonesia, are justly famous for being the home of multiple spices including cloves and nutmeg. In a world in which few people bathed and most meals were simple, these aromatics had enormous appeal. Within the region metals such as gold, tin, and silver were also traded, and cotton textiles were extremely popular because they were so well suited to the climate.

The long-distance slave trade in the Indian Ocean wasn't as large as in the Islamic world, probably because most societies were able to source slaves and other types of laborers locally. Moreover, the societies around the Indian Ocean didn't encourage the freeing of slaves as did contemporary societies in the Islamic world. As a result, they did not have to replenish their slave populations.

The European voyages across these oceans around 1500 weren't the first chapter of globalization for the region. One thousand years earlier local mariners were already regularly traversing the sea routes later "discovered" by da Gama and Magellan. Nor did European mariners introduce long-distance commerce, which was well established at the time of their arrival. What the Europeans wanted to do, and eventually did do, was cut out the middlemen and avoid paying duties to rulers. In Africa, the Europeans gained direct access to the sources of gold and slaves, and in the Spice Islands they found out how to purchase spices, woods, and other aromatics without going through middlemen.

The most surprising journeys around the year 1000 took place between the Malay Peninsula and Madagascar on the east coast of Africa some 4,000 miles (6,500 km) away (just under the 4,400 miles, or 7,000 km, of Columbus's first voyage). Although Madagascar is only some 250 miles (400 km) off Africa's east coast, the language of the islands, Malagasy, is related to Malayic languages and not—as you'd expect—to the Bantu family of languages predominant in Africa and along the East African coast.

Malagasy turns out to be in the same language group as Malay, Polynesian, Hawaiian, and the indigenous language of Taiwan. These Malayo-Polynesian languages have much in common: the Hawaiian word for "forbidden" is *kabu*, while the Tahitians pronounce the same word as "tabu" (the origin of "taboo" in English). The peoples who settled the Pacific between 1000 BC and AD 1300 spoke languages in this family, as did those who went all the way to Madagascar.

To linguists, then, it was clear that settlers speaking Malayo-Polynesian languages arrived in Madagascar before anyone from East Africa. Similarly, DNA tests on the modern population of Madagascar have shown that they have both Southeast Asian and African ancestors.

Only recently have archeologists established the date when the peoples speaking Malayic languages came to Madagascar. They analyzed 2,433 charred seeds from eighteen archeological sites located on both the island of Madagascar and the East African mainland, which were dated between 650 and 1200. The East African coastal sites contained the seeds of sorghum, pearl and finger millets, cowpeas, and the baobab tree, all typical African crops, while the seeds found on Madagascar, such as rice, mung beans, and cotton, all originated in Southeast Asia. Some Madagascar sites produced only the remains of rice seeds, which point to the presence of presumably Asian settlers who ate a heavy rice diet. The voyagers also brought animals. Cats arrived in the 500 and 600s, chickens in the late 700s, and cattle, sheep, and goats in the 800s. The Malay settlements on Madagascar were well established by 1000.

Because no one has found any boat remains in the Indian Ocean, archeologists don't know what kind of vessels the early sailors used to go to Madagascar. The earliest written records about how their Polynesian counterparts crossed the seas date to the late 1700s, when Captain James Cook arrived in Hawaii and Polynesia.

In Cook's day South Sea islanders were voyaging hundreds of miles into the Pacific. Their vessels? Two canoes tied together that carried a single sail. The islanders used coconut fiber rope to lash the canoes to a wooden frame, on which they could place heavy loads of cargo. On Tahiti, Cook met a local navigator named Tupaia who called himself *arioi*, a word for a priest with a deep knowledge of local geography. Cook drew up a map of 130 different destinations to which Tupaia knew how to sail; the most distant was New Zealand.

Archeologists are not certain whether the Polynesians used double canoes around AD 1000. Most people assume that the ancient voyagers speaking Malayo-Polynesian languages used similar vessels whether they went to Madagascar or deep into the Pacific, but the world's most prominent scholar of ancient Southeast Asian boats, the French archeologist Pierre-Yves Manguin, has challenged this view. He believes that they used double canoes in the Pacific but Southeast Asian boats in the Indian Ocean. He focuses on what is known about boats made in Southeast Asia. There, boatbuilders hewed planks from trees, carved knobs on the interior of the planks, drilled holes into the knobs, and tied the planks together with cord. This is called the lashed-lug technique.

Manguin reasons that the sailors going from the Malay Peninsula to Madagascar used vessels whose wooden planks were joined together in this way. With multiple masts and sails, these vessels have been archeologically recovered in the South China Sea and Southeast Asian waters. The Phanom Surin shipwreck, the largest boat of this type found so far, measured some 115 feet (35 m) long.

At present we have no way of knowing whether these early sailors used double canoes or larger boats with multiple sails. We are certain that Polynesian navigators ventured east into the Pacific at the same time as the Malay voyages to Madagascar. Starting from Melanesia, the Polynesians gradually fanned out, reaching Fiji, Samoa, Hawaii, Easter Island (Rapa Nui), and New Zealand, the last place on earth to be occupied by humans, in around AD 1300. The settlers left behind shards of distinctive pottery, which make it possible to trace their route, though controversy still surrounds the exact date when each island was settled.

There are always two camps: the proponents of a long chronology who see the settlement of a given place as occurring earlier, and those in favor of a short chronology who believe in more recent occupation. For example, the long chronology proponents put the settlement of New Zealand at AD 1000, while the short chronology suggests AD 1300. The disparity between the long and short chronologies can be as much as 1,000 years. A 2011 study of over 1,434 carbon dates for forty-five different islands concluded that the short chronology dates are more accurate because they rely on materials such as seeds, twigs, and leaves, which live a few decades at most—as opposed to charcoal, which can survive for hundreds of years and therefore often provides misleadingly early dates.

The most recent chronology favored by many goes like this. In

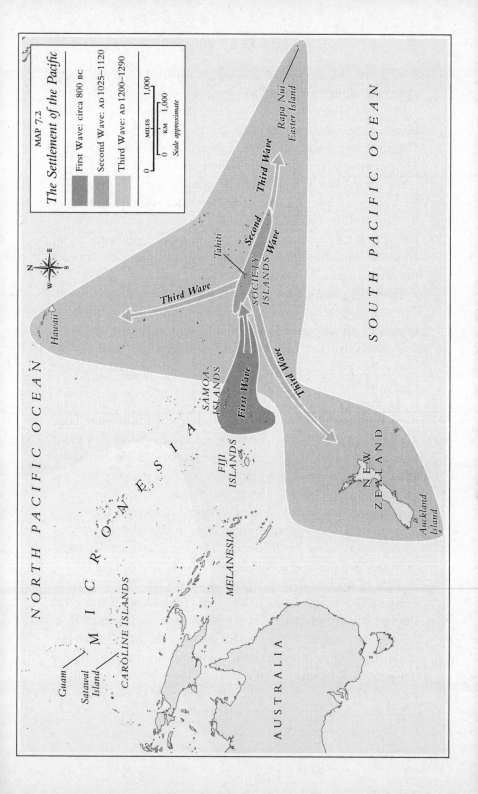

MAP 7.2
The Settlement of the Pacific

First Wave: circa 800 BC
Second Wave: AD 1025–1120
Third Wave: AD 1200–1290

MILES 1,000
0
KM 1,000
0
Scale approximate

NORTH PACIFIC OCEAN

SOUTH PACIFIC OCEAN

Guam
Satawal Island
CAROLINE ISLANDS

M I C R O N E S I A

MELANESIA

AUSTRALIA

FIJI ISLANDS

SAMOA ISLANDS

First Wave

Third Wave

SOCIETY ISLANDS WAVE

Tahiti

Second

Third Wave

Third Wave

Rapa Nui
Easter Island

Hawaii

NEW ZEALAND

Auckland Island

around 800 BC the ancient Polynesians departed from Melanesia, to the east of the Philippines, and reached Samoa. There they stayed 1,800 years before, in AD 1025–1120, they sailed to the Society Islands, located at the center of the Pacific Triangle, which connects Hawaii, Easter Island, and New Zealand. And between 1190 and 1290 they moved simultaneously in three directions: north to Hawaii, southwest to New Zealand, and east to Easter Island, or Rapa Nui. Each of these journeys is more than 2,500 miles (4,000 km) long.

Why did the Polynesians decide to explore the entire Pacific just after 1000? Possible answers include an environmental crisis, a sudden breakthrough in technology (perhaps the invention of the double canoe), or even an El Niño event, such as increased winds, which would have facilitated travel to more distant islands. The new chronology explains why various tools, such as fishhooks from distantly dispersed Pacific islands, look so similar: the Polynesians who had left the Society Islands around 1190 carried identical items with them, whether they headed for Hawaii, Easter Island, or New Zealand.

In the late 1700s, Cook's men noticed that the Polynesians were traveling great distances on fishing expeditions for large mammals, probably orca or bottlenose dolphins. When they made their map together, Cook realized how knowledgeable Tupaia was about local geography, but Cook didn't record precisely how the Polynesian found his way around the islands.

Detailed information about Polynesian navigation techniques came in the late twentieth century from anthropologists working on the more remote Pacific islands. These scholars recorded traditions that had died out on the more centrally located islands.

One of the best informed mariners was Mau Piailug. He was born in 1930 and grew up on the Micronesian island of Satawal in the Caroline Island chain, where he learned how to navigate from tribal elders. In 1983 Piailug taught the basic principles of this traditional system to Steve Thomas, a visiting American. Using no navigational instruments at all, Piailug closely observed the flight paths of birds, and clouds, and the movement of the waves (he could describe eight different varieties of ocean swells).

Piailug began his lessons by drawing a circle on the ground to represent the night horizon and using stones to indicate where fifteen different stars rose and set. Having memorized the sequences of stars on voyages he had taken to the Caroline Islands, the Philippines, and Guam, Piailug was also able to recite the order of stars for journeys that he himself had never taken to North and South America, Tahiti, Samoa, and Japan. Piailug knew the courses of more than 150 stars and how their location on the circle changed each season. Piailug received international acclaim in 1976 when he successfully sailed the 2,600-mile (4,200 km) journey from Hawaii to Tahiti on a reconstructed double canoe built to celebrate the U.S. Bicentennial. It was the first time he had done the journey, and he used no navigational instruments.

Yet, sustained storms could cause even seasoned mariners like Piailug to go off course. In 2003, at the age of seventy-one, he embarked on a 250-mile (400 km) voyage between two islands. When a typhoon blew through and he failed to show up at his destination after two weeks, his family contacted the Coast Guard, which finally located him. He explained that, despite the delay due to the typhoon, he knew exactly where he was. Refusing their help, he resumed navigating by the traditional system and arrived home safely.

Piailug's information about traditional navigation explains how sailors might have gone from the Malay Peninsula all the way to Madagascar. If they kept a certain star in view at dawn and at dusk, they could follow the latitude roughly 6 degrees south of the equator. Beginning at the Sunda Strait (between Sumatra and Java) and sailing west to the Chagos Islands, it was a straight shot across the rest of the Indian Ocean to the Seychelles, which lay to the north of Madagascar. The mariners either traveled in double canoes with a sail, or, if Pierre-Yves Manguin proves to be correct, in large wooden vessels with multiple sails.

These voyages resulted in the settlement of many remote islands throughout the Pacific as well as Madagascar. We know that the Malayo-Polynesian boats carried men and women, as well as rats, pigs, and dogs, because both humans and the animals reproduced and populated the various islands they inhabited. The settlers brought plants, like the sweet potato, breadfruit (a seedless fruit that had a breadlike texture when baked), and taro (an edible root that must be pounded before it can be eaten), and their impact on the previously unoccupied islands where they landed was sudden and lasting.

People who remained in Southeast Asia also plied the sea and through their travels encountered all the major civilizations around them—but mainly India. Even today the influence of India on Southeast Asia is obvious in the architecture and religious life on the islands of Indonesia and the mainland countries including Cambodia, Thailand, and Vietnam.

If we could travel back in time, we would observe locals wearing Indian cotton textiles and eating food inspired by Indian cuisine. Evidence of the early penetration of Indian culture into Southeast Asia takes the form of Sanskrit and Tamil inscriptions and stone images of the Buddha dating to between AD 300 and 600. When missionaries from North India arrived in Southeast Asia, they encountered groups who worshipped spirits believed to live in mountains, caves, trees, rocks, and other features of the landscape. In addition, guardian spirits watched over individual households and villages, as did ancestral spirits. After 600, Hindu deities, particularly the main two gods, Shiva and Vishnu, also came to be worshipped in the region.

At this time, the largest political units in Southeast Asian society were villages and chiefdoms. Population density was low throughout the region: in 1600, there were around 14 people per square mile (5.5 people per sq km), less than one seventh of the population density of China (not including Tibet). The populations would have been even lower in earlier centuries, with the densest pockets in locales where wet rice was intensively cultivated such as the Red River Delta of Vietnam.

People living in chiefdoms hunted animals and gathered wild plants. Villagers engaged in swidden agriculture, meaning that they cut and burned plants in a wooded area to clear a space for crops. When the fields were depleted of nutrients, they shifted to a new place, so swidden agriculture is also sometimes called shifting agriculture. Whether they cultivated crops, hunted and gathered, or did both, Southeast Asians were accustomed to moving from place to place and assembling and disassembling temporary homes, which were usually built above the ground on stilts.

Indian missionaries who worked as royal advisors were often literate in Sanskrit, Tamil, and other Indian languages. Introducing Indian alphabets, they taught local leaders how to record gifts to temples and to correspond with other leaders. Sometimes scribes wrote inscriptions in Sanskrit or Tamil, and sometimes they used the letters from one of the Indian alphabets to record the sounds of local languages. These inscriptions are the most important source for this early period. An earlier generation of scholars portrayed this movement of Indian culture into Southeast Asia as solely the result of Indian initiative, but in fact many Southeast Asian rulers decided which aspects of Indian culture to adopt.

Like leaders elsewhere in the year 1000, Southeast Asian leaders converted to a universal religion to enhance their power. Both Buddhism and Hinduism gained many princely adherents. Especially appealing was the Buddhist ideal of the chakravartin donor-king. Popular among the grasslands peoples of North Asia such as the Kitan, it proved to be just as powerful in Southeast Asia. The chakravartin ideal wasn't limited to Buddhism; Hindus also believed that talented leaders were able to rule over large realms only because of divine support.

The adoption of these new religions led to the construction of some of the world's most stunning monuments, including Borobudur in central Java, the Brihadisvara temple to Shiva in Thanjavur, India, and Angkor Wat in Cambodia. The size and beauty of these religious sites still inspire awe today, and every visitor wonders how the respective societies managed to build such imposing monuments. These societies developed a distinctive pattern of governing that we will call "temple states" because of the importance of ritual and the pivotal role of temples in organizing these large construction projects.

Rulers of temple states came to power in the usual way—by outsmarting their rivals and defeating them in battle—but once in power they didn't depend exclusively on force to govern. They encouraged their subjects to associate them with the main deities of Buddhism, Hinduism, or both. Carrying out the ideals of chakravartin rule, monarchs donated gifts and land to temples, where their subjects regularly saw their rulers performing rituals.

Since these temple states depended so heavily on an individual ruler's charisma and ability to project his power, their reach fluctuated enormously. When rulers of temple states were strong, they participated in larger networks, presenting gifts to temples that were farther away and receiving offerings from rulers of distant realms. They were able to raise large armies and dispatch naval expeditions across the oceans. When rulers were weak, their networks shrank. As a result, these states expanded and contracted just as a balloon inflates and deflates.

Several temple states were especially important around the year 1000. The Srivijaya empire was based in southern Sumatra, about 300 miles (500 km) directly south of Singapore and near the modern Indonesian city of Palembang. In India, the Cholas on the tip of South India gained regional dominance in the late 800s. And the kings of the Angkor dynasty in Cambodia, who built the famous temple complex of Angkor Wat, outlasted both the Srivijayans and the Cholas.

The Srivijaya empire arose in the same period that the Malay mariners sailed to Madagascar around 600 or 700. It prospered from its position near the Strait of Malacca. Sometime before 350, ships traveling from the Arabian Peninsula to China discovered a new route. Before 350, they did the trip in two stages, stopping in modern Thailand, carrying cargo overland across the Isthmus of Kra, and reloading the cargo on vessels bound for China. After 350, ship owners started to make one long voyage rather than suffering cargo loss by portaging the goods overland. The new route went through the Strait of Malacca and required dropping anchor there for six months to wait for the monsoon winds to change. Even though the wait was tedious, the ship's crew didn't have to unload, carry cargo overland, and reload it.

We know about this change from a Chinese monk named Yijing who took this route on his way to India in 671 (and several more times in the 680s and 690s). Yijing's travels between China and India via the Strait of Malacca remind us that merchants weren't the only people going from one port to another in the region. Monks traveled all over, sometimes so that they could study with eminent teachers, and sometimes in response to invitations from rulers. These Buddhists offered a powerful combination of spells, rituals, and initiations, all practices that mark Esoteric Buddhism. Rulers hosted these Buddhists because they hoped that the holy men could strengthen their kingdoms.

The rulers of Srivijaya prospered by encouraging and taxing the maritime trade in the Malacca Strait. Because the empire didn't keep any records that have survived, most of what we know comes from official Chinese sources. The description of Srivijaya from the dynastic history of the Song is a good example. Like Wikipedia entries today, the Chinese descriptions of foreign lands followed a set formula, which included the country's most important products, the local currency system (the residents of Srivijaya exchanged gold and silver for the goods they wanted; they didn't use coins), and a chronological account of the most important events in the history of that place, almost always providing a list of tribute-bearing delegations. Among the various items the Srivijaya ruler presented to the Song dynasty emperor were elephant tusks, rhinoceros horns, rock crystal, and aromatics such as frankincense, all Southeast Asian goods in great demand among the Chinese, royal and commoner alike. A different Chinese source reports that the ruler of Srivijaya maintained a monopoly on frankincense and sandalwood and that government officials conducted sales of those goods to foreign merchants.

Chinese and Arab visitors portray the Srivijayan capital as a conventional city. For nearly a century, archeologists searched all over Sumatra for its ruins but with no success. Eventually they realized that Srivijaya probably never had a fixed capital. The only permanent structures were brick towers for offerings to the Buddha. The ruler could always shift to a new site if shipping facilities were destroyed in battle or in a storm.

Canoes were crucial to the functioning of the Srivijaya kingdom. Kings dispatched them upriver with orders to subordinate chieftains when they needed men for expeditions, and the men paddled their boats downriver to the capital to gather by the appointed time. When the tide was going out, paddlers could cover 50 miles (80 km) in just a few hours. Around 900 one Arab writer witnessed a fleet of 1,000 vessels gather in response to such a summons from the king.

Different types of boats crossed the oceans at the time of Srivijaya's dominance. One was the Southeast Asian lashed-lug boat. The other was a dhow—a vessel with planks sewn together with coconut fibers. Because of their flexible hulls, dhows were less likely to come apart if dashed on rocks. The primary shipbuilding centers for dhows were on the Arabian Peninsula and the Horn of Africa, and their main users were Muslim merchants.

We know what dhows were like around the year 800 because a sunken dhow measuring 60 feet (18 m) long and all its cargo was recovered offshore of the Indonesian island of Belitung, east of the port city of Palembang. (A modern replica, the *Jewel of Muscat*, made on the basis of the Belitung wreck, is on display in a Singapore museum, and recently archeologists have unearthed another dhow, the Phanom Surin shipwreck, a vessel measuring 115 feet [35 m] long and dating slightly later.)

Because the Belitung vessel was looted for a full year before being commercially excavated, and the remnants were sold to the Singapore government for $32 million, some archeologists believe that any data from the excavation is suspect. They believe that the payment of money encouraged unscientific excavation techniques, even though the excavation company hired professional archeologists who worked with the Indonesian military to prevent further theft. Oblivious to the challenges of excavating in a region with so many unprotected shipwrecks, these critics were able to block an exhibition about the wreck at the Sackler Museum, part of the Smithsonian, in 2012. Still, despite their objections, the critics all accept the authenticity of the objects from the shipwreck.

The Belitung ship was built of wooden planks from Africa sewn together on the Arabian Peninsula, perhaps near Oman, where dhow vessels are still made today. The boat sank sometime after 826 (one pottery vessel on board gives the date). It carried large quantities of iron goods, silver ingots, gold vessels, bronze mirrors, and ceramics—all typical Chinese exports at the time. But the quantity of ceramics surprised even the most experienced archeologists. They unearthed 60,000 small plates, fired in kilns in Changsha, Hunan, in the wreck.

Some of the Belitung ceramics look as though they have Arabic script on them, but upon closer inspection it turns out that the script isn't real Arabic. It just looks like it. (Experts call this pseudo-Arabic.) Ingenious Chinese craftsmen wanted to sell to consumers in the Abbasid empire, and they used Abbasid ceramics as models, but these potters didn't know enough Arabic to get the lettering right. That didn't stop the Chinese from mass-producing ceramics for Muslim consumers who viewed Chinese ceramics as superior because they were nearly translucent, had thin walls, and rang when struck.

In response to the threat of Chinese imports, Abbasid potters developed a new technology, called lusterware, sometime after 750. They applied a second layer of silver and copper to glazed pots that had already been fired once. This made the pots shiny, and they appealed to consumers because people living all along the East African coast imported them. This allowed the Abbasid potters to retain some of their market share, but in the end their lusterware copies couldn't match the sheen of the high-fired Chinese glazes. Globalization operated then just as it does now.

The Belitung ship also carried some high-end goods such as four cups and three dishes all made of solid gold. One cup is the largest gold object made in traditional China ever found outside its borders. A ceramic pouring vessel, called a ewer, measured over one yard (1 m) tall and had an intricate dragon whose mouth opened to allow wine to be poured from it. Representing the highest-quality art objects circulating among the top echelons of Chinese society, these items are so finely crafted that they may have been gifts from the Tang emperor to an Islamic ruler, perhaps in return for goods offered as tribute. If not tribute goods, these objects were shipped to the Middle East for sale.

Since the design of the ceramics suggests that the boat was on its way to a port in the Islamic world, it was most likely headed for Basra or Oman. Leaving Guangzhou between December 826 and late March 827 (or perhaps a year or two later), the ship caught the monsoon winds as they blew in a southern direction. Under smooth conditions, this ill-fated boat might have completed the journey from Guangzhou to Belitung in less than a month. The ship sank at Belitung before it could go on to the Malacca Strait.

The Belitung vessel wasn't the only type of ship engaged in long-distance trade. Other contemporary ship designs—eleven different types, in fact—appear on stone panels at the world-famous Borobudur temple in central Java. Stone reliefs of merchant ships with outriggers provide more detail about the construction of these Southeast Asian vessels than any other contemporary depictions. A short walk from the monument brings you to the Samudra Raksa Museum. It houses a seagoing vessel that was reconstructed on the basis of a drawing from a Borobudur stone panel. This vessel successfully completed a voyage to Madagascar in 2003–2004.

Borobudur was built by the Shailendra kings, who intermarried with the rulers of Srivijaya. The kings also supplied Srivijaya with rice, an important commodity for provisioning visiting ships and their crews as they waited for the wind to shift.

Borobudur is the largest Buddhist monument anywhere in the world. Dating to around 800 and constructed entirely of stone, the nine-level monument rises over 100 feet (31.5 m) tall. The bottom layer of the monument sank below ground even when first built, possibly because of a volcanic explosion or earthquake. This layer depicts a hell for those who don't observe Buddhist precepts.

Visitors start their tour at the ground level and then walk in a full circle to view the stone panels on one level. When they finish, they climb a flight of stairs to go up to the next level. It's a 3-mile (5 km) walk to see the stone panels showing 1,460 different scenes. Most depict the former existences of the Buddha. In one place, the Buddha appears as a sea captain shipwrecked on an island inhabited by female ogres. In another scene, the Buddha saves a ship from a storm and a sea monster.

One relief introduces us to Javanese markets. It shows a marketplace in which there are more female vendors than male vendors, a pattern confirmed by written sources. Javanese markets met at regular intervals, often every five days or so, and the king appointed market officials to oversee the activities of part-time traders, including farmers, weavers, and metalworkers, who cultivated or made the goods they sold, and traders who devoted themselves full time to selling others' goods. The king granted the right to collect commercial taxes to merchant guilds who then transferred the revenues to temples.

At the top of the monument, visitors come upon seventy-two bodhisattva statues. A bodhisattva has attained enlightenment but chooses to stay in this existence to help others; Buddhist believers often prayed to them to obtain help with their problems. Each bodhisattva sits inside a bell-shaped stone structure with holes for viewing. Above the seventy-two bodhisattvas there used to be a single tower, which probably held a relic of the Buddha, perhaps a small bone or a small piece of glass resembling a preserved body part. Clay tablets in many different languages found at Borobudur testify to the site's draw as a regional pilgrimage center.

At the time that Borobudur was constructed around 800, full-time merchants were already involved in long-distance regional trade; they imported iron vessels and silk thread from China. Java produced far more rice than its population could consume, which enabled it to trade its surplus rice for cloves, sandalwood, and nutmeg from neighboring islands. Although safflower and black pepper originated in South India, the Javanese learned how to cultivate both crops. Java went on to become China's main supplier of black pepper, and Java and Bali both provided Chinese weavers with safflower dye, immensely popular because it turned textiles a deep rose-red. The Javanese and Balinese merchants successfully competed for market share in the agricultural sector and pushed their Indian competitors out.

Southeast Asian potters tried to do the same in the manufacturing sector. Like the Islamic potters who copied Chinese exportware, Javanese ceramicists switched from making pots with a paddle and anvil to using a potter's wheel. Although they replicated the exact shapes of Chinese wares, they, too, were unable to match the eye-catching sheen of the high-fired Chinese ceramics, just as Chinese potters failed to write Arabic letters correctly.

Inscriptions report that slave traders raided communities along the coast and then moved the captives to a new island. The legal code discusses the conditions under which debtors could enslave themselves to moneylenders and explains how they could purchase their freedom. Still, there is no evidence of a long-distance trade in slaves.

Thirty miles (50 km) from Borobudur is the Prambanan monument, which has many scenes from the great Indian epic the Ramayana depicting scenes in the life of Rama, who was worshipped as a Hindu deity. Built some fifty years before Borobudur, Prambanan was clearly a Hindu temple. The local kings probably saw no conflict between the two religions and made contributions to both Buddhism and Hinduism, quite possibly at the same time. The Shailendra rulers on Java financed these monuments by taxing both wet-rice agriculture and commerce, and they may have received some contributions from their in-laws, the Srivijayan rulers, too.

Pilgrims to Borobudur stopped on the islands around the Malacca Strait. There they would have encountered sailors from ships traveling from the Islamic world that had to lay anchor and wait for the monsoon winds to shift before they could continue on to China. Because no wrecks going in that direction have yet been found, we must consult other sources to learn what the Chinese imported. Islamic merchants sold frankincense and myrrh, both aromatics harvested by making cuts in tree bark and then allowing the sap to harden before removal. Small amounts of frankincense or myrrh could perfume the air even in large rooms.

Muslim merchants used dhows to ship these aromatics directly from the Arabian Peninsula to China. Early on, those taking the Persian Gulf–China route largely bypassed Southeast Asia without taking on or dropping off much cargo. In modern trade parlance, the ultimate end-users weren't in Southeast Asia but mainly in the Middle East and China.

Over time, merchants switched to products from Southeast Asia. They began to substitute resin from a pine grown in northern Sumatra for the frankincense brought from the Arabian Peninsula. The Sumatran pine resin wasn't as fragrant as frankincense, but it was much cheaper.

Similarly, merchants originally buying Middle Eastern myrrh shifted to the cheaper Sumatran benzoin storax, a solid gum from the *Styrax officinalis* tree, which also grew on the northwest coast of Sumatra. Like myrrh, it gave off a pleasantly intense fragrance when burned. This shift in sourcing patterns from the Middle East to Southeast Asia shows that product substitution was already a common phenomenon, as middlemen were constantly on the lookout for cheaper places to source commodities.

Camphor was another distinctive product in high demand in China because its crystallized form repelled insects and served as a powerful decongestant. It even made an excellent embalming fluid. Camphor and benzoin grew in the same region in Sumatra, so the same workers could harvest the two crops and the same ships could carry them to Chinese consumers.

At first glance the late shift to Southeast Asian commodities doesn't make sense: why would merchants start by shipping goods from far away Arabia and then centuries later change to nearer sources? Surely it would have made more economic sense to start by selling commodities from a location closer to China. The answer has a modern ring: initially Southeast Asia lacked the infrastructure and specialized suppliers to support international trade.

Merchants needed someone to organize the harvesting, processing, and shipping of these resources to the coast, where ships could pick them up. Eventually, different peoples began to work together to collect these woods and tree gums. Usually one group harvested a certain product in the upland forests, another carried it downriver to a port on small boats, while a third group lived on the shore and loaded goods onto oceangoing vessels.

The increase in Chinese demand had a direct impact on the indigenous peoples who harvested the aromatic woods as well as those who shipped the goods to the ports. Before the merchants began to stop in Southeast Asia, many of these indigenous groups had lived as hunters and gatherers who collected different forest products for their own consumption. Eventually, they became deeply enmeshed in a sophisticated and quasi-industrial system of agro-farming. They had to work full-time to export goods to Chinese purchasers whom they'd never meet. Yes, this was before the introduction of steam ships or electricity, but in this way globalization transformed the lives of these indigenous peoples who never left home.

Sometime around 900, trade throughout the entire region slowed down. Attacks on foreign merchants residing in China certainly contributed to the trade hiatus. In 879, as the Tang dynasty was weakening, a rebel named Huang Chao led a massive uprising that explicitly targeted the Muslim merchants who were the key actors in the trade just as did the anti-foreign riots that occurred slightly later in Cairo and Constantinople. The number of foreigners killed in the city of Guangzhou is recorded variously as 80,000 or 120,000. Whatever the actual death toll, Muslim traders pulled out of China, some moving to Southeast Asia, and their departure temporarily suspended the Indian Ocean trade.

But by the year 1000 the maritime trade had resumed. In 1016, the Chinese ranked four countries as their most important trading partners and permitted them each to send delegations of up to twenty people. They had done business with the Arab lands, Srivijaya, and Java for centuries at this point, but the fourth power—the Chola empire of South India—was new. The first Chola delegation had arrived in China in 1015, about half a century after the Chola dynasty's founding. For the next three centuries, Chola's rulers and merchants were active throughout South India, the Thai and Malay Peninsulas, parts of the Indonesian Archipelago, and as far as the South China coast.

Surpassing other kingdoms on the east and west coast of India, the Cholas became one of the most powerful kingdoms in South Asia, rivaled only by Mahmud's Ghaznavid dynasty, lying far to the north in modern Afghanistan. The careful management of water was key to the Cholas' success. The Cholas constructed large tanks and irrigation channels to bring water to the fields. Rather than collect taxes directly from their subjects, the Chola rulers asked them to contribute a share of the rice harvest to the temples they financially supported. The rulers exercised the greatest power in the lowland river valleys where farmers grew rice in heavily irrigated fields. They had much less control in areas where cultivators practiced dry agriculture, herded animals, or hunted for forest products.

Enthusiastic patrons of Hinduism, the Cholas worshipped Shiva. Hinduism stressed public worship in temples and daily private worship at home. In his capital at Thanjavur, Rajaraja I gave large grants of land to the royal Brihadisvara temple to Shiva. This temple, like the one at Somnath that Mahmud of Ghazna raided, had an innermost chamber containing a stone lingam phallus.

When Rajaraja I took the throne in 985, he directly controlled the immediate vicinity of the capital in Thanjavur and other large cities in his domain, but many villages surrounding the cities were essentially independent. He conquered a broad swath of territory in South India and succeeded in invading the island of Sri Lanka as well. He also projected power through a network of local temples subordinate to the Shiva temple in Thanjavur who acknowledged the Chola kings as their spiritual overlords.

Rajaraja I, like other rulers, conducted diplomacy through temple patronage. He believed that the best way to solidify ties with allies was to allow them to construct temples in his territory, and he demonstrated his support by making contributions to the temples his allies paid for. In 1005 the ruler of Srivijaya established a Buddhist monastery and financed a Hindu temple on its grounds in Nagapattinam, the most important port in the Chola realm. Both Rajaraja I and his son Rajendra dedicated the tax income from neighboring villages to support these structures, which were still standing in 1467 when some shipwrecked Burmese monks worshipped at the site. These types of temple donations helped to bind the far-flung states in South and Southeast Asia together.

In 993 Rajaraja I invaded Sri Lanka, a predominantly Buddhist island only 35 miles (55 km) from the southern tip of India. The Chola conquests resulted in direct rule of a few important cities in Sri Lanka, where Rajaraja I built Shiva temples. He exercised sufficient control to collect tolls from traders who carried goods along the main roads but not enough to collect other types of taxes that required more staff.

Conquest brought tangible benefits. Rulers and soldiers alike both obtained plunder. The Hindu Chola armies looted the Buddhist monasteries, as a later Buddhist chronicle describes in detail: "The Cholas seized the Mahesi, the jewels, the diadem that the King had inherited, the whole of the royal ornaments, the priceless diamond bracelet, a gift of the gods, the unbreakable sword and the relic of the torn strip of cloth. . . . Breaking open the relic chambers, they carried away many costly images of gold, etc., and while they violently destroyed here and there all the monasteries, like blood-sucking yakkha [spirits] they took all the treasures of Lanka for themselves." The Chola Hindu rulers saw the Buddhists in Sri Lanka as their enemies. Their rationale for attacking Buddhist temples in Sri Lanka closely resembled Mahmud of Ghazna's for raiding Hindu temples in North India: to acquire plunder from temples in a different religious tradition.

In the hands of skilled rulers like Rajaraja I, the Cholas established contacts with distant powers. In 1012, Rajaraja I's son Rajendra joined him as a co-ruler, and the two reigned together before Rajaraja I died in 1014. At this point, the balloon began to deflate. Rajendra's capital city, which he boastfully named City-of-the-Chola-Who-Conquered-the-Ganges, never replaced his father's more glorious city of Thanjavur.

Few primary sources from the Cholas survive today: only inscriptions written on stone or copper plates. Anything else, such as palm leaves with writing on them, has perished in South India's hot and humid climate. The inscriptions are mostly short texts, each recording a gift by a group, sometimes a merchant guild, to a temple in the name of the ruler. Did the Chola king force the donors to give those gifts? Or did the donors initiate the gift and then credit the ruler? We just don't know.

These differing possibilities underlie the varying assessments of Chola strength by different scholars. Those who see the Cholas as a powerful state identify the king as the key actor; those who credit the donors with exercising the main initiative minimize the king's role. This split in opinion is widest concerning the Chola inscription with the boldest boast of all: that of Rajaraja I's son Rajendra, who claimed to have sent a fleet in 1025 to conquer the Srivijaya capital.

Rajendra carved this inscription on the western wall of his father's Shiva temple: "Rajendra having dispatched many ships in the midst of the rolling sea and having caught the king of Kadaram, together with the elephants in his glorious army, took the large heap of treasures which that king had rightfully accumulated; captured with noise the arch called Vidyadhara torana at the war-gate of his extensive capital, Srivijaya." Subtract the florid phrasing, and the point is simple: Rajendra captured the king of Srivijaya, his elephants, and an arch in his capital, and looted his capital.

What actually happened? It's conceivable that Rajendra *did* send a fleet to such a distant place, but that his forces left no trace in Sumatra. It's more likely that a merchant guild going to Sumatra brought along some mercenary guards to protect their merchandise, and when attacked, the guards successfully repulsed the attack.

All rulers used inscriptions to heighten their glory; Rajendra was no different from others in that respect. One king in Burma, the ruler of the Pagan dynasty, claimed that his representative persuaded the Chola ruler to give up Hinduism and convert to Buddhism. (This never happened.)

Importantly, Rajendra's inscription about the expedition to Srivijaya mentions thirteen different places in Southeast Asia (five probably on the Malay Peninsula, four probably on Sumatra, one in the Nicobar Islands, and three still unidentified). The detailed knowledge of Rajendra's scribes about the geography of Sumatra and the Malay Peninsula confirms that the Indian Ocean pathways linked the Chola domain with Southeast Asia.

Other temple inscriptions listing donations specifically from merchant guilds help us to understand how their members gained that geographic knowledge. The guilds had existed in India in earlier periods, and they flourished under the Cholas. They had a diverse membership, both local and non-Indian, who sold different commodities but joined together so that they could receive privileges from the ruler: sometimes they paid lower taxes, and sometimes they collected taxes on his behalf.

Merchant guilds were key to the Chola expansion. Groups of Tamil-speaking merchants joined together to trade in Southeast Asia and China. They specialized in high-profit goods: gold, pepper, various Southeast Asian aromatics, and high-grade printed cottons. The residents of both India and Southeast Asia preferred cotton textiles to silk because cotton was so much more comfortable in the heat. The guilds organized the production of cotton through all stages from cultivation to dyeing and weaving and the final stages of block printing.

One such merchant guild, named the Five Hundred, was based on the east coast of South India. A 1050 inscription from Mysore claims that the guild members traveled all over India, Malaya, and Persia to trade a large number of goods: elephants, horses, sapphires, pearls, rubies, diamonds, and other gemstones, cardamom and cloves, sandalwood, camphor, and musk. The sheer variety of goods impresses: the Indian Ocean route was a major pathway, and the multiple goods being traded underline its maturity. The list is surprising for another reason: today's scholars often describe the route from the Malay Peninsula to India as lying along the Maritime Silk Route, but silk wasn't the main good traded along it. It wasn't even the main textile: cotton was.

The ornate language of the full guild inscription, which runs some three pages in its English translation, includes some surprising boasts for a group of Hindu merchants: "like the elephant, they attack and kill; like the cow, they stand and kill; like the serpent, they kill with poison; like the lion, they spring and kill." Their pride points to a key source of their strength: with the dues they received from their members, they hired mercenaries to protect their shipments.

As a series of weaker kings succeeded Rajendra, more air

escaped from the Chola balloon. The Cholas began to retreat from Sri Lanka in the 1060s and formally withdrew in 1070. The Cholas and Srivijaya were rivals at this time, as Chinese records attest, and each claimed to be superior to the other. After several incidents in which each power vied for higher status than its rival, Chinese protocol officials reached a final decision to downgrade the Cholas to subordinates of Srivijaya. As they weakened in the thirteenth century, the Chola rulers ceded chunks of territory to their neighbors.

The Chola merchant guilds always paid lip service to their rulers, but it turned out that they didn't need the rulers to succeed in their business endeavors. Even as the dynasty declined, Tamil merchant guilds remained active in Burma, Thailand, and China. In China they supported an active expatriate community in the port city of Quanzhou, as Tamil-language inscriptions and remnants of Hindu temples show.

The Angkor empire, based in modern Cambodia, was a temple state contemporary with Srivijaya and the Cholas. The name of the dynasty was derived from the Sanskrit word for city, and the city that became its capital in the late 800s also took the name Angkor. Located in modern-day Cambodia near the city of Siem Reap, the temple district of Angkor Wat is one of the largest monuments on earth, with hundreds of temples occupying a core area of 75 square miles (200 sq km).

The Angkor dynasty was founded in 802 and continued well after 1400. Each of its successful rulers extended the dynasty's influence over a larger region. The founder of the dynasty, Jayavarman II, who came to the throne in 802, succeeded in conquering considerable territory. The balloon deflated during the reign of his successor and filled up again when powerful rulers came to the throne. Jayavarman VII, who ruled from 1181 to 1218, was the last great builder at the site.

Many of the features of the Angkor temple state will sound familiar. Aspiring to the ideal of chakravartin donor-kings who generate merit by giving money and gifts to the Buddhist order, the Angkor kings gave financial support to Buddhist temples as well as Hindu temples to Shiva and Vishnu. Most rulers chose a single deity for their patronage. Almost all the temples receiving royal support were built with stone, not wood. They housed inscriptions written in both Sanskrit and the local Khmer language. Similarly, local artists modified primarily Indian iconography to depict deities. The king's subjects made offerings to the stone lingam phalluses housed in shrines and temples all over the kingdom.

Although many use the name Angkor Wat to refer to the whole site, in fact it is the name of just one temple complex among some two dozen—such as Angkor Thom, Banteay Srei, and Ta Prohm—and many other smaller complexes. (The word "wat" is a Buddhist term; that particular temple began as a Hindu temple and came to be known as Angkor Wat only after 1400.) It's too far to walk from one temple to the next. The strong sun, brutal even in the winter month of December, doesn't help. But visitors can bike, take a motor scooter, or get around by taxi.

A new survey technique called lidar (short for "light detection and ranging") has transformed our understanding of Angkor. Laser guns mounted on planes or helicopters bombard a site with pulses and use software that records only the pulse bouncing back from the earth's surface. By eliminating any vegetation, lidar produces an unusually precise map of the actual shape and contours of the ground—including the remains of walls and temples—normally obscured by the dense tropical forest.

Lidar surveys of Angkor have captured the outlines of canals, earthworks, dams, and ponds—all part of the irrigation system—that are very hard to detect even when walking through the jungle. Without these crucial waterworks, the king's subjects could never have cultivated the wet rice that underpinned the entire economy.

Although earlier investigators assumed that the areas outside the temple complexes were uninhabited, as they are today, lidar shows that they were full of dwellings packed together on dense city streets. By combining lidar scans with information from inscriptions, archeologists have dramatically increased their estimates of Angkor Wat's population to 750,000 residents.

Stunning temple murals also provide information about how people lived. The justifiably famous stone bas-reliefs at Bayon depict religious scenes from Hindu epics and Buddhist texts and occasionally offer glimpses of daily life. Viewers even observe Khmer and Chinese residents (each with distinct hairstyles) gambling on fighting cocks.

These scenes point to a major change in the direction of commerce. Although Southeast Asian rulers and commoners alike continued to worship Indian deities, they had less direct contact with South Asia after 1000. Instead, China became the major trade destination, and the number of Chinese merchants increased as Indian merchants gradually withdrew from the region. Boats laden with goods traveled back and forth to China as the region's residents supplied more and more goods to China's voracious consumers.

The shift in trade toward China affected Southeast Asian localities in different ways. The Javanese and Balinese began to import Chinese bronze coins to use as small change in the eleventh century, and by the thirteenth century, when supplies from China ran low, they copied Chinese coins for their own use. In ports all over the region, Chinese merchants came to outnumber Indian merchants, especially after the Mongol conquest of South China in the 1270s, when many Chinese moved permanently to Southeast Asia. The thirteenth century was also the time of the earliest Muslim graves in northern Sumatra, where Islam eventually became firmly established.

In 1290, after the Mongols had conquered China, a Chinese envoy named Zhou Daguan visited Angkor on behalf of the Mongol emperor Khubilai Khan. Minister Zhou noticed many things and produced one of the most detailed surviving accounts. He listed the various goods exported from China to Cambodia as well as in the other direction. Like everyone else in Southeast Asia the Cambodians imported vast quantities of Chinese ceramics. Zhou's list includes some raw materials—mercury, saltpeter, sandalwood—but the sheer variety of manufactured items stands out: tin goods, lacquered and copper trays, umbrellas, iron cooking pots, baskets, wooden combs, needles, and rush mats. China's industry may not have been powered by electricity, but it had sizable enterprises capable of churning out large quantities of mass-produced goods for export.

Here is Zhou's list of what the Cambodians exported to China: kingfisher feathers, elephant tusks, rhinoceros horns, beeswax, aloeswood, cardamom, gamboge-tree resin (a yellow dye for textiles), lacquer, Chaulmoogra oil (a medicine for skin diseases), and blue and green peppercorns. The many forest products might give the misleading impression that the people of Cambodia maintained their traditional ways as they gathered these raw materials. In fact, it took sophisticated logistics and quasi-industrial processing to prepare all these natural goods for export. Professional full-time hunters, Zhou explains, lured male kingfishers into their nets by using a female to attract them; on a good day they might snare three to five kingfisher birds, on a bad day, none at all.

At the time of Zhou Daguan's visit, Cambodia's major rival was Vietnam, which gained its independence from China in 1009. Located on a major trade route running along the coast of the Gulf of Tonkin, it supplied many of the same goods as Cambodia to Chinese consumers living to the north. Fiercely independent, the Vietnamese emulated the Chinese more than any other Southeast Asian country, holding their own version of the civil service examinations.

Situated among the islands near Ha Long Bay in the Red River Delta, Van Don emerged as the most important port in northern Vietnam sometime after 1100. Merchants there sold the products of the highland forests to merchants from all over the Indian Ocean. Chinese merchants were particularly important because they settled in large numbers and influenced the local peoples, who adopted Chinese clothing, food, and tea.

In 1406, when the third emperor of the Ming dynasty discovered that he had supported a usurper to the Vietnamese throne, he authorized an invasion. For twenty years, Ming occupiers attempted to govern Vietnam as a province of China. They established offices throughout the country that taxed merchants, salt, and fishing.

The Ming even established an office near Van Don to collect pearls, an item always in demand in China. A contemporary source describes the facility: "The Ming set up a pearl fishing compound to collect them. They forced thousands of people to work each day. In those days the Ming were endlessly demanding. They made the people collect all local products: pepper, aromatics, white deer, white elephants, nine-tailed tortoises, hanging-down birds, white-cheeked monkeys, snakes, and other animals as well. These they took back to China." This passage gives a visceral sense of what it was like to be a producer in a globalized economy: working outside all day long, the Vietnamese locals gathered plants and animals all destined for China. When the Ming dynasty withdrew in 1427, a Vietnamese dynasty resumed governing, but the economy continued to produce for Chinese consumers.

The globalized economy of Southeast Asia took shape over 500 years. For thousands of years the residents of Southeast Asia and India had crossed the Indian Ocean, and the intensity of those connections only increased with time as consumers all over the region, and particularly in China's ports, purchased the spices and the aromatic resins and woods native to India and Southeast Asia. Traffic on some routes was more intense in some periods than in others, but the overall trend was clear. Before 1000 most of the pathways linking Southeast Asia to the outside world led to India. But starting around 1000, the entire region reoriented so that it could supply China, the subject of the next chapter.

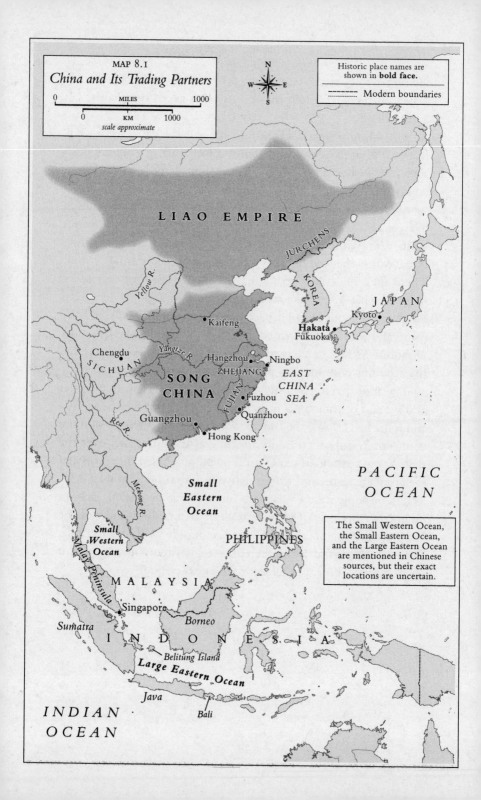

MAP 8.1
China and Its Trading Partners

0   MILES   1000

0   KM   1000

scale approximate

N
W   E
S

Historic place names are
shown in **bold face**.

- - - - - - - Modern boundaries

LIAO EMPIRE

JURCHENS

Yellow R.

KOREA

JAPAN

Kyoto

• Kaifeng

Hakata
Fukuoka

Chengdu •

Yangtze R.

Hangzhou •

• Ningbo

SICHUAN

ZHEJIANG

*EAST
CHINA
SEA*

SONG
CHINA

FUJIAN

Fuzhou •

Red R.

Guangzhou •

Quanzhou •

• Hong Kong

*Small
Eastern
Ocean*

PACIFIC
OCEAN

Mekong R.

*Small
Western
Ocean*

PHILIPPINES

Malay Peninsula

M A L A Y S I A

The Small Western Ocean,
the Small Eastern Ocean,
and the Large Eastern Ocean
are mentioned in Chinese
sources, but their exact
locations are uncertain.

Singapore •

Borneo

Sumatra

I N D O N E S I A

Belitung Island •

Large Eastern Ocean

Java

Bali

INDIAN
OCEAN

CHAPTER EIGHT

The Most Globalized
Place on Earth

The Chinese had more extensive trade ties to foreign countries than any other people in the world in 1000. China exported high-end ceramics and other manufactured items halfway across the globe to its customers in the Middle East, Africa, India, and Southeast Asia, and suppliers in those countries supplied goods for Chinese consumers. China's international contacts were so extensive that they affected people at all social levels—not just the residents of Chinese port cities but also those living deep in the hinterland. The Chinese weren't experiencing a preparatory phase for globalization. They lived in a globalized world, pure and simple. And that world reached maturity during the three hundred years of the Song dynasty (960–1276).

Some of the goods the Chinese purchased in large quantities are familiar. Pearls and cat's eye gemstones served as jewelry or decorations for clothing. Craftsmen transformed ivory tusks and rhinoceros horns into beautiful objects for display in homes. Coconut and jackfruit were tropical fruits that couldn't be grown in China, and along with black pepper, cloves, nutmeg, and cardamom, they added flavor to cooked dishes. The one manufactured good that the Chinese imported in large quantities was woven rattan mats from the southern tip of Malaysia, near modern Singapore.

The most common import from Southeast Asia was aloeswood. Aloeswood was harvested from the Aquilaria tree that grew all along the coast of mainland Southeast Asia and on the islands of Indonesia. When invaded by a certain mold, the tree produces a fragrant resin, and wood from affected trees also gives off a pleasant odor. The Chinese placed chips of aloeswood in metal holders; when lit, they burned slowly, imparting a fragrance to the air. Many recipes for perfume began with a large quantity of aloeswood because it blended so well with other fragrances.

In the period before the consumption of aromatics exploded, their use was limited to the top echelons of society. We obtain a glimpse of this elite consumption in *The Tale of Genji*, a novel written around the year 1000 by Lady Murasaki, a court woman who lived in Kyoto, then the capital of Japan.

Born to a low-ranking aristocratic family, probably in the early 970s, Lady Murasaki was married in her mid-twenties, at a slightly late age, as a secondary wife to a much older man. After she gave birth to one daughter, her husband died, widowing her in her early thirties, and she lived for another decade or so. Like Shakespeare, Lady Murasaki was a much better writer than anything in her biography would suggest she should have been. *The Tale of Genji* isn't the world's first novel—certain writings in Greek and Latin lay claim to that title—but we can call it the world's earliest psychological novel because the author describes the feelings of multiple characters in such exquisite detail.

The Tale of Genji depicts a hermetically sealed world of courtiers living in and around the Kyoto Imperial Palace in a space of just 10 square miles (26 sq km). Lady Murasaki set her novel in the early 900s, about a century before she was writing. Her *Tale* recounts the friendships, amorous adventures, and eventual death of Genji, the son of an emperor who has removed him from the line of succession so that Genji can never become the monarch.

Most relevant to our story, the lead characters in the novel—the imperial family, the regent's family, and high-ranking aristocrats—devoted considerable attention to aromatics, making their own blends, which they used to impart unusual fragrances to their clothing and to scent the air. These aromatics originated in the Islamic world and Southeast Asia and were transshipped via

Song dynasty China to the port of Fukuoka (then called Hakata), Japan's gateway to the outside world.

In this rarefied world, the mark of a gentleman was his own distinctive scent. Genji's friends—and his many lovers—knew him by his odor, which was so powerful that it lingered long after he left the room. Making perfume wasn't a task for servants: Genji spent hours grinding spices and different woods together until he obtained the perfect combination.

The women also perfumed their clothing. They remained inside their houses and gardens almost all the time, except for rare outings to temple fairs. As in Japan today, even the rich lived in simple houses with no tables or chairs. Everyone sat and slept on tatami mats.

At one point, when Genji was planning a lavish birthday party for his daughter, the Akashi Princess, he decided to hold a contest for the best fragrance. After gathering multiple boxes and jars to serve as suitably elegant containers, he began to work on his own blends. Judging some samples of fragrant wood newly arrived from China to be slightly inferior, he combined them with older, higher-quality aromatics. (One of the novel's recurring themes is the longing for the past.) His recipe mixed cloves with aloeswood because aloeswood made the perfect base for a blend. Once the mixture was ready, he buried a batch near a stream to intensify the fragrance.

Most of the birthday party guests submitted perfumes linked to a specific season: a fragrance smelling of plum blossoms evoked spring, while Genji's blend was autumnal. Each person's individual scent, the product of their own odor and whatever blend they used to steam their clothing, would have varied with the season. One court woman opted instead to make a blend so strong that it could be detected from a hundred paces away. When the time came to judge, Genji's half-brother Sochinomiya didn't choose a winner but praised the different blends, conveying a deep connoisseurship of the multiple scents that these palace dwellers encountered daily.

Lady Murasaki's novel provides an unusual level of detail about the place of aromatics in the lives of the Japanese imperial family, and the Chinese emperor and aristocrats at court would also have recognized each other by their personal scent. Because many of the fragrance-bearing substances were wood or resins, the Chinese and the Japanese did not use liquid perfume or lotion that often. They preferred to use the wood or resin in its natural state, often burning mixtures of them to impart fragrance to the air. They steamed their clothing in the smoke of different woods, attached sachet bags containing fragrance to their clothing, and bathed in scented water. They also filled their houses with furniture and storage containers made from fragrant woods.

Aromatics enjoyed great popularity because the Chinese devoted enormous energy to changing the way that things smelled and tasted. People didn't bathe often, and it was difficult to clean silk clothing. The poor had so few clothes, usually made of ramie, hemp, and other bast fibers, that washing them wasn't practical.

Aromatics were much more important in the world of 1000 than they are nowadays, when the primary use of scented candles and incense is to perfume the air. Not many of us do that very often (the primary consumers of incense sticks today are temple goers in East Asia). In the year 1000 the superwealthy—the imperial families of Japan and China—consumed huge quantities of aromatics. And by far the largest market for them was in China.

The Chinese language had a single catchall term for "aromatics" (*xiang*), which included fragrant tree gums, scented woods and tree resins, and perfume preservatives such as musk and ambergris. Some had only one function: musk, the dried gland of Tibetan musk deer, and ambergris, a grayish substance contained in whale intestines, intensified fragrances and made them last longer. Similarly, frankincense and myrrh, both tree resins from the Arabian Peninsula, gave off a strong fragrance when burned. Others were more versatile: sandalwood, from India or Java, could be used to make furniture or boxes, to alter a perfume's scent, and to flavor food and medicine.

China's extensive trade with the Indian Ocean region began well before the year 1000. The first goods the Chinese imported in the first and second centuries AD were largely decorative items such as Sri Lankan pearls, elephant ivory, and colorful bird feathers like those from the bright blue kingfisher. Only the emperor and his wealthiest courtiers could afford those. The demand for fragrant woods, tree resins, and incense arose after 500, signaling a shift from court-centered demand for rare commodities to a broader consumer base.

China had many thriving port cities, but its main hub of trade was Guangzhou, sometimes called Canton, which lies just north of Hong Kong on China's southeast coast. Ships set off from Guangzhou moving southward along the coast of Vietnam and through the Malacca Strait. They traveled west from there, reaching India's west coast, and proceeded to the Arabian Peninsula. Once they passed Oman, they unloaded their cargo at the Persian Gulf ports of Siraf, in modern Iran, or Basra, in modern Iraq. The Persian Gulf–China maritime route, with the additional leg to East Africa, had taken shape by the 700s and 800s. At this time most of the ships moving along this route originated in the Arabian Peninsula, India, or Southeast Asia (ships of Chinese design assumed a major role after 1000).

Merchant ships carried Chinese ceramics to East Africa, and, as was often true when new pathways opened up, information about northeast Africa reached China early on. Duan Chengshi, who died in 863, knew enough about the Berbera coast east of modern Djibouti to sketch the slave trade there: "The people of this country capture and sell their own countrymen to foreign merchants at prices many times higher than they would obtain at home." He added that the region also exported elephant tusks and the perfume intensifier ambergris. Some fictional tales set in the port of Guangzhou tell of dark-skinned slaves from Southeast Asia or Africa, who were skilled swimmers and credited with magical powers.

At the time that Duan was writing, the predecessor dynasty to the Song, the Tang dynasty (618–907), appointed a maritime trade superintendent to collect customs duties in Guangzhou, but the dynasty never created a state monopoly on imported goods.

Tang trade policy consisted of inspecting foreign ships when they arrived; trade court officials, often eunuchs, selected what they wanted for the court (one Arab observer reports they took 30 percent of each ship's cargo) and allowed the traders to sell the remaining goods.

After the Tang dynasty ended in 907, China broke up into different regions, each with its own ruler. The trade between China and Southeast Asia paused around this time, when the attacks on Muslims by the Huang Chao rebels prompted many foreign merchants to leave Guangzhou.

Most of the ships traveling among the Islamic world, Southeast Asia, and China before 1000 were either dhows or lashed-lug vessels made in Southeast Asia. One lashed-lug vessel, which sank off the Indonesian port of Intan, offers a precious snapshot of China's trade with Southeast Asia when the trade began to revive in the early tenth century. Traveling from Belitung island to northwest Java, this Indonesian-made ship carried a large quantity of valuable metals—including gold coins, 145 Chinese lead coins (some bearing dates of 918), tin currency made in the Malay Peninsula, metal Buddhist figurines (to be melted down to make coins), tin and bronze ingots, and finally roughly 400 pounds (190 kg) of silver.

The quantity of silver from the Intan wreck was enormous, almost the entire annual production from one of China's most productive mines. Inscriptions on the silver ingots provide a crucial clue about their purpose: the tax office of a regional ruler issued them, most likely for the purchase of Southeast Asian aromatics.

A second ship sank off the coast of Java near the modern town of Cirebon sometime around 970. This lashed-lug ship measured some 100 feet (30 m) long, and it carried an astonishingly large load of 600,000 ceramics (almost all Chinese). The capacity of the Cirebon ship has been estimated at between 200 and 270 tons (225–300 metric tons). Assuming that such ships traveled between China and Indonesia multiple times a year, we can see how extensive commerce between the two regions was even before 1000.

As the trade between China and Southeast Asia recovered, Chinese boatbuilding technology began to improve, and Chinese-built sailing ships took on a more important role in the maritime trade. A key breakthrough occurred around 1000, when Chinese metallurgists learned to anneal iron wire and to make magnetic needles; floating such a needle on water created a shipboard compass that allowed Chinese mariners to find magnetic north. Other navigational instruments, such as the astrolabe, used all over the Islamic world, required clear skies, but the compass worked in all types of weather, giving Chinese navigators a huge advantage.

Chinese boatbuilders also used metal nails to attach wooden planks together, and their ships had separate compartments for passengers and for cargo. Bulkheads and watertight compartments increased buoyancy and made Chinese ships better able to survive storms. If the ship sprang a leak, it affected just one section—not the entire craft, as was the case for either dhows or lashed-lug vessels.

The famous world traveler Ibn Battuta (who observed 600 slave girls crossing the Sahara) praised the advantages of Chinese ships. On a dhow, all the passengers gathered together on the deck, while on a Chinese ship they could occupy compartments separated by wooden walls. Ibn Battuta loved the genuine privacy they offered. At one point he insisted on shifting his possessions from a larger ship to a smaller Chinese one so that he could enjoy the company of several concubines traveling with him.

As Chinese ships assumed a more important role in maritime shipping around 960, when the Song dynasty was founded, the emperor continued to receive tribute missions from surrounding countries. The tribute system, which had been in existence for over 1,000 years, provided a framework for China's neighbors to send gifts, usually local products, to the Chinese emperors and for emperors to reciprocate with gifts, often silk textiles, in return.

Early in the dynasty, the Song dispatched officials to the countries of Southeast Asia to recruit tribute missions. Song envoys armed with fill-in-the-blank forms recorded the name of the ruler, his country, and the expected gifts. Because the ruling dynasty used the tribute system to gain prestige, in many instances, the gifts the Chinese emperor bestowed were worth more than those presented by the tributaries. This is why so many foreign merchants posed as tribute bearers when they arrived in China. Regulations required Chinese trade officials to reject impostors, but some merchants, especially those from unfamiliar places, managed to evade detection.

Song regulations from the 970s specify that envoys who brought tribute were entitled to visit the Song capital at Kaifeng so that they could present their gifts to the emperor in person. The same regulations stipulated that merchants who engaged in ordinary trade should remain in the port where they landed. During the 1030s, the tribute voyages came to a temporary halt. After that year, although it hosted the occasional tribute mission, the Song government shifted primarily to taxing foreign goods.

The scale of the maritime commerce prompted the Song dynasty to break with the fiscal practices of earlier dynasties and to tax international trade aggressively. The new tax system of the dynasty was complex but ingenious. The officials who created it, like all those who design taxes, sought the highest revenues possible.

Each port had a top trade official, called the Superintendent of Maritime Trade, who supervised all foreign merchants coming to his port and issued licenses to Chinese merchants leaving his jurisdiction to sail to foreign lands. The superintendent was responsible for collecting the new taxes and forwarding them to the imperial government in the northern city of Kaifeng. Guangzhou was such an active trade port that in 971 the Song dynasty appointed the first superintendent to serve there. Unlike the Tang authorities, who had named only one trade superintendent, also in Guangzhou, the Song government named other superintendents in the southern ports of Hangzhou and Ningbo in the next twenty years, a sign of how important the revenues from international commerce were to the new dynasty.

The dynasty's tax officials established three new taxes. First, after a ship arrived in port, trade officials boarded the vessel so that they could estimate the overall value of the cargo. They confiscated a portion, usually between 10 and 20 percent of the cargo's value. Direct confiscation allowed officials to obtain the items the central government—effectively the emperor and his household—required.

Trade officials collected a second tax on "fine goods," or high-value imports such as pearls, large elephant tusks, and ambergris, by buying them at an artificial rate lower than prevailing market prices. This regulation effectively granted the government a monopoly on all fine goods, and Song dynasty trade officials established markets for these goods all over the empire. Many of these goods went to wholesalers, but individuals could also make small-scale purchases.

The third tax was on "coarse goods," or the bulk goods, often larger blocks of fragrant wood, which constituted the remainder of the cargo. Once the foreign merchants had paid the tax on the coarse goods, they were granted permission to sell them direct to Chinese purchasers, and they sometimes conducted sales at dockside.

As one might expect, the rates changed often, and merchants protested when the direct requisitions were too high or the rates paid for the fine goods too low. Sometimes the traders won: in 995, the government backed down and told trade officials to stop buying goods at artificially low prices or selling at excessively high rates. Much like today, such unfair trade practices could and did destroy international merchants' incentive to trade. At one point when the cash-strapped government raised the direct confiscation to 40 percent, far higher than the usual 10 or 20 percent rate, foreign merchants simply stopped coming to Chinese ports.

The war with the Liao dynasty in 1004 ended with the 1005 Treaty of Chanyuan. Although it called for the careful patrolling of the border trade between the Liao and Song dynasties, in reality the border between the two states was permeable. Horses, whose sale the Liao forbade, made it to Song territory, and some salt, books, maps, weapons, and coins traveled north to the Liao realm in spite of a Song dynasty government order banning their export.

The Song banned the export of coins to the Liao territory because bronze coins with a high copper content remained the primary currency used within the Song realm, and finance officials feared their loss would damage the economy. Chinese coins were round with a square hole that allowed them to be strung together—originally in bunches of 1,000, later, in the high 700s—so they could be counted more easily. Coins had disadvantages: heavy, they were difficult to transport across great distances, and copper supplies couldn't always keep up with demand.

Because the copper shortage was particularly acute in the northwestern province of Sichuan, in the 980s the government issued iron coins, which were even heavier than bronze ones. It took one and a half pounds of iron coins to purchase a pound of salt. Following a rebellion in 993–994 triggered by economic difficulties, local merchants took the revolutionary step of replacing iron coins with promissory notes written on paper. Concerned about possible abuses, local officials limited the right to issue paper notes to just sixteen particularly credit-worthy merchants. But when some of those merchants defaulted, local officials began to issue paper money in 1024. That was the world's first paper money, but since it circulated only in the region of Sichuan, its impact was limited.

During the decades that officials in Sichuan were experimenting with paper money, the Liao and the Song signed the Treaty of Chanyuan. The resulting border controls drastically limited Song dynasty trade with the north. But because the army needed horses (the Chinese never succeeded in raising horses as fast and powerful as those from Asia's grasslands), they purchased many horses from different kingdoms to the northwest. Horses were the most important overland import over the course of the Song dynasty.

Chinese merchants sent ever-greater numbers of ships to the south and the west, to Southeast Asia, India, the Middle East, and East Africa, where no hostile enemy prevented trade. The Chinese profited greatly from the export of high-grade textiles and high-fired ceramics. Metal exports were important, too, whether in the form of unprocessed cylinders and ingots or processed goods such as iron cauldrons, woks, and mirrors. The steady flow of revenue from exports financed the flourishing aromatics trade.

The metropolis of Quanzhou in particular profited from that trade. On China's southeast coast, just opposite Taiwan, Quanzhou was home to many non-Chinese residents. South Indians financed a Buddhist temple in the 980s. The main mosque in Quanzhou, the Mosque of the Prophet's Companions, was first built in 1009 or 1010. Over 200 gravestones with Arabic inscriptions have surfaced in Quanzhou, far more than in any other Chinese city before 1500, and the Arabic-speaking Muslims of Quanzhou formed China's largest foreign community at the time.

This level of contact, with outsiders and locals living side by side, was unusual for a Chinese city, so much so as to trigger comment by officials. In the neighborhood for international merchants in the south of the city, "there were two types of foreigners, dark and light," one observer noted, pointing to the diverse origins of the city's merchant community.

Quanzhou had become a major international port by 1000. Government regulations stipulated that all goods coming into China had to go through a port with a designated Superintendent of Maritime Trade, but Quanzhou prospered because compliance wasn't total (it never was in the premodern world, just as it isn't today). Before Quanzhou was named a trade superintendency, smuggling was rife. One observer noted "The sea-going merchant vessels return each year in groups of twenty ships carrying various goods and forbidden goods in quantities as great as mountains." Finally in 1087 the government named the first Superintendent of Maritime Trade for the port of Quanzhou.

From this point on, Guangzhou and Quanzhou were the two most important Chinese ports, and they received ships coming from Southeast Asia and beyond. A third port, Ningbo, grew in importance because it was the primary port for vessels headed for Japan and Korea. Although Song China and Japan didn't have a formal relationship that allowed them to exchange tribute, ships frequently sailed between the Chinese port of Ningbo and the Japanese trade office based in the port of Fukuoka, the only market officially open to foreign merchants. Ships coming from the Liao realm north of Song China also landed at Fukuoka.

Writing in 1117, Zhu Yu, the son of a trade official in Guangzhou, provides many vivid descriptions of port life. To prevent smuggling, government officials posted lookouts along a 200-mile

(320 km) stretch of the coast approaching Guangzhou to spot any arriving ships. Zhu Yu explains how the ships navigated. Knowing the outline of the coast, they could determine their course at night from the stars and during the day from the sun's shadow. They also used a long string with a hook at the end of it to test the mud from the sea bottom because skilled mariners could determine their location from its odor and consistency. And, when visibility was poor, they could consult a compass.

The high penalties—smugglers of even the smallest amount of goods risked having all their goods confiscated—were meant to discourage smuggling. Just as Song laws directed, the Superintendent of Maritime Trade confiscated one tenth of the cargo and then categorized the remaining cargo into fine and coarse goods.

Zhu Yu is the only writer in the Song dynasty who mentions slaves brought from other countries. He explains that some were originally crewmen captured by pirates and that they possessed an unusual skill: "the foreign slaves are good at swimming; they enter the water without closing their eyes." The slaves knew how to fix leaks in ships by using "wadding to repair the ship's exterior."

The slaves had difficulty adjusting to Chinese ways. Since they were accustomed to eating raw food, cooked food gave them such severe diarrhea that some died. Zhu Yu tells us the slaves "are black as ink. Their lips are red, and their teeth are white. Their hair is curly as well as yellow." Yellow? This word in Chinese can indicate the color of aging hair, but it is also possible that the slaves suffered from a nutritional disorder called kwashiorkor, which is caused by a severe lack of protein. Sometimes those who eat only raw foods suffer from this disorder, which can leave their hair rust-colored.

Those slaves who adapted to Chinese food eventually learned to comprehend spoken Chinese commands, but none ever mastered the language themselves. Zhu's understanding of cultural adjustment mirrored that of his contemporaries: viewing cuisine as a crucial element of Chinese identity, they had difficulty believing that anyone who had not eaten Chinese food since birth could ever learn to speak the language properly.

Zhu's detailed account of the foreign slaves is puzzling. If the Chinese were importing large numbers of slaves, surely someone else would have mentioned them. Perhaps the slaves he described were the personal slaves of expat Islamic merchants living in Guangzhou.

The Chinese didn't need to import slaves. They had their own massive labor supply. The sources give no hint of a labor shortage. Recall that China's population boomed during the Song, exceeding 100 million at the time Zhu was writing.

Zhu Yu also helps us to understand the dramatic increase in the consumption of aromatics: the Chinese used them to make foods and drinks. "The custom today is when guests arrive to drink tea and when they leave to drink soup," Zhu Yu explains. "Containing medicinal ingredients and a little sweetener and fragrance, the soup can be warm or cool. The use of sweet herbs is the custom throughout the empire."

Those at the top of society continued to use aromatics in refined ways. One official was particularly fond of burning incense: "every day that he was in his office, he would get up and before starting work would light two incense burners and place his official robes on top of them. On leaving the house, he would gather up his sleeves. When he sat down, he would loosen his sleeves, emitting an intense fragrance that filled the entire room." This practice spread among Chinese officials.

Sometimes the wealthy consumed enormous quantities of aromatics on a single occasion. During the reign of Emperor Huizong, between 1100 and 1126, the imperial family switched from unscented candles to candles that contained a chunk of aloeswood or camphor along with a piece of ambergris to intensify the fragrance. At the palace the scented candles were "lined up in two rows, each several hundred candles long, which lit up the room very brightly and emitted a dense cloud of fragrance. If you looked for anything comparable in the empire, you'd never find it." The tale has a wistful quality as the writer is looking back on an extravagant period at court that came to a sudden end in 1126.

That was the year of an invasion by a confederation of northern peoples headed by the Jurchen—originally a people subject to the

Kitan Liao. The Jurchen lived in northeast China near the modern border with North Korea. Just as the Kitan leader Abaoji created a powerful tribal confederation by winning the allegiance of different peoples around 900, the Jurchen leader Aguda did precisely the same after 1100 and founded the Jin dynasty in 1115.

At first the Song allied with the Jurchen Jin in the hope of defeating the Kitan Liao and recovering the territory that they had ceded to them in the Treaty of Chanyuan. But as soon as the Jurchen had vanquished the Liao, they turned on the Song. Conquering all of China north of the Huai River in 1127, including the Song capital Kaifeng, the Jurchen forces captured both the former emperor Huizong and the ruling emperor Qinzong. As the Song empire collapsed, the Jurchen victors forced the two former emperors, along with many of their wives and courtiers, on a long and humiliating march to the north, where both men eventually died.

The loss of the north further encouraged Chinese trade with Southeast Asia. The new emperor, Gaozong, gained his position because he was one of the few Song dynasty princes the Jurchen did not capture. He established a capital in the southern city of Hangzhou, itself already an important trade entrepôt. (Chinese historians refer to the second half of the Song dynasty as the Southern Song because the capital was located in the south.) Hangzhou—about 100 miles (160 km) southwest of modern-day Shanghai—was the only coastal port ever to serve as the Chinese empire's capital, showing the importance of maritime trade to the Song dynasty.

Initially, it wasn't clear whether Emperor Gaozong or the dynasty would survive. Wartime made it difficult to collect taxes, especially agrarian taxes, traditionally the main source of revenue for Chinese dynasties. Emperor Gaozong realized that taxing foreign trade offered a solution to the budget shortfall. He noted, "The profits from overseas trade are the greatest. If the trade is handled in the right way, the profit can easily reach millions of coins. Isn't the revenue from trade better than taking it from the people? I should pay more attention to overseas trade so that I can bring some slight relief to the people." It was remarkable for the Chinese emperor to notice how heavily the burden of agrarian taxes fell on his subjects and even more remarkable for him to attempt to lighten their burden by taxing international trade.

Indeed, the proportion of government revenue from taxes on international trade peaked at 20 percent in the years just after 1127, when the Song was particularly desperate for tax revenues. Eventually, when the dynasty regained its footing and reestablished its agrarian base, the tax on international trade returned to about 5 percent of overall revenue, the level where it had been before the fall of the north.

The situation stabilized in 1141 when Emperor Gaozong signed a treaty with the Jin dynasty that set Song payments to the Jurchen at an even higher level than those they had given to the Liao dynasty: 250,000 ounces of silver and 250,000 bolts of silk, both paid annually. The treaty with the Jin dynasty wasn't as successful in keeping the peace as the Treaty of Chanyuan with the Liao dynasty had been. Still, although each side periodically attacked the other, neither side managed to shift the border between North and South China.

Despite the loss of the North and the high annual payments paid to the Jurchen, the residents of South China enjoyed nearly two centuries of unequaled prosperity as the Chinese continued to import ever larger quantities of aromatics from Southeast Asia.

Emperor Gaozong appreciated aromatics so much that he developed his own brand of incense to give to favored courtiers. Archeologists have recovered one square of incense inscribed with four Chinese characters in his calligraphy saying "may the country flourish and antiquity be restored." Each square had a small hole drilled into an upper corner so that his officials could hang it on their belts. The imperial recipe? Of course, aloeswood was the main ingredient, with flower petals and camphor from Borneo for fragrance and musk to intensify the odor.

Ingenious Chinese merchants developed new ways to increase sales of aromatics. Street vendors experimented with adding multiple fragrances to enhance the taste of snacks and sold both lotus root and water flavored with aloeswood. Enterprising stall owners steamed stalks of raw sugarcane in the smoke of musk, the costly aromatic made from the glands of Tibetan deer. Even the poorest consumers could afford a taste of these delicacies at market stands.

The use of frankincense was particularly widespread. The central government stored the imported aromatic in warehouses. In 1175, realizing that they had too great a supply on hand, officials set prices artificially high and required purchasers to buy large quantities, triggering a rebellion in central China on the border of modern Hunan and Guizhou provinces.

Frankincense, along with other imported aromatics like cloves and putchuck, appear in medical prescriptions for the first time in the tenth and eleventh centuries, and in the twelfth and thirteenth centuries more and more druggists prescribed myrrh, borax, and black pepper. Most Chinese prescriptions consisted of different herbs and aromatics ground into a fine powder that patients boiled in water to make a medicinal tea. Before the year 1000 the only imported good regularly appearing in prescriptions was ginseng from Korea, but prescriptions after 1000 regularly call for multiple imported components.

Aromatics weren't just luxury products for the most well-to-do. People from all walks of life bought snacks at markets and visited healers to obtain medicines made from various imported aromatics. In 1076 the government established the first public pharmacy in the world. The main branch was in the Kaifeng capital, and later on branch pharmacies opened throughout the empire. One department of the pharmaceutical government agency purchased the ingredients for prescriptions and packaged different ingredients, while the other ran the drugstores that sold directly to the populace.

Incense makers also blended imported fragrances. Of 300 recipes contained in the thirteenth-century book *Mr. Chen's Guide to Incense*, 66 percent called for sandalwood, 61 percent for musk, 47 percent for aloeswood, 43 percent for camphor, 37 percent for cloves, and 13 percent for frankincense. Making their first appearance around 1300, incense sticks were another sign of the use of incense by the poor, who could more easily afford a single stick containing far less incense than an entire cake.

As the consumption of aromatics spread throughout society, the rich, as they so often do, developed even more extravagant ways to display their wealth. In the winter, the wealthy partitioned off "warming rooms," or spaces that could be heated individually. One man built three warming rooms made entirely from aloeswood. He ordered specially carved benches with holes in them. With incense coils lit under them, the fragrance permeated the rooms. He used the same technique on a boat built entirely from Chinese cedar. The well-to-do in Song dynasty China lived comfortably indeed.

As the aromatics trade boomed, many people made fortunes: Chinese and foreign merchants living in Quanzhou and Guangzhou as well as Chinese officials who managed the sales of fine and coarse goods. The wealthy financed entire ships, and men and women with less money could purchase shares. If a voyage succeeded, all stood to make a handsome profit.

The aromatics trade was so lucrative that it attracted the less-wealthy members of the imperial family. Sometime after 1100, the imperial clan—all the emperor's male descendants and their families—had become too numerous to live in the capital of Kaifeng. The revenues from a single city couldn't cover the cost of the generous stipends paid to each male. Accordingly, the imperial family broke into three different branches, one of which stayed in Kaifeng.

After the fall of the North in 1127, the Kaifeng branch moved to the new capital in Hangzhou, while the two other branches looked for cities sufficiently prosperous to support them. The western branch, which had about 200 people, chose Fuzhou, a port in northern Fujian province, while the southern branch, with some 400 members, opted to move farther south down the coast to Quanzhou, where they became deeply involved in the aromatics trade.

Already on its way to becoming the most important port in China, Quanzhou surpassed Guangzhou sometime around 1200. The city's population of one million in 1080 reached 1.25 million by the 1240s, putting it on a par with Baghdad and slightly smaller than the two capitals of the Song dynasty Kaifeng (960–1126) and Hang-zhou (1127–1276), whose populations were each around 1.5 million.

The prosperity of Quanzhou and other nearby ports spilled over to the entire province of Fujian, enabling the province's residents to shift away from subsistence farming so that they could produce goods for commercial markets. Like the residents of Southeast Asia who harvested aromatics for the Chinese, the people in Fujian adjusted to the challenges of living in a globalized economy. They stopped growing their own food. They discovered that they could make more money if they cultivated cash crops like lychees, sugarcane, and glutinous rice, or if they grew local textile fibers like ramie and hemp. They came to purchase food for their families at local markets with the money they earned. Many gave up agriculture altogether. Some worked in silver, copper, iron, and lead mines. Some fished. And some made salt by diverting ocean water into pans and letting it evaporate.

The ceramics industry absorbed the largest share of the labor force. Entrepreneurs built dragon kilns that stretched over 300 feet (100 m) up the sides of hills. Producing between 10,000 and 30,000 vessels in a single firing, such kilns employed hundreds, if not thousands, of laborers. Attaining the highest temperatures anywhere in the world, these kilns produced shiny, easy-to-clean ceramics treasured in Africa, the Middle East, India, and Southeast Asia. We don't think of these kilns as industrial simply because they didn't use steam or electric power (they burned wood or charcoal), but these enterprises were just as large and complex as the first factories of the Industrial Revolution. Fully 7.5 percent of Fujian's population of five million—some 375,000 people—were involved in making export ceramics in the twelfth and thirteenth centuries.

A shift in Song monetary policy had a dramatic effect on its international trade partners. When Song government officials first issued paper notes in 1024, they had limited their use to the province of Sichuan, but in 1170 the Song government established a permanent system of paper notes backed by silver. Overnight, cumbersome bronze coins fell out of use, and merchants seized the opportunity to export huge quantities of coins to Japan. The main goods the Japanese exported to China were lumber, sulfur, mercury, and gold, all raw materials.

At first the Japanese government banned the Chinese coins but then changed policy in 1226 and allowed their use, and by 1270 Chinese bronze coins became the de facto currency throughout the Japanese Archipelago. Chinese coins also circulated widely in Java during the twelfth and thirteenth centuries, and the Javanese minted copies of Chinese coins. The use of Chinese coins in Japan and Java shows how deeply integrated the economies of East and Southeast Asia had become.

The people living along China's southeast coast were the most deeply affected by globalization because so many major ports were located there, but globalization reached those living in the interior as well. One coastal market in Shaoxing offered "jades, white silks, pearls, rhinoceros horns, renowned perfumes and precious medicines, silk damasks, and goods made of lacquer and of rattan," an impressively wide range of goods that we'd expect from vendors in a seaport not too far from modern Shanghai. But at one market deep in the interior, some 1,000 miles (1,600 km) to the west, in Chengdu, Sichuan, consumers could buy "mica and frankincense the color of sparkling crystal, aloeswood and sandalwood wafting their fragrant scents." The availability of goods from abroad wasn't quite at the level of today's Ikea—the markets didn't meet every day and the prices of most imported goods were high—but it was closer than you might imagine.

In 1225, Zhao Rukuo, a member of the imperial clan and the Superintendent of Maritime Trade in Quanzhou, wrote a book about China's foreign trade entitled *Record of Various Foreign Peoples*. He drew on both historical records and his conversations with people living in Quanzhou. Superintendent Zhao displayed deep knowledge of China's longtime trading partners like Korea, Japan, and Vietnam as well as much more distant places like Sicily, Somalia, and Tanzania.

Earlier trade superintendents must have also spoken with foreign merchants, as we know from government regulations speci-

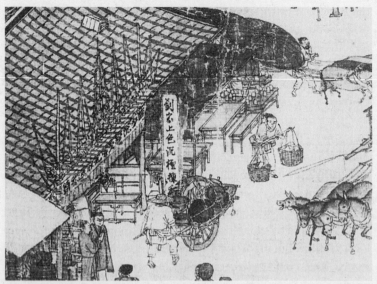

劉家上色沉檀揀香

Cultural Relics Press, China

This detail from a scroll depicting a Chinese city shows a furniture store that specializes in imported woods. The sign announces "The Liu Family's Top-Quality Aloeswood, Sandalwood, and Frankincense."

fying how often officials should host dinners for visiting merchants, but we don't know what they learned. Walking around modern Quanzhou, you can see many places where Superintendent Zhao might have interviewed foreign merchants. Multiple small canals still crisscross the city, and one leads right up to the former trade superintendent's office, now a local Daoist temple. The main street where foreign merchants lived is but a short walk away.

Superintendent Zhao's book has two sections. Following earlier geographic writings, the first part gives a capsule history of fifty-three places and their products. The second section was completely new. Proceeding commodity by commodity, it identifies the different countries that produced the item, and explains variations in quality. As the quantities of goods coming into China from Southeast Asia increased, traders realized that they had to distinguish between higher- and lower-quality goods, and the difference often lay in determining where a certain good came from. These traders were Zhao's target audience. As trade superintendent, he spent long hours talking to foreign merchants and boiled their testimony down to tell his audience what they wanted to learn.

China enjoyed a large trade surplus, Superintendent Zhao revealed. While exporting the world's highest quality textiles, ceramics, and metal goods, China imported a narrower range of products—foreign woods, resins, and spices, most from Southeast Asia, some from the Middle East. Superintendent Zhao's book focused on the maritime trade, so he does not mention the continuing overland imports of horses, so desperately needed by the army, from the northwest.

The imports of aromatics were extremely important because all social levels consumed them. They imparted pleasant fragrances to people's bodies, clothing, and air in rooms. They were also a crucial ingredient in drinks, snacks, and foods. Because so many medical prescriptions included them, they were a necessity for many people.

Superintendent Zhao's book gives much more than commercial information. Consider his poignant description of the capture of slaves on Madagascar: "In the West there is an island in the sea with many wild men with bodies as black as lacquer and frizzy hair. They are tricked by offers of food and captured. They are traded as slaves to the Arabian countries, where they fetch a high price. They work as gatekeepers. People say that they do not miss their kin." The final comment would have surprised Chinese readers with their strong family system: we can almost hear Zhao wondering whether this was actually possible.

Superintendent Zhao's account of elephant hunting is even more detailed: "People don't dare get close to the elephants. Hunters use bows of extraordinary strength and shoot poisoned arrows. When hit by an arrow the elephant runs away, but before he's gone one or two miles, the poison takes effect and the animal dies. The hunters follow him, remove the tusks from his carcass, and bury them in the ground." Once they have ten or more tusks, they sell them to Arab merchants who transport them to Srivijaya, Superintendent Zhao explains. The best elephant tusks from the Arabs are three times as large and whiter than those from Southeast Asia, which tend to have a reddish tint. Zhao doesn't realize that the superior tusks are from Africa. Because Arab merchants dominated the lucrative ivory trade, he thinks they sourced the high-quality tusks in their native land.

Foreign trade was so important during the Song that math textbooks covered the topic. One word problem, from 1247, asks the reader to determine the shares due to four partners who invested in a ship that sailed to Southeast Asia and back. "Assume that there is a sea-going junk which has been to the customs station and cleared of its obligations. Apart from the goods to be paid to the owner of the ship there remain 5,088 Chinese ounces [over 400 pounds or 188 kg] of aloeswood, 10,430 bundles of black pepper, each weighing 40 catties [52.5 pounds or 23.8 kg], and 212 pairs of elephant tusks." The choice of aloeswood, black pepper, and elephant tusks—all important commodities in the trade with Southeast Asia—is apt.

The problem goes on to explain that Partners A, B, C, and D borrowed different amounts from each other, which adds to the challenge. You can solve the problem only with matrices, which shows that the Chinese were using linear algebra by this time.

A ship that sank just outside Quanzhou in the 1270s offers a real-life example of what a ship's cargo financed by multiple partners would have looked like. Measuring 79.4 feet (24.2 m) long by 30 feet (9.15 m) wide, the ship was recovered by archeologists who excavated 5,300 pounds (2,400 kg) of aromatic woods including aloeswood and sandalwood; five quarts (4.75 l) of black pepper; ambergris from Somalia; 6.3 grams (.22 oz) of frankincense; and 8.8 pounds (4 kg) of mercury. All the items in the cargo were important goods in the Southeast Asian trade with China, and the dominance of aromatics is just as we'd expect. The ship was also carrying some Chinese coins, the latest of which was dated 1271, so it sank in that year or not too long afterward.

Divided into thirteen separate wooden compartments, the ship was clearly manufactured in China; the workmen carved a constellation of seven small holes and one large one—perhaps a depiction of the Big Dipper—at the two ends of the keel, or main

The Chinese-language 1987 site report about the Quanzhou shipwreck.

Unlike craft made elsewhere, Chinese boats had watertight compartments, a technological breakthrough in boatbuilding. This innovation restricted the damage from leaks to just one section of a boat.

beam running along the bottom of the ship. These carvings were a traditional Chinese means of seeking divine protection. Archeologists found evidence of boat repairs using the lashed-lug technique, a sign that the ship had traveled to Southeast Asia and back.

The ship also contained ninety-six wooden labels giving the names of individuals, shops, places, and commodities. Tied to different crates, these allowed investors, the crew, and the captain to identify which goods belonged to which owner. One quarter of the tags bore an unusual label: "southern family," which puzzled everyone until a local historian realized that the term referred to the southern branch of the imperial clan, the primary investors in the vessel.

It seems most likely that the ship departed Quanzhou in the early 1270s when the port was still under the rule of the Southern Song dynasty. The trade superintendent at the time was a powerful man of Arab descent named Pu Shougeng. His ancestors had moved from Guangzhou to Quanzhou sometime around 1200, and he became the Quanzhou trade superintendent about 1266. Assuming office during the dynasty's protracted collapse, Pu concurrently served as pacification commissioner, a position that gave him command of a small army, which he could supplement with the militias controlled by locally powerful families.

The Mongols, who had already gained control of North China, launched intermittent raids on South China with their navy. After they captured the Song capital of Hangzhou in 1276, the last Song emperor, a small boy, fled to Quanzhou, where the Mongol navy attacked and dealt the final blow to the Song dynasty.

Anticipating a Mongol victory, Trade Superintendent Pu switched his allegiance, probably in 1277, when he killed some of the imperial clansmen residing in the city.

It seems likely that the ill-starred ship returned to Quanzhou with all of its cargo around this time. Unearthed in a shallow bay near Quanzhou, the ship sank with its hull undamaged and no sign that anyone on board had died or that the ship had sprung a leak. Someone did remove the mast and all the wood above the surface of the water, presumably to sell it or use as fuel. Because it contained so much of its original valuable cargo, it's possible that it was deliberately scuttled—because the ship captain realized that the Mongols had overthrown the Song imperial family? For whatever reason, those who sank the ship never came back to retrieve the goods, and, like the buried hoards of silver coins in Eastern Europe, the ship lay untouched until archeologists found it.

Killing the last boy-emperor of the Song in 1279, the Mongols conquered all of China. They took over as the successor to the Song dynasty and ruled China as the Yuan dynasty. Trade with Southeast Asia continued to flourish under Mongol rule. Marco Polo claimed to have visited Quanzhou in the 1280s or 1290s, and his account contains echoes of reliable information. He calls Quanzhou "Zaiton," an Arabic name meaning "city of olives." "The total amount of traffic in gems and other merchandise entering and leaving this port is a marvel to behold. . . . I assure you that for one spice ship that goes to Alexandria or elsewhere to pick up pepper for export to

Christendom, Zaiton is visited by a hundred. For you must know that it is one of the two ports in the world with the biggest flow of merchandise." The other was the former Song capital of Hangzhou.

Polo reports that all ships entering the harbor pay "10 percent duty on all their wares, including gems and pearls, that is to say a tithe on everything." This is the same one-tenth customs duty that Song officials initiated at the start of their dynasty in 960. "Payment for the hire of ships, that is for freight, is reckoned at the rate of 30 percent on small wares, 44 percent on pepper, and 40 percent on aloeswood and sandalwood and all bulky wares." The percentages are all plausible, but Polo makes a crucial mistake: these aren't shipping charges but the varying taxes levied on fine and coarse goods. The Mongols collected the same three taxes on foreign ships as had Song dynasty officials. After paying these taxes, Polo explains, the merchants "make such a profit that they ask nothing better than to return with another cargo."

Polo commits other errors. He mentions "beautiful" and "cheap" porcelain that acquires its "sheen" from being buried in the ground "for thirty or forty years," because he doesn't understand kiln technology. The Muslim traveler Ibn Battuta also reported that the Chinese buried ceramics underground when he visited the Muslim quarter of Quanzhou before returning home to Morocco. Few people outside China understood how such high-quality ceramics were made.

Chinese trade with Southeast Asia continued to boom under Mongol rule, as we can see from a list included in a Guangzhou gazetteer of sixty-nine different foreign products, forty from Southeast Asia, traded in 1300. The nine most costly were ivory, rhinoceros horn, crane crests, pearls, coral, a greenish mineral (perhaps a type of jade), kingfisher feathers, and turtle and tortoise shells. The depth and range of the list makes perfect sense for the most heavily frequented sea route in use before the arrival of the Europeans in the 1500s.

As information about foreign countries traveled alongside goods, the Chinese learned more about Southeast Asian geography. The Guangzhou gazetteer's author divided the waters of the South China

Sea into the Small Western Ocean (the section of the South China Sea near the Malay Peninsula), the Small Eastern Ocean (the Sea of Sulu east of Borneo), and the Large Eastern Ocean (the Java Sea), and explained which countries were located near each body of water.

As knowledgeable as Chinese mariners were about the geography of Southeast Asia, India, the Arabian Peninsula, and Africa, they didn't venture east of the Philippines into the Pacific because they believed that the world ended there. As Superintendent Zhao explained in 1225, "still farther east [of Java] is where the Ultimate Drain empties. People don't live beyond this point."

The Ultimate Drain was the name of the place where the Chinese thought all the ocean's waters flowed back into the earth. The Chinese wrote about the Ultimate Drain as early as the third century BC, when the great Chinese philosophical text Zhuangzi explains: "Of all the waters of the world, none is as great as the sea. Ten thousand streams flow into it—I have never heard of a time when they stopped—and yet it is never full. The water leaks away at the Ultimate Drain—I have never heard of a time when it didn't—and yet the sea is never empty."

Superintendent Zhao quotes a long passage from a late-twelfth-century book that locates the legendary drain in a specific place: "On the southwest quadrant of the Southern Sea, there is a big ocean called the Vietnam Sea. Three currents meet there." The source continues: "Boats coming from the south always encounter the confluence of these three currents." It seems likely that the author was referring to the start of the Kuroshio Current, which was somewhere slightly to the west of Luzon, between Taiwan and the Philippines.

The risks to mariners who traveled so far were great: "If they catch a gust of wind, they can be saved. If they are becalmed, there is the danger that the boat cannot escape and will break apart where the three currents meet. . . . That is the place where the Ultimate Drain pours into the Nine Underworlds." The location of the Ultimate Drain was far to the east, beyond anywhere that the Chinese reader would have known about.

The Chinese fear of the Ultimate Drain parallels the Roman

idea of the Torrid Zone that Portuguese navigators gradually disproved as they made their way down the west coast of Africa. Contrary to what the ancient Roman geographer Ptolemy had written, they found no region so hot that humans couldn't survive. Unlike the Portuguese navigators, Song observers continued to believe in the dangers of the Ultimate Drain; perhaps that is why the Chinese didn't sail past the Philippines farther into the Pacific until after European mariners had pioneered the route.

The Chinese aromatics trade with Southeast Asia continued to increase after the end of Mongol rule. After the founding of the Ming dynasty in 1368, a single tribute shipment to the court was so large that it comprised eighty tons of tropical goods, primarily pepper and sappanwood.

China's most extensive ocean voyages occurred between 1405 and 1433 when the Ming dynasty sponsored seven voyages led by Admiral Zheng He. An imperial fleet of 317 ships carrying 28,000 men went from China to Southeast Asia, then India, and on to Iraq. Some of the ships broke away from the main fleet and went as far as Mombasa on the east coast of Africa. We know this because both written and archeological evidence of these voyages survives in the form of Chinese coins found overseas, Chinese historical records, and—most convincing of all—Chinese-language inscriptions carved onto stone tablets in Sri Lanka and Calicut, India.

Admiral Zheng's largest ships were 200 feet (61 m) long, dwarfing Christopher Columbus's ships, probably a mere 100 feet (30 m) long (surprisingly, we don't know the precise dimensions of Columbus's ships). While Admiral Zheng's full fleet had 317 ships, Columbus traveled with only 3.

Admiral Zheng's ships went through the Malacca Strait along the coast of the Arabian Peninsula and India, covering 8,000 miles (13,000 km). If they crossed the Indian Ocean directly, the route was only 6,500 miles (10,500 km). If you add the 4,700-mile (6,500 km) leg from Basra, in Iraq, to Sofala, Mozambique, on the east coast of Africa, the length of the trip is even more noteworthy, especially given that Columbus traveled only some 4,400 miles (7,000 km) on his first voyage.

In short, Zheng He's voyages were on a much larger scale than Columbus's. And the goal of the voyages? To proclaim the power of the third emperor of the Ming dynasty.

The size of the Chinese fleet, and the extent of government sponsorship, may have been new in the 1400s, but the route wasn't. Zheng He was on the Persian Gulf–China sea corridor. Zheng He's men weren't exploring; they were traveling on familiar routes around Southeast Asia and across the Indian Ocean to India, Arabia, and Africa that Chinese ships had been sailing since 1000.

The government-sponsored voyages ended in 1433, but private traders continued to ply these waters in the following centuries. The economy of the entire Indian Ocean region was fully commercially integrated before the European voyages of discovery in the 1500s, and it was afterward, too. Starting in the mid-1400s, the Portuguese concentrated on exporting gold from Africa to Europe. But once they gained control of the Spice Islands in 1520, they realized that there was far more money to be made there than in Africa. Of course there was. Since 1000 Chinese rulers, merchants, and middlemen had all prospered by tapping that very source of wealth.

Epilogue

And so our tour of the world comes to an end. We've followed the pathways first opened in 1000 and observed their impact over the next 500 years. After 1500 a new chapter—a European chapter—of world history begins. For more than 400 years, Europeans relied on more advanced weaponry to move into preexisting trade pathways whenever possible and to create new ones when not.

In 1497 Vasco da Gama traveled south along the West African coast and rounded the Cape of Good Hope. At the time of his voyage, the Portuguese already realized that it was life-threatening for them to go into the interior of Africa, because, as nonnatives, they had no resistance to malaria. Whenever a group of Portuguese ventured inland from the coast, the casualties were enormous. It made much more sense for the Europeans to establish coastal ports where they could rest, stock up on supplies, and purchase whatever goods they needed—primarily slaves and gold—from the interior. In this first phase of imperialism, the Portuguese empire resembled a necklace consisting of beads—the ports of Cape Town, Mombasa, and Mogadishu, among others—strung along the African coastline.

That's why El Mina—the early trading fort on the coast of Ghana—was an important test case. It demonstrated the feasibility of conducting trade from a coastal base to which Portuguese ships could sail directly, obtain the goods they desired, and return home. After the Portuguese established El Mina, African entrepreneurs moved existing trade routes in the interior to the coast so that traders could deliver gold and slaves to the Atlantic ports.

This wasn't the first time that Africans changed their trade routes: when, around 1000, Sijilmasa replaced Zuwila as a key node of trade in North Africa, the major trans-Saharan gold and slave trade route also shifted west.

After da Gama rounded the Cape of Good Hope, he was no longer pioneering a new maritime route. He joined the much frequented Persian Gulf–China maritime route connecting East African port cities with Indian Ocean ports. Once on that route, it was easy to find a pilot to guide his four ships across the Indian Ocean to the port of Calicut, famed for its spices. The name of the pilot who joined da Gama at Malindi was Malemo Cana (possibly Canaca), and the two sources who mention him say that he was a Moor who could speak some Italian.

The route connecting China with Africa was the longest and most heavily traveled sea route before 1492, and aromatics were the most important commodity carried on it. After 1492, traffic on the transatlantic route from Europe to the Americas and the trans-pacific route from the Americas to the Philippines surpassed the Persian Gulf–China route, but some trade still continued along it.

As they constructed their empire in the Americas, the Spanish took over the Aztec capital of Tenochtitlan and established Mexico City as their capital. Columbus recognized the sophistication of the existing American trade network when, in 1502, he encountered the enormous canoe carrying high-quality textiles, obsidian knives, copper bells, and wooden swords, which all circulated between the Yucatan Peninsula and the Caribbean.

Columbus had no way of knowing about the indigenous trade routes connecting the Maya north to the American Southwest and the Mississippi River Valley and south to Panama and the Andes, but the Spaniards who followed him to the Americas took full advantage of those preexisting pathways to build new empires in Mexico and Peru.

In 1519, when Cortés arrived in Mexico, he befriended an Aztec noblewoman named Malinché who had been captured by the Maya. Fluent in both Mayan and the Nahuatl language of the Aztecs, she helped Cortés negotiate alliances with different tribes seeking to overthrow the Aztecs. With her help, the Spanish were able to conquer the Aztec capital in just two years. Farther south, the Inca empire turned out to be as vulnerable as the Aztecs, but for a different reason—Pizarro, approaching by sea from Panama, arrived in the middle of a succession dispute about who would become the next leader of the Inca—and was able to capitalize on the disarray to establish control.

None of the Spanish—certainly not Columbus—realized it, but they were all carrying deadly germs to which the Amerindians had no immunity. The long period of isolation after the first prehistoric settlers arrived left the indigenous peoples of the Americas deeply vulnerable to European diseases such as smallpox, the flu, and even the common cold.

Because no census data survives, historians don't agree on the population of the Americas in 1492—estimates range from a low of 10 million to a high of 100 million. Our first more reliable information comes in 1568 from a Spanish census. Only some 2 million Amerindians in the agrarian heartlands of Mexico and Peru survived the massive outbreaks of disease brought by the Europeans. (Perhaps an additional million in remote areas were also able to make it). These mass deaths paved the way for European colonists.

In the 1600s, Britain, the Netherlands, and France replaced the Spanish and the Portuguese as the main European powers, and their countrymen settled North America. Locals taught the Europeans many survival skills that contributed to their success in these radically different environments. Remember: the Vikings withdrew from northeastern Canada around 1000 and from Greenland after 1400 because they found the environment too harsh.

Squanto (his full name was Tisquantum) made it possible for the Pilgrims to make it through the first winter at Plymouth. Less well known, though, is that prior to the arrival of the Pilgrims, Squanto had been kidnapped in 1614 by an English explorer who brought him to Europe and sold him as a slave in Spain. Squanto managed to escape and return to the region of Cape Cod. When the pilgrims encountered him, he could already speak English.

Da Gama's pilot Malemo Cana. Malinché. Squanto. These intermediaries are all major figures in recent historical accounts of European expansion, but we don't always fully grasp their significance. Yes, they helped Europeans learn about and ultimately gain control of their home societies. But more was going on than that. They offered access to the system of pathways and trade networks constructed entirely by the indigenous peoples long before the arrival of the Europeans. These intermediaries allowed the Europeans to plug into those local networks, and to do so quickly.

Europeans reached some places in the world much later than others. When James Cook arrived in the South Seas in the late 1700s, he realized the importance of the priest Tupaia's knowledge of traditional Polynesian navigation and geography. Together, the two men made a map of the region, a crucial aid that enabled Cook to find his way to the many islands spread all over the Pacific. Cook's voyages launched the settlement of Australia and New Zealand by the British.

Imagine, for a moment, a world in which the European voyages of the 1490s and the resulting settlement of many continents never occurred. What would that world have been like? Surely the tempo of world trade would have continued to increase. Already in 1225, the Chinese trade official Zhao Rukuo listed forty-one different products sold in the Mediterranean, East Africa, India, and Southeast Asia, all markets for China's exports.

Sa'di, a Persian observer writing some thirty years later, in 1255, described meeting a merchant on the island of Kish in the Persian Gulf. A wealthy man, the trader possessed 150 camels and 40 slaves and servants. After boasting all night long of his travels and acquaintances in foreign lands, he admitted that he still wanted to take one more business trip. He would start in the Fars region of modern Iran: "I want to take sulfur from Fars to China, for I hear it commands a tremendous price there. From there I will take Chinese goblets to Anatolia, Anatolian silks to India, Indian steel to Aleppo, Aleppan crystal to the Yemen, and Yemeni swords to Fars."

This was quite an itinerary: Iran to China to the Anatolian

region of modern Turkey to India to Syria to Yemen and then back to Iran. The merchant's plan entailed buying a certain good in one place, selling it in the next town, and using the proceeds to finance the onward leg of his journey. It doesn't seem that he actually made the trip, but he knew about all these distant places and their products, and the lengthy trip he proposed was entirely feasible.

As the merchant's proposed route shows, the trade pathways across the Middle East continued to evolve even after the Abbasid empire broke apart and independent rulers took over different regions. Scholars and poets traveled on these pathways in search of patronage from different rulers, and male and female students studying at madrasas used them as well. Millions of slaves imported from Africa, Eastern Europe, and Central Asia were also forced to move along these routes to the main markets at Cairo, Baghdad, and other major cities.

Without Columbus's and da Gama's voyages and subsequent European settlements, we can assume that the circles of trade would have opened ever wider as merchants discovered yet more goods made in one location and desired by consumers in another. It was really only a matter of time before existing trade networks in Afro-Eurasia and the Americas would have reconnected with one another. The Vikings had already crossed the North Atlantic briefly in 1000, and their subsequent logging trips indicate their ability to return anytime they liked. Just as the Chinese hunger for sea slugs prompted their fishermen to continue moving south until they arrived in Australia sometime around 1500, the persistent Chinese desire for aromatics would've pushed mariners to conquer their fear of the Ultimate Drain and voyage past the Philippines farther into the Pacific.

But the European voyages actually did occur, and Europeans settled both the Americas and Australia. Historians traditionally distinguish between the first wave of European settlement around the world after 1500 and a second wave, powered by the innovations of the Industrial Revolution, that allowed the Europeans to go farther inland and establish greater control. The steamship provided faster and more reliable transportation than the sailing ship, and the first European steamships crossed the Atlantic in the 1820s and 1830s. The placement of cannon on their decks transformed those steamships into gunboats, which enabled the British navy to win the Crimean War and two Opium Wars with China. In 1857, another invention, the telegraph, allowed the British to put down a mass mutiny in India by informing British officers where troops were most needed.

The British were able to transport their troops by railroad, the most important technological innovation of the 1800s. Trains moved troops anywhere the European powers had laid tracks. The discovery that daily doses of quinine prevented malaria came in the 1850s. These technological innovations underpinned a new wave of colonization, not just along the coast, but deep into the interior of Africa in the late 1800s.

As powerful as they were, the Europeans didn't colonize the entire planet. One of the largest places to escape was China, which the European powers divided into different economic spheres, each under the control of a different country, while maintaining the fiction of continued rule by the Qing dynasty.

Historians have puzzled over why the Industrial Revolution occurred in England but not in China, which had an advanced economy much earlier than England. Without using either steam power or electricity, the Chinese had achieved manufacturing on a large scale. Some of the largest enterprises, such as the giant dragon kilns that produced thousands of pottery vessels in a single firing, dated back to 1000. Consumer demand for those ceramics and Chinese silks powered Chinese economic growth for centuries.

A key difference between England and China was that China had no labor shortage. With a surplus population, China needed machines that used less cotton, not less labor, to produce a bolt of cloth. And such machines do not exist.

China and Britain were at comparable levels of economic development before the Industrial Revolution. Only after 1800 did Britain's economy take off and leave China behind. The Industrial Revolution ushered in more than a century during which Europe drove the world economy.

When did the age of European dominance come to an end? Perhaps in 1945 with the close of World War II, when America emerged so much wealthier than Great Britain, Germany, or France. Or perhaps in the early 1960s, when the former colonies of Great Britain, France, and Germany gained independence. One could even make the case for 1973–1974, when OPEC implemented its first oil embargo. In any event, it's certainly over now.

What can the world of 1000 teach us about globalization? Obviously, our current world differs in myriad ways. Among the most striking differences: the world is much more crowded now than it was then. It now has a population nearing 8 billion, while in 1000, 250 million people enjoyed plenty of elbow room.

People today know a great deal about the peoples on earth, even those residing in distant parts of the globe, whereas in 1000 they were encountering them for the first time.

We live in a world filled with all kinds of sophisticated machines, while our ancestors lived with hardly any mechanization. The differences between the most high-tech nations and the least high-tech are huge and grow daily, while in the past the most technologically sophisticated countries had only a slight edge.

If you strip away all the gadgets and technology, people remain very much themselves. And as our ancestors responded to the changing world in 1000 in a variety of ways, we have to study what they did so that we can better tackle the future that lies before us.

The strategies that worked in the past should still succeed today. The scholars who did their best to learn about all the countries of the globe helped to prepare their countrymen for their first encounters with people from those other places. The inventors who came up with innovative products and the merchants who brought them to emerging markets opened up new pathways and contributed to economic prosperity in their homelands.

Globalization in 1000 brought benefits, but it also produced winners and losers as it does today. In 879 the Huang Chao rebels targeted foreign merchants living in Guangzhou, then China's largest port. In 996 the residents of Cairo rioted against the expat merchants from Amalfi, Italy. And in 1181 the residents of Constantinople murdered thousands of Italian merchants in the Massacre of the Latins. In each instance, the root causes were the same. The locals resented the wealth of the foreign expats and believed that the outsiders had profited at their expense.

Despite these protests, many seized the new opportunities offered by increased contact. The Chinese excelled at manufacturing paper, silks, and ceramics, which they sold throughout Eurasia. Merchants supplying China found new aromatics in Southeast Asia that replaced the more expensive myrrh and frankincense of the Arabian Peninsula.

Trade provided a continuing incentive to catch up. The potters of the Islamic world may never have matched the high temperatures of Chinese kilns that produced such shiny porcelains, but they never stopped trying. Middle Eastern lusterware ceramics found buyers at home and in Africa, allowing those potters to retain some of their market share.

Those who successfully adapted to change didn't always possess sophisticated technology. The Thule were able to move all the way from Alaska to eastern Canada and then to Greenland because of their superior ability to hunt seals—even in winter. This skill set allowed the Thule to displace the Norse settlers, who were less able to adapt to the harsh conditions and retreated back to Iceland.

The Thule provide a valuable reminder: those who ultimately succeed aren't always the people living in the richest, highest-tech countries. The inhabitants of the most advanced lands have certain advantages; it has to be easier to stay ahead when you begin ahead. But close attention to one's environment and the willingness to wait for the right moment can reap dividends as well.

The most important lesson we can learn from our forebears is how best to react to the unfamiliar. Some Vikings killed the indigenous people sleeping under canoes without even checking to see if they were dangerous. On other continents, those who encountered strangers took their time, greeted strangers patiently, and traded their belongings for whatever goods their new acquaintances offered. Some of the most successful learned new languages and forged trading relationships across huge distances. True, globalization didn't benefit everyone who experienced it. But those who remained open to the unfamiliar did much better than those who rejected anything new. That was true in the year 1000, and it's just as true today.

Acknowledgments

The idea for this book came to me as I was finishing my book on the Silk Road and realized that the Karakhanids took Kashgar in 1006, only a year after the Liao and Song dynasties signed the Treaty of Chanyuan in 1005. Given that the Norse landed at L'Anse aux Meadows just around 1000, I wondered if the three events were related, and eventually I realized that regional expansion at that time lay behind all three.

Work began in earnest in spring 2014 when Anders Winroth, a medieval European historian who specializes in the Vikings, and Mary Miller, a pre-Columbian art historian with expertise on the Maya, and I met to prepare a seminar that we had agreed to co-teach entitled "Circa 1000." The fun started when Mary showed us the photographs of the Chichén Itzá blondies and asked Anders if they looked like Vikings. Since then Mary and Anders have unstintingly shared their ideas and materials, and the students in the seminar provided an excellent sounding board.

Mary introduced me to two more experts on Mesoamerica, who both gave generously of their time and expertise: Andrew Turner, who has now joined Mary Miller at the Getty Research Institute, in March 2017 led the "Circa 1000" seminar on a trip to Tula, Mexico City, and Chichén Itzá, where he skillfully introduced the complex iconography of the Maya. Michael D. Coe, professor emeritus in Yale's Anthropology Department, was happy to talk about anything related to the Maya or to his second love, Angkor Wat, at his or our house or over a lobster roll in Branford Harbor. Once when he and I were talking about how the North Atlantic Gyre might have carried the Norse to Chichén Itzá, he remembered reading something about Africans who washed ashore on the Yucatan Peninsula. That night, at 10 p.m., he sent me a PDF with the passage in the Spanish friar Alonso Ponce's writings. His delight—both at finding the passage and helping me—was palpable. His death at the age of 90 in September 2019 marked the end of an extraordinarily prolific career in Maya studies.

The Yale History Department maintains a high level of collegiality, and many colleagues answered my queries quickly and in detail. Special thanks go to Paul Bushkovitch, Paul Freedman, and Francesca Trivellato, and to two colleagues in Religious Studies, Phyllis Granoff and Koichi Shinohara.

A different group of teachers introduced me to the Arabic language: Sarab al-Ani and Elham Alkasimi in New Haven and Nevine Mikhail in Singapore. For two and a half years, Michael Rapoport, an extraordinarily gifted Arabist, did his best to teach me Classical Arabic. Comparing the original passages with published translations, he checked and redid many of the translations of Arabic sources in this book.

I was lucky enough to spend time away from Yale in the course of writing. Mira Seo and Emanuel Mayer hosted me at Yale-N.U.S. College in Singapore; Lu Xiqi welcomed me to Xiamen University in China, where Chen Qinfen, Lu Chenyao, Lin Changzhang, and Ge Shaoqi made our stay a productive one; Frantz Grenet invited me to speak at the Collège de France, where Étienne de la Vaissière and Valérie Kean provided crucial feedback; Frantz Grenet and Dominique Barthélemy invited me to a conference devoted to the year 1000 that was held in Les Treilles, France; and Naomi Standen hosted me at the Institute for Advanced Study at the University of Birmingham.

Naomi Standen and Catherine Holmes had just finished editing a pathbreaking volume entitled *The Global Middle Ages*, which has since been published as *Past & Present* Supplement no. 13 (November 2018). In an act of unusual scholarly generosity, Naomi and Catherine invited their volume's multiple authors to Birmingham to critique the rough draft of *The Year 1000*. Despite its being the busy start of the semester, some ten colleagues came for a day of intensive and productive conversation, which I was able to continue in one-on-one meetings in Birmingham, Durham, Oxford, and Sheffield.

Many people helped with editing, revising, and notes. Jan Fitter wields her scalpel with greater accuracy and kindness than any other editor I've ever known. In the summers of 2018 and 2019 the intrepid and indefatigable Luke Stanek copyedited, tracked down notes, and resolved (and raised) countless queries, particularly about climate history. Wei Tai Ting provided valuable research assistance early on, while Christopher Sung did yeoman service with the notes. Near the end of the writing process, Matthew Coffin, Emily Giurleo, and Nancy Ryan made key suggestions for improving chapter drafts. Alexander Laurent transformed lousy shots into publishable photos, Kate Qian Zhang advised on ocean gyres, Amelia Sargent contributed crucial drawings, and Richard Stamelman graciously tightened captions.

Michael Meng, Haruko Nakamura, and the Sterling Library curators provided excellent research assistance, while the staff of the Council of East Asian Studies—Nick Disantis, Amy Greenberg, Injoong Kim, Stephanie Kim, and Richard Sosa—resolved all kinds of problems, often daily.

My editor, Rick Horgan, and my agent, Andrew Stuart, believed in *The Year 1000* since my first emails to them, and their support—and their standards—never wavered. Fred Chase meticulously and sensitively copyedited the manuscript, and Emily Greenwald and Beckett Rueda had key roles in transforming the manuscript from typescript to finished book.

Jim Stepanek helped to conceive, write, and polish this book, and he made all the travel fun and rewarding (often by renting bicycles, which is why our time in Angkor was a high point). At one point near the end of the process he joked that he'd spent 12,000 hours on the book, surely a low-ball estimate entirely in keeping with his trademark optimism.

As always, our kids helped out. The idea for the prologue came from Claire, who, on a long flight, eavesdropped on a conversation about a Song dynasty Chinese city that sounded totally modern. One time Bret asked me about something that happened after 1500, and he suggested adding an epilogue to fill in readers about those developments. Lydia texted, "Maybe my contribution is that I advised you not to write any more -*logues*?" but yet she found time to select photographs.

The names of still others who read drafts, answered queries, and suggested materials appear before the endnotes to individual chapters. I am indebted to them and many others whose names aren't here due to space constraints.

Want to Learn More?

Chapter One: The World in the Year 1000

John Man's *Atlas of the Year 1000* (2001) guides the reader around the different regions of the world at this time. R. I. Moore's *The First European Revolution, c. 970–1215* (2000) remains the best introduction to Europe. Seamus Heaney's translation of *Beowulf* is many people's favorite. For the Maya, see Michael D. Coe and Stephen Houston, *The Maya*, 9th ed. (2015). For a thoughtful discussion of the Liao, Jin, and Song dynasties, see Dieter Kuhn, *The Age of Confucian Rule: The Song Transformation of China* (2011).

Those interested in ocean currents and their effects should consult Tom Garrison and Robert Ellis's unusually clear *Oceanography: An Invitation to Marine Science*, 9th ed. (2016). For the latest information about demography, see Massimo Livi-Bacci, *A Concise History of World Population* (2017).

A collection of essays published in November 2018 as Supplement no. 13 to *Past & Present*, entitled *The Global Middle Ages*, and edited by Catherine Holmes and Naomi Standen, presents a cutting-edge view of the field by an extremely talented group of scholars.

Chapter Two: Go West, Young Viking

The two Vinland sagas are the place to begin. The translation by Magnus Magnusson and Hermann Pálsson entitled *The Vinland Sagas: The Norse Discovery of America* (1965) offers an excellent introduction, informative notes, and a helpful glossary. Just as valuable (and an incredible car trip if you drive as we did) is the museum at L'Anse aux Meadows on the northern tip of the Canadian island of Newfoundland. Helge and Anne Stine Ingstad, *The Viking Discovery of America* (2001), tells how they found the site.

Anything by the lead investigator at L'Anse aux Meadows, Birgitta L. Wallace, is worth reading, particularly her article "The Norse in Newfoundland: L'Anse aux Meadows and Vinland," *Newfoundland Studies* 19.1 (Spring 2003): 5–43. The exhibit catalogue, *Vikings: The North Atlantic Saga*, edited by William W. Fitzhugh and Elizabeth I. Ward in 2000, remains a classic, for both the high quality of the photographs and the information in the essays.

Chapter Three: The Pan-American Highways of 1000

Start with a visit to Chichén Itzá. If you can tolerate crowds, go for the spring or fall equinox (March 21 and September 21), days that draw tens of thousands to the site. Otherwise try to visit before it gets too hot in the summer (and definitely take a swim in a cenote to cool off). Cahokia Mounds, Chaco Canyon, and Mesa Verde are well worth seeing, as are the surrounding smaller sites such as Salmon Ruins if you have time.

Popol Vuh is one of the few traditional Mayan texts to survive. Dennis Tedlock's translation is the best, and the YouTube version entitled *The Popol Vuh, Mayan Creation Myth* (in seven segments) is informative.

The best books about the Maya and Mesoamerica are all by Michael D. Coe. Start with the most recent edition of *The Maya* or *Mexico*. Timothy Pauketat, the leading archeologist writing about Cahokia Mounds, has edited multiple volumes on North American archeology, including the first-rate *The Oxford Handbook of North American Archaeology* (2012). Justin Jennings's book, *Globalizations and the Ancient World* (2010), which examines the impact of ancient Mesopotamian, Mississippian, and Wari cities on the surrounding countryside, is both original and fascinating.

Want to Learn More?

Chapter Four: European Slaves

For detailed maps showing where the Vikings went in Eastern Europe, see John Haywood, *The Penguin Historical Atlas of the Vikings* (1995). For general introductions to the Scandinavians, see the two books by Anders Winroth: *The Age of the Vikings* (2014) and *The Conversion of Scandinavia: Vikings, Merchants, and Missionaries in the Remaking of Northern Europe* (2012).

Simon Franklin and Jonathan Shepard, *The Emergence of Rus, 750–1200* (1996), remains the best introduction to the subject, and the *Russian Primary Chronicle* makes an excellent companion volume. The rooms in the Hermitage Museum in St. Petersburg devoted to the Rus give a visceral sense of their material culture.

James E. Montgomery has translated the complete account of Ibn Fadlan, *Mission to the Volga*, in *Two Arabic Travel Books*, ed. Philip F. Kennedy and Shawkat M. Toorawa (2014). The Hollywood film *The Thirteenth Warrior* isn't very accurate, but how often do you have a chance to see Antonio Banderas play an Arab envoy from the early 900s?

Paul Kingsworth's novel *The Wake* re-creates the English world before and after 1066; the author uses a language he created with some Old English vocabulary that becomes increasingly charming as you get used to it. A. B. Yehosha's novel, *A Journey to the End of the Millennium*, takes place in the France and Germany of 1000, while Robert Lacey and Danny Danziger's history, *The Year 1000: What Life Was Like at the Turn of the First Millennium: An Englishman's World* (1999), delivers exactly what the title promises.

Chapter Five: The World's Richest Man

Three excellent books on Africa appeared just as this book neared completion: François-Xavier Fauvelle-Aymar, *Golden Rhinoceros: Histories of the African Middle Ages*, trans. Troy Tice (2018); Michael A. Gomez, *African Dominion: A New History of Empire in Early and*

Medieval West Africa (2018); and the exhibition catalogue edited by Kathleen Bickford Berzock, *Caravans of Gold, Fragments in Time: Art, Culture, and Exchange Across Medieval Saharan Africa* (2019).

The forthcoming second volume of *The Cambridge World History of Slavery* promises to completely revise our understanding of the topic. In the meantime, readers should consult the *Encyclopaedia of Islam* for first-rate scholarly articles on anything related to Islam.

The medieval neighborhoods of Cairo are intriguing to stroll around; a professional guide such as Enass Saleh can make them come alive. See also Jonathan Bloom, *Arts of the City Victorious* (2008); Bloom and his frequent coauthor (and wife) Sheila Blair are gifted interpreters of Islamic art who both write beautifully.

The four volumes of *The Travels of Ibn Battuta* as translated by H. A. R. Gibb are absorbing; Ross Dunn's *The Adventures of Ibn Battuta* (2012) provides the best introduction, while Tim Mackintosh-Smith's *Travels with a Tangerine* (2012) recounts his adventures as he retraced Ibn Battuta's steps. (Natives of Tangiers, such as Ibn Battuta, were called Tangerines, and the fruit is named for the city.)

Chapter Six: Central Asia Splits in Two

You can visit many places discussed in this chapter. Uzbekistan offers different Samanid structures, with Ismail Samani's mausoleum in Bukhara as the stand-out example. The Inner Mongolia Museum in Hohhot has the world's best collection of Liao dynasty artifacts, and other regional archeological museums, especially the Beita Museum in Chaoyang, are quite interesting. Kyoto's museums display beautiful Heian objects and paintings, and the Byodoin Temple lies in the nearby suburb of Uji, the site of many scenes in *The Tale of Genji*. (Dennis Washburn's translation of the novel is particularly gripping in light of the #MeToo movement.) The National Museum in Seoul is the best single-stop collection of Korean art, and the Haeinsa Monastery with its thousands of printing blocks is a UNESCO World Heritage site.

The latest scholarship on the Liao dynasty appears in a special issue entitled *Perspectives on the Liao* of *The Journal of Song-Yuan Studies* 43 (2013), while in 2007 the Asia Society hosted an exhibit entitled "Gilded Splendor" with a first-rate catalogue and website with a well-researched virtual tour of the tomb of the Princess of Chen.

Dick Davis's translation of *Shahnameh* is wonderfully accessible, and the online *Encyclopædia Iranica* represents the highest level of scholarship on all topics touching on the Persian language and Iranian civilization. Amin Maalouf's novel *Samarkand*, a fictionalized account of the life of Omar Khayyam, conveys a vivid sense of the city around 1000, and Omar Khayyam's poems in the Rubaiyaat have been a classic since first translated into English in the mid-1800s. Vladimir Minorsky translated both the anonymous geographical text *The Limits of the World*, under its Persian title, *Hudud al-'Alam*, and the writings of al-Marwazi. For an inspired introduction to Asia, see Peter Frankopan's *The Silk Roads: A New History of the World*.

Chapter Seven: Surprising Journeys

Shipwreck museums are all over the Southeast Asian region. The most impressive artifacts from the Belitung shipwreck are on display in the Asian Civilizations Museum in Singapore, and you can see other items from the shipwreck in the city's casinos and hotels. To understand life on a dhow, watch the documentary *Sons of Sinbad*, about the *National Geographic* photographer Marian Kaplan, who wrote about her voyage from Oman to East Africa in 1974. Steve Thomas's *The Last Navigator*, an account of his studies with Mau Piailug, remains the most readable study of Polynesian seafaring. The Samudra Raksa Museum, a short walk from the Borobudur monument, contains the replica boat that was built using traditional shipbuilding techniques on the basis of the stone panels at Borobudur.

Of the sites mentioned in the chapter, Angkor Wat in Cambodia is by far the most extensive, and you need at least five days, ideally a week, to visit the most important temples. The best guide, *Angkor and the Khmer Civilization* (2018), is by the indefatigable Michael D. Coe, who branched out from his studies of Mesoamerica to study similar terrain in Southeast Asia; his coauthor, Damian Evans, has pioneered the use of lidar. The temples at Borobudur and Thanjavur, both in excellent condition today, illuminate the workings of temple states.

Chapter Eight: The Most Globalized Place on Earth

Of all China's coastal ports, Quanzhou preserves many buildings and much of the city layout from the Song dynasty, and walking around the streets and visiting temples and the mosque from then is unforgettable. The Maritime Museum is a must-see, as is the museum devoted to the 1270s shipwreck, which is located on the grounds of Kaiyuan Monastery. The city, although close to Xiamen, is a little off the beaten track, and can be difficult to negotiate if you don't have a Chinese speaker with you. The best scholarly studies of Quanzhou remain the essays in the volume edited by Angela Schottenhammer entitled *The Emporium of the World: Maritime Quanzhou, 1000–1400* (2001). The top scholars in the field are John Chaffee, Hugh Clark, Huang Chunyan (writing only in Chinese), and Billy So. For a general introduction to Chinese history, see my *Open Empire*, 2nd edition (2015).

The Southern Song dynasty capital of Hangzhou is much more developed than Quanzhou. There you can visit an excavated dragon kiln and see the high-fired ceramics it produced, and also walk along an underground street from the 1200s. The Qingming scroll, finished sometime before 1186, is a painting over 5 yards (5 m) long, which many call China's *Mona Lisa*. The scroll offers a detailed view of an idealized Chinese cityscape; multiple reproductions and introductions on YouTube are available, and the Beijing Palace Museum sometimes displays the painting in the autumn.

Notes

Prologue

5 **This book is the first to recognize these as "globalization":** Manfred B. Steger wrote a helpful introduction, which sees time-space compression as the key to globalization, and focuses, like most books, on the 1970s. Some analysts have detected globalization before 1000: Justin Jennings argues that ancient Mesopotamia, Cahokia, and the Wari culture all saw cities influencing the surrounding countryside. Earlier scholars, particularly David Northrup and John Man, have remarked on the importance of the year 1000, while Janet Abu-Lughod identified the Mongol period as marking the key step toward greater integration. C. A. Bayly defined globalization as "a progressive increase in the scale of social processes from a local or regional to a world level," and he believed that the first phase, which he called archaic globalization, occurred after 1500.

See Steger, *Globalization: A Very Short Introduction* (2009); Jennings, *Globalizations and the Ancient World* (2011); Northrup, "Globalization and the Great Convergence: Rethinking World History in the Long Term," *Journal of World History* 16.3 (2005): 249–67; Man, *Atlas of the Year 1000* (2001); Abu-Lughod, *Before European Hegemony: The World System A.D. 1250–1350* (1989); Bayly, "'Archaic' and 'Modern' Globalization in the Eurasian and Africa Arena, c. 1750–1850," in *Globalization in World History*, ed. A. G. Hopkins (2002).

6 **"slapped":** Magnus Magnusson and Hermann Pálsson (trans.), *The Vinland Sagas: The Norse Discovery of America* (1965): 100.

7 **92 percent:** Jon Emont, "Why Are There No New Major Religions?," *The Atlantic* (August 6, 2017).

Chapter One: The World in the Year 1000

9 **one quarter and one third:** James C. Lee and Wang Feng, *One Quarter of Humanity: Malthusian Mythology and Chinese Realities, 1700–2000* (1996): 6 (Figure 1.1).

10 **sustained prosperity:** Andrew M. Watson, "The Arab Agricultural Revo-

lution and Its Diffusion, 700–1100," *Journal of Economic History* 34.1 (1974): 8–35; Watson, *Agricultural Innovation in the Early Islamic World: The Diffusion of Crops and Farming Techniques, 700–1100* (1983). Paolo Squatriti has demonstrated that Watson's original thesis about the spread of crops throughout the Islamic world has stood the test of time in his "Of Seeds, Seasons, and Seas: Andrew Watson's Medieval Agrarian Revolution Forty Years Later," *Journal of Economic History* 74.4 (2014): 1205–20.

10 **35 to 40 million:** Andrew Watson, "A Medieval Green Revolution," in *The Islamic Middle East, 700–1900: Studies in Economic and Social History,* ed. A. L. Udovitch (1981): 29–58, 30; Charles Issawi, "The Area and Population of the Arab Empire: An Essay in Speculation," in the same volume, 375–96, 387.

10 **"cerealization":** R. I. Moore, *The First European Revolution, c. 970–1215* (2000): 30–39, 30 (doubling of population), 33 (population of Córdoba), 46–48 (cerealization).

11 **Medieval Warm Period:** H. H. Lamb, "The Early Medieval Warm Epoch and Its Sequel," *Paleogeography, Paleoclimatology, Paleoecology* 1 (1965): 13–37.

11 **Medieval Climatic Anomaly:** PAGES 2k Consortium, "Continental-Scale Temperature Variability During the Past Two Millennia," *Nature Geoscience* 6 (2013): 339–46. For a map of the world showing cooling and warming trends as well as drought and wet periods, see the online Medieval Warm Period mapping project led by Sebastian Lüning: http://t1p.de /mwp. See also the essays by Quansheng Ge et al. about China, and Christian Rohr et al. about Europe, in the *Palgrave Handbook of Climate History,* ed. Sam White et al. (2018).

11 **Ongoing research:** Alexander F. More, "New Interdisciplinary Evidence on Climate and the Environment from the Last Millennium," unpublished paper delivered at the conference, "Histoires de l'an mil," Fondation des Treilles, France, September. 9–14, 2019.

11 **60 percent:** Valerie Hansen, *The Open Empire: A History of China to 1800,* 2nd ed. (2015): 239.

11 **the Byzantine empire was the most prosperous power:** Cécile Morrisson, "La place de Byzance dans l'histoire de l'économie médiévale (v. 717–1204): méthodes, acquis, perspectives," in *Richesse et croissance au Moyen Âge. Orient et Occident* (Monographies de Travaux et Mémoires 43), ed. D. Barthélemy and Jean-Marie Martin, (2014): 11–30.

12 *al-jabr:* Sonja Brentjes, "Al-jabr," *Encyclopaedia of Islam,* 3rd ed. (2007).

12 **Most people referred to the year by the reign:** Uta C. Merzbach, "Calendars and the Reckoning of Time," *Dictionary of the Middle Ages* (1983) 3: 17–30.

12 **Various itinerant preachers:** Robert E. Lerner, "Millennialism, Christian," *Dictionary of the Middle Ages* 8: 384–88; Norman Cohn, *The Pursuit of the Millennium: Revolutionary Messianism in Medieval and Reformation Europe and Its Bearing on Modern Totalitarian Movements,* 3rd ed. (1970).

12 **10–15 million:** Tom Clynes, "Exclusive: Laser Scans Reveal Maya 'Megalopolis' Below Guatemalan Jungle," *National Geographic* (February 1, 2018). Available online.

12 **The Maya city of Tikal:** Michael D. Coe and Stephen Houston, *The*

Maya, 9th ed. (2015): 73, 84 (early agriculture), 126 (Tikal population), 176 (Chichén Itzá).

13 **more than 50 percent:** Massimo Livi-Bacci, *A Concise History of World Population* (2017): 25.

13 **Paris had a population:** William W. Clark and John Bell Henneman, Jr., "Paris," William A. Percy, "Population and Demography," in William W. Kibler et al., *Medieval France: An Encyclopedia* (1995): 698–707, 751–52.

14 **the city of Jenne-jeno:** Conrad Leyser, Naomi Standen, and Stephanie Wynne-Jones, "Settlement, Landscape and Narrative: What Really Happened in History," *The Global Middle Ages,* ed. Catherine Holmes and Naomi Standen, *Past and Present,* Supplement 13 (2018): 232–60.

16 **Subsequent geographers:** Travis E. Zadeh, *Mapping Frontiers Across Medieval Islam: Geography, Translations, and the 'Abbāsid Empire* (2011).

17 *1421:* Gavin Menzies, *1421: The Year That China Discovered America* (2008).

17 **"One of them":** Ishaan Tharoor, "Muslims Discovered America Before Columbus, Claims Turkey's Erdogan," *Washington Post* (November 15, 2004); entry for October 29, 1492, *Journal of the First Voyage of Christopher Columbus,* ed. Julius E. Olson and Edward Gaylord Bourne (1906): 133.

17 **"Biruni Discovers America":** Frederick S. Starr, *Lost Enlightenment: Central Asia's Golden Age from the Arab Conquest to Tamerlane* (2014): 375–78.

17 **earth was a sphere:** Saiyid Samad Husain Rizvi, "A Newly Discovered Book of Al-Biruni: 'Ghurrat-uz-Zijat,' and al-Biruni's Measurements of Earth's Dimensions," in *Al-Biruni Commemorative Volume,* ed. Hakim Mohammed Said (1979): 605–80, 617.

18 **He suspected that most of the opposite side of the globe:** Fuat Sezgin (ed.), *The Determination of the Coordinates of Positions for the Correction of Distances Between Cities: A Translation from the Arabic of al-Biruni's Kitab Tahdid Nihayat al-Amakiin Litashih Masafat al-Masakin by Jamil Ali* (1992): 102–10, which translates 136–46 of al-Bīrūnī, *Kitāb Taḥdīd nihāyāt al-amākin li-taṣḥīḥ masāfāt al-masākin,* ed. P. Bulgakov (Frankfurt, 1992).

18 **the elephants became bishops:** Helmut Nickel, "Games and Pastimes," *Dictionary of the Middle Ages* (1985): 5: 347–53.

19 **walrus ivory:** Anibal Rodriguez, Museum Technician, American Museum of Natural History, personal communication, March 11, 2015.

19 **150 miles in a single day:** John Howland Rowe, *Inca Culture at the Time of the Spanish Conquest* (1946): 231–32.

19 **10 and 20 miles per day:** Ross Hassig, *Aztec Warfare: Imperial Expansion and Political Control* (1995): 66.

19 **normal rate for a march:** U.S. Department of the Army Techniques Publication, "Foot Marches (FM 21-18)" (April 2017): Section 2-41.

20 **60 miles per day:** Ashleigh N. Deluca, "World's Toughest Horse Race Retraces Genghis Khan's Postal Route," *National Geographic News* (August 7, 2014); H. Desmond Martin, *The Rise of Chingis Khan and His Conquest of North China* (1950): 18.

20 **macaw feathers:** Stephen H. Lekson, "Chaco's Hinterlands," in *The Oxford Handbook of North American Archaeology,* ed. Timothy R. Pauketat (2012): 597–607, 602–3.

Notes

20 **17 mph:** Anders Winroth, *The Age of the Vikings* (2014): 72.

20 **speeds about half that:** Ben R. Finney, *Hokule'a: The Way to Tahiti* (1979); Ben Finney, *Voyage of Rediscovery: A Cultural Odyssey Through Polynesia* (1994): 127.

20 **rowboats can travel in any direction:** Mark Howard-Flanders, experienced mariner, Branford, Connecticut, personal communication, September 1, 2017.

21 **The Greenland Current:** Birgitta Wallace, "The Norse in Newfoundland: L'Anse aux Meadows and Vinland," *Newfoundland Studies* 19.1 (2003): 5–43, 8.

21 **"the wind dropped":** Keneva Kunz (trans.), *Vinland Sagas: The Icelandic Sagas About the First Documented Voyages Across the North Atlantic*, ed. Gísli Sigurdsson (2008): 4.

22 **more than 100 miles in a day:** http://oceanservice.noaa.gov/. See also the very helpful website https://earth.nullschool.net/ on which you can look up winds and currents on any given day.

22 **the men were vulnerable to scurvy:** Cassandra Tate, "Japanese Castaways of 1834: The Three Kichis" (posted July 23, 2009), http://www.history link.org/File/9065; Frederik L. Schodt, *Native American in the Land of the Shogun: Ranald MacDonald and the Opening of Japan* (2003).

22 **boats can go much faster:** Tom Garrison and Robert Ellis, *Oceanography: An Invitation to Marine Science*, 9th ed. (2016): 230 (monsoons), 232 (Figure 8.19a and b: monsoon patterns), 251 (Figure 9.3: North Atlantic Gyre), 255 (Figure 9.8 a and b: surface currents).

23 **"This sea route":** George F. Hourani, *Arab Seafaring in the Indian Ocean in Ancient and Early Medieval Times*, revised and expanded by John Carswell (1995): 61 (route in greatest use), 74 (sailing times).

23 **The direction of the current:** Robert Delfs, well-known underwater photographer based in Indonesia, personal communication, October 2015.

23 **Chinese consumers loved sea slugs:** Wang Gungwu, Emeritus Professor of History, National University of Singapore, personal communication, October 2015; C. C. McKnight, *The Voyage to Marege': Macassan Trepangers in Northern Australia* (1976); Derek John Mulvaney, "Bêche-de-mer, Aborigines and Australian History," *Journal of the Royal Society of Victoria* 79.2 (1966): 449–57.

24 **magnetic shipboard compasses:** Robert K. G. Temple, *The Genius of China: 3,000 Years of Science, Discovery, and Invention* (1986): 148–57.

24 **Mau Piailug:** Steve Thomas, *The Last Navigator: A Young Man, an Ancient Mariner, and the Secrets of the Sea* (1987).

24 **When the weather was clear:** Mau Piailug obituary, *Washington Post* (July 21, 2010).

24 **The men in Beowulf's warband:** Seamus Heaney (trans.), *Beowulf: A New Verse Translation* (2001).

25 **Small warbands:** Ben Raffield, "Bands of Brothers: A Re-appraisal of the Viking Great Army and Its Implications for the Scandinavian Colonization of England," *Early Medieval Europe* 24.3 (2016): 308–37, 314 (size of bands), 317 (women), 325 (different ethnicities).

25 **Warband leaders who succeeded:** Jonathan Karam Skaff, *Sui-Tang China and Its Turko-Mongol Neighbors: Culture, Power, and Connections, 580–800* (2012): 12–15, 75–104; Timothy Reuter, "Plunder and Tribute in the Carolingian Empire," *Transactions of the Royal Historical Society*, 5th Series, 35 (1985): 75–94; Naomi Standen, "Followers and Leaders in Northeastern Eurasia, ca. Seventh to Tenth Centuries," in *Empires and Exchanges in Eurasian Late Antiquity: Rome, China, Iran, and the Steppe, ca. 250–750*, ed. Nicola di Cosmo and Michael Maas (2018): 400–18.

25 **sometime around 900:** Gwyn Jones, *A History of the Vikings* (1968): 290.

25 **network of global pathways:** John Man, *Atlas of the Year 1000* (2001).

Chapter Two: Go West, Young Viking

My colleague Anders Winroth has generously suggested key readings for the past twenty years, even as he remains skeptical of the historic value of the sagas. Chris Callow, University of Birmingham, and Conrad Leyser, Oxford, also did their best to explain the skeptics' position to me.

28 **Scholars still debate:** Keneva Kunz (trans.), *The Vinland Sagas: The Icelandic Sagas About the First Documented Voyages Across the North Atlantic*, ed. Gísli Sigurdsson (2008): 5–10 (Leif's voyage), 31–32 (Gudrid's singing), 45 (Karlsefni's encounter).

28 **Humans could be killed with iron weapons:** Annette Kolodny, *In Search of First Contact: The Vikings of Vinland, the Peoples of the Dawnland, and the Anglo-American Anxiety of Discovery* (2012): 58 (meaning of "Skraeling"), 59 (iron weapons), 60 (Wabanaki Alliance), 272 (Wayne Newell), 274 (noisemakers).

29 **prisoners of war or purchased slaves:** Ben Raffield, "Bands of Brothers: A Re-appraisal of the Viking Great Army and Its Implications for the Scandinavian Colonization of England," *Early Medieval Europe* 24.3 (2016): 308–37, 325.

30 **Gudrid . . . is as virtuous as Freydis is wayward:** Nancy Marie Brown, *The Far Traveler: Voyages of a Viking Woman* (2006).

30 **centuries-long process:** Anders Winroth, *The Conversion of Scandinavia: Vikings, Merchants, and Missionaries in the Remaking of Northern Europe* (2012).

31 **Salme, Estonia:** Heather Pringle, "New Visions of the Vikings," *National Geographic* 231.3 (March 2017): 30–51, 39.

31 **the introduction of the square sail:** John Haywood notes that there are runestones with pictures of square sails dating to the 600s from the Danish peninsula. See his *The Penguin Historical Atlas of the Vikings* (1995): 9–10.

32 **modern replicas of Viking ships:** Max Vinner, *Boats of the Viking Ship Museum* (2017): 20–21.

32 **small bronze statue of the Buddha:** Dieter Ahrens, "Die Buddhastatuette von Helgö," *Pantheon* 22 (1964): 51–52; Scott Ashley, "Global Worlds, Local Worlds, Connections and Transformations in the Viking Age," in

Notes

Byzantium and the Viking World, ed. Fedir Androshchuk et al. (2016): 363–87, 364, 372.

32 **Oseburg ship:** Thorleif Sjøvold, *The Viking Ships in Oslo* (1985): 22.

33 **Warships:** Five different ship frames are on display in the Viking Ship Museum in Roskilde, Denmark.

33 **large quantities of cod bones:** James H. Barrett and David C. Orton (eds.), *Cod and Herring: The Archaeology and History of Medieval Sea Fishing* (2016).

33 **Norse sailed to Iceland:** The Settlement Exhibition Reykjavík 871±2 Museum dates the earliest known settlement on Iceland by matching it to an ice core from Greenland.

34 **It's likely that they were first composed:** Erik Wahlgren, "Vinland Sagas," *Medieval Scandinavia: An Encyclopedia* (1993): 704–5.

34 **They want to stress the creativity:** Jesse Byock, Professor of Old Norse and Medieval Scandinavian Studies, UCLA, personal communication, August 23, 2017.

34 **These deniers are convinced:** Sverrir Jakobsson, "Vinland and Wishful Thinking: Medieval and Modern Fantasies," *Canadian Journal of History/Annales canadiennes d'histoire* 47 (2012): 493–514; Jerold C. Frakes, "Vikings, Vinland and the Discourse of Eurocentrism," *Journal of English and German Philology* 100.1 (April 2001): 157–99.

34 **the anecdote soup theory:** Theodore M. Andersson lists seven types of anecdotes (for example, biographical accounts) that circulated orally: *The Growth of the Medieval Icelandic Sagas (1180–1280)* (2006). See also Margaret Cormack, "Fact and Fiction in the Icelandic Sagas," *History Compass* 5.1 (2007): 201–17.

34 **two sagas agree about the main events:** *Erik's Saga* has Thorvald die after Karlsefni arrives in Vinland, while the *Greenlanders' Saga* puts his death before Karlsefni lands.

35 **contact or trickle-trade:** Robert W. Park, "Contact Between the Norse Vikings and the Dorset Culture in Arctic Canada," *Antiquity* 82 (2008): 189–98.

36 **Innu:** Ralph T. Pastore, "Archaeology, History, and the Beothuks," *Newfoundland Studies* 9.2 (1993): 260–78; Ralph Pastore, "The Collapse of the Beothuk World," *Acadiensis: Journal of the History of the Atlantic Region* 19.1 (1989): 52–71.

36 **artifacts at L'Anse aux Meadows:** Birgitta Wallace, *Westward Vikings* (2006): 21–23 (detailed discussion of dating), 25, 29–30 (those who proposed L'Anse aux Meadows as a Viking site), 38–48 (detailed description of each structure), 78 (estimate of population), 87–88 (Beothuk and Innu at L'Anse aux Meadows).

36 **Hugging the coast:** Birgitta Wallace, "L'Anse aux Meadows: Leif Eriksson's Home in the Americas," *Journal of the North Atlantic*, Special Volume 2 (2009): 114–25, 116 (sixteenth-century trade route), 120 (animal bone evidence), 121 (Cartier and Chaleur Bay).

37 **"sent on shore part of their people":** Ramsay Cook, *The Voyages of Jacques Cartier* (1993): 19–21.

38 **"brought down among a group of men":** Henry Rowe Schoolcraft

(1793–1864), *Historical and Statistical Information Respecting the History, Condition and Prospects of the Indian Tribes of the United States*, Volume 1 (1851): 85.

40 **"the people there are greenish":** Adam of Bremen, *History of the Archbishops of Hamburg-Bremen*, trans. Francis J. Tschan, introduction by Timothy Reuter (2002): 218–19.

40 **"Beyond that island":** A few other manuscripts in Icelandic, dated between 1121 and 1400, also mention Vinland. Ari Thorgilsson (born 1067), *Book of the Icelanders* (Íslendingabók), written in 1127 is one of the most important.

41 **But they never put their theories to the test:** W. A Munn, *Wineland Voyages: Location of Helluland, Markland and Vinland* (1946 reprint of 1914 privately printed pamphlet).

42 **"We let out a holler":** Anne Stine Ingstad, *The New Land with the Green Meadows* (2013): 169.

42 **Other objects:** Helge Ingstad and Anne Stine Ingstad, *The Viking Discovery of America: The Excavation of a Norse Settlement in L'Anse aux Meadows, Newfoundland* (2001): 105–9 (meaning of Vinland), 137 (foundry), 157 (needle sharpener and spindle whorl), 160 (pin).

43 **generic name like "land of meadows":** Erik Wahlgren, "Fact and Fancy in the Vinland Sagas," in *Old Norse Literature and Mythology: A Symposium*, ed. Edgar C. Polomé (1969): 44, 52–53.

43 **discovery of three butternuts:** Birgitta Wallace, "The Norse in Newfoundland: L'Anse aux Meadows and Vinland," *Newfoundland Studies* 19.1 (2003): 10 (sagas), 11 (no fields nearby), 18–19 (shipbuilding), 25 (planned departure), 26 (butternuts).

44 **After careful study:** Erik Wahlgren, *The Vikings and America* (1986): 11–15 (expeditions to northern Greenland), 163–64 (location of Vinland). For other possible locations, see the chart, "Suggested Locations of Places Mentioned in the Vinland Sagas," in Kunz, *Vinland Sagas*, 66–67.

46 **It was minted between 1065 and 1080:** Svein H. Gullbekk, "The Norse Penny Reconsidered: The Goddard Coin—Hoax or Genuine?," *Journal of the North Atlantic* 33 (2017): 1–8; Steven L. Cox, "A Norse Penny from Maine," in *Vikings: The North Atlantic Saga*, ed. William W. Fitzhugh and Elizabeth I. Ward (2000): 206–7; Gareth Williams, British Museum, email, July 11, 2016.

47 **textiles preserved in ice from the Greenland site:** Joel Bergland, "The Farm Beneath the Sand," in Fitzhugh and Ward, *North Atlantic Saga*, 295–303, 300.

47 **One group traveled:** Magnus Magnusson and Hermann Pálsson (trans.), *The Vinland Sagas: The Norse Discovery of America* (1965): 21 (expeditions to northern Greenland), 22 (1379 killing), 23 (1492 pope's letter), 42–43 (Columbus).

47 **An ivory figurine:** Museum of History, Ottawa, Canada, accession no. KeDq-7:325.

48 **The Norse began to abandon their settlements:** PAGES 2k Consortium, "Continental-Scale Temperature Variability During the Past Two Millennia," *Nature Geoscience* 6 (2013): 339–46.

Notes

48 **All these technologies:** Robert W. Park, "Adapting to a Frozen Coastal Environment," in *The Oxford Handbook of North American Archaeology*, ed. Timothy R. Pauketat (2012): 113–23.

48 **The Norse population in Greenland:** Niels Lynnerup, "Life and Death in Norse Greenland," in Fitzhugh and Ward, *North Atlantic Saga*, 285–94.

49 **It was just another account:** Roberta Frank, English Department, Yale University, personal communication, July 12, 2016.

50 **Sigurdur Stefansson:** Biørn Jonsen of Skarsaa, Description of Greenland and the Skálholt Map, Det Kongelige Bibliotek. Skálholt Map #431.6 (1590), www.myoldmaps.com.

Chapter Three: The Pan-American Highways of 1000

Three Yale colleagues shared their knowledge generously: the late Michael D. Coe, professor emeritus of Anthropology, Yale University; Mary Miller, professor of the History of Art, now director of the Getty Research Institute; and Andrew Turner, a postdoctoral curator at the Yale University Art Gallery, now also at the Getty Research Institute. John E. Kelly of Washington University graciously gave me a tour of the Cahokia site on April 11, 2015; Michelle Young, also from Yale, offered an incisive critique of the Andes section; and Caroline Dodd Pennock, University of Sheffield, suggested major revisions to the argument.

53 **Chichén Itzá:** Geoffrey E. Braswell, "What We Know, What We Don't Know, and What We Like to Argue About," Yale Brownbag Archaeological lunchtime talk (December 8, 2017).

53 **largest Maya ball court:** Mary Miller, *The Art of Mesoamerica: From Olmec to Aztec* (2012): 224.

55 **sap from morning glory flowers:** Laura Filloy Nadal, "Rubber and Rubber Balls in Mesoamerica," in *The Sport of Life and Death: The Mesoamerican Ballgame*, ed. E. Michael Whittington (2002): 21–31.

55 **Clearing the temple:** Earl H. Morris, *The Temple of the Warriors: The Adventure of Exploring and Restoring a Masterpiece of Native American Architecture in the Ruined Maya City of Chichén Itzá, Yucatan* (1931): 62.

55 **Many wall paintings at the Temple of the Warriors depict conquest:** Michael D. Coe and Stephen Houston, *The Maya*, 9th ed. (2015): 126, 163, 174–98 (Terminal Classic), 182, 201 (events of 987), 201–15 (Chichén Itzá description), 214–19 (Mayapán), 242 (white roads).

55 **Invaders had gray skins:** Ann Axtell Morris did a watercolor of the murals at the Temple of the Warriors and accompanied them with a black-and-white rendering of the still visible drawings. She filled in the missing figures by copying similar figures from other parts of the mural, showing the care with which she worked. Earl H. Morris, Jean Charlot, and Ann Axtell Morris, *The Temple of the Warriors at Chichen Itza, Yucatan*, Publication No. 406 (1931): I: 386–95, II: plate 139 (Maya village being raided); plate 146 (naval battle); plate 147b (captive with beads in his hair); plate 147c (captive shown in color plate); plate 159 (Maya village at peace).

56 **A second has beads:** Compare the murals at the Bonampak site in the Mexican city of Chiapas near the Guatemala border.

56 **Maya blue:** Also known as attapulgite, the scientific name of this clay is hydrated magnesium aluminum silicate hydroxide.

56 **"emphasize a difference of tribe":** Morris et al., *The Temple of the Warriors*, I: 402.

56 **an extreme solution:** J. Eric S. Thompson, "Representations of Tlalchitonatiuh at Chichén Itzá, Yucatan, and at Baul, Escuintla," *Notes on Middle American Archaeology and Ethnology* 19 (1943): 117–21. See also Donald E. Wray, "The Historical Significance of the Murals in the Temple of the Warriors, Chichén Itzá," *American Antiquity* 11.1 (1945): 25–27.

57 **This is precisely when the paintings were done:** Beniamino Volta and Geoffrey E. Braswell, "Alternative Narratives and Missing Data: Refining the Chronology of Chichén Itzá," in *The Maya and Their Central American Neighbors: Settlement Patterns, Architecture, Hieroglyphic Texts, and Ceramics*, ed. Geoffrey E. Braswell (2014): 356–402, 373–74 (Table 13.1 of inscriptions), 377–83 (dating).

58 **Las Monjas:** John S. Bolles, *Las Monjas: A Major Pre-Mexican Architectural Complex at Chichén Itzá* (1977): 198 (photo of the boat mural in room 22 taken in 1934), 199 (Adela Breton painting of the mural), 202–3 (Jean Charlot watercolor of the mural).

58 **Although many published drawings:** Søren Nielson, Head of Maritime Craft Reconstruction, Viking Ship Museum in Roskilde, Denmark, email, June 7, 2018.

58 **Chumash:** Jeanne E. Arnold, "Credit Where Credit Is Due: The History of the Chumash Oceangoing Plank Canoe," *American Antiquity* 72.2 (2007): 196–209; Brian Fagan, "The Chumash," in *Time Detectives* (1995).

58 **"some were driven back":** Magnus Magnusson and Hermann Pálsson (trans.), *The Vinland Sagas* (1965): 51.

59 **Xequechakan:** Ernest Noyes (trans.), "Fray Alonso Ponce in Yucatán" (Tulane), *Middle American Research Series*, Publication No. 4 (1934): 344–45.

60 **thirty tools:** Bruce J. Bourque and Steven L. Cox, "Maine State Museum Investigation of the Goddard Site, 1979," *Man in the Northeast* 22 (1981): 3–27, 18 (seal and mink teeth).

61 **Ramah chert:** Kevin McAleese, "Ancient Uses of Ramah Chert," 2002, http://www.heritage.nf.ca/articles/environment/landscape-ramah-chert.php.

61 **other contemporary sites:** Bruce J. Bourque, "Eastern North America: Evidence for Prehistoric Exchange on the Maritime Peninsula," in *Prehistoric Exchange Systems in North America*, ed. Timothy G. Baugh and Jonathan E. Ericson (1994): 34–35.

61 **"mobile farmers":** Elizabeth Chilton, "New England Algonquians: Navigating 'Backwaters' and Typological Boundaries," in *The Oxford Handbook of North American Archaeology*, ed. Timothy R. Pauketat (2012): 262–72.

61 **Algonquians:** Ronald F. Williamson, "What Will Be Has Always Been:

The Past and Present of Northern Iroquoians," in *The Oxford Handbook of North American Archaeology*, 273–84.

61 **Ohio:** Bernard K. Means, "Villagers and Farmers of the Middle and Upper Ohio River Valley, 11th to 17th Centuries AD: The Fort Ancient and Monongahela Traditions," in *The Oxford Handbook of North American Archaeology*, 297–309.

62 **Beans came to the Mississippi Valley:** Deborah M. Pearsall, "People, Plants, and Culinary Traditions," in *The Oxford Handbook of North American Archaeology*, 73–84.

62 **corns, beans, and squash:** Alice Beck Kehoe, *America Before the European Invasions* (2002): 177 (Cahokia filed teeth), 178 (corns, beans, and squash).

62 **residents didn't depend solely on cultivated crops:** Timothy R. Pauketat, *Ancient Cahokia and the Mississippians* (2004): 7–9.

62 **Cahokia:** Justin Jennings, *Globalizations and the Ancient World* (2011): 83–84 (Cahokia population), 87–88 (Cahokia's regional influence), 92–95 (Spiro).

62 **The different mounds, which are the distinguishing feature:** Robert L. Hall, "The Cahokia Site and Its People," in *Hero, Hawk, and Open Hand: American Indian Art of the Ancient Midwest and South*, ed. Richard F. Townshend (2004): 93–103.

63 **chunkey stones:** Timothy R. Pauketat, *Cahokia: Ancient America's Great City on the Mississippi* (2009): 31–36 (trade), 36–50 (chunkey), 69–84 (Mound 72), 92–98 (twin legends).

63 **20,000 shell beads:** Melvin L. Fowler, "Mound 72 and Early Mississippian at Cahokia," in *New Perspectives on Cahokia: Views from the Periphery*, ed. James B. Stoltman (1991): 1–28.

64 **Pottery vessels:** John E. Kelly, "Cahokia as a Gateway Center," in *Cahokia and the Hinterlands: Middle Mississippian Cultures of the Midwest*, ed. Thomas E. Emerson and R. Barry Lewis (1991): 61–80, 75.

64 **Spiro, Oklahoma:** Townshend, *Hero, Hawk, and Open Hand*, 150, 157.

64 **This obsidian was so unusual:** Alex W. Barker et al., "Mesoamerican Origin for an Obsidian Scraper from the Precolumbian Southeastern United States," *American Antiquity* 67.1 (2002): 103–8.

64 **Mesoamericans altered their teeth:** Gregory Perino, "Additional Discoveries of Filed Teeth in the Cahokia Area," *American Antiquity* 32.4 (1967): 538–42.

65 **traces of chocolate:** Michael Bawaya, "A Chocolate Habit in Ancient North America," *Science* 345.6200 (2014): 991.

65 **Popol Vuh:** Dennis Tedlock, *Popol Vuh: The Definitive Edition of the Mayan Book of the Dawn of Life and the Glories of Gods and Kings* (1996).

65 **Not always visible:** Ruth M. Van Dyke, "Chaco's Sacred Geography," in *In Search of Chaco: New Approaches to an Archaeological Enigma*, ed. David Grant Noble (2004): 79–85.

66 **Pueblo Bonito:** Thomas C. Windes, "This Old House: Construction and Abandonment at Pueblo Bonito," in *Pueblo Bonito*, ed. Jill E. Neitzel (2003): 14–32, 15.

66 **purpose of the great houses:** David Grant Noble, *Ancient Ruins of the*

Southwest: An Archaeological Guide (1991): 27 (Mesoamerican trade goods at Chaco), 73, 115 (great houses and roads).

66 **migrants from southwestern Colorado:** Michael A. Schillaci, "The Development of Population Diversity at Chaco Canyon," *Kiva* 68.3 (2003): 221–45.

66 **deliberately notched teeth:** Christy G. Turner II and Jacqueline A. Turner, *Man Corn: Cannibalism and Violence in the Prehistoric American Southwest* (1999): 128–29, 476 (Figure 5.7).

66 **traded the turquoise to obtain tropical birds:** Stephen Nash, "Heated Politics, Precious Ruins," *New York Times* (July 30, 2017): TR7–9.

67 **excavated macaw skeletons:** Exhibit label at the Salmon Ruins Museum and Research Library, Bloomfield, New Mexico, 87413 (visited March 21, 2016); Tori L. Myers, "Salmon Ruins Trail Guide" (2013): 9, 15.

67 **theobromine:** Patricia L. Crown and W. Jeffrey Hurst, "Evidence of Cacao Use in the Prehispanic American Southwest," *Proceedings of the National Academy of Sciences of the United States of America* 106.7 (2009): 2110–13; W. Jeffrey Hurst, "The Determination of Cacao in Samples of Archaeological Interest," in *Chocolate in Mesoamerica: A Cultural History of Cacao*, ed. Cameron L. McNeil (2006): 104–13.

67 **Chocolate was first domesticated:** Zach Zorich, "Ancient Amazonian Chocolatiers," *Archaeology* (January/February 2019): 12.

67 **processing of chocolate:** Sophie D. Coe and Michael D. Coe, *The True History of Chocolate*, 3rd ed. (2013): 21–24.

70 **collapse of Maya society:** Douglas J. Kennett et al., "Development and Disintegration of Maya Political Systems in Response to Climate Change," *Science* (2012): 788–91.

70 **wheel:** Richard W. Bulliet, *The Wheel: Inventions and Reinventions* (2016): 36–41.

70 **Milky Way:** Joel W. Palka, *Maya Pilgrimage to Ritual Landscapes: Insights from Archaeology, History, and Ethnography* (2014): 81; Angela H. Keller, "A Road by Any Other Name: Trails, Paths, and Roads in Maya Language and Thought," in *Landscapes of Movement: Trails, Paths, and Roads in Anthropological Perspective*, ed. James E. Snead et al. (2009): 133–57, 145.

71 **Sacred Cenote:** C. W. Ceram, *Gods, Graves, and Scholars: The Story of Archaeology*, trans. E. B. Garside (1953): 379, 385.

71 **Maya books:** See https://arstechnica.com/science/2016/09/confirmed -mysterious-ancient-maya-book-grolier-codex-is-genuine/.

71 **sacrificed human beings:** Friar Diego de Landa, *Yucatan: Before and After the Conquest*, trans. William Gates (1978): 17 (Maya merchant prince), 90 (Sacred Cenote).

71 **Edward Herbert Thompson:** Clemency Chase Coggins and Orrin C. Shane III (eds.), *Cenote of Sacrifice: Maya Treasures from the Sacred Well at Chichén Itzá* (1984): 24–25.

72 **the Merchant God L:** Simon Martin, "The Dark Lord of Maya Trade," in *Fiery Pool: The Maya and the Mythic Sea*, ed. Daniel Finamore and Stephen D. Houston (2010): 160–62.

73 **bells:** Dorothy Hosler, "Metal Production," in *The Postclassic Mesoamerican*

Notes

World, ed. Michael E. Smith and Frances F. Berdan (2003): 159–71, 163; Warwick Bray, "Maya Metalwork and Its External Connections," in *Social Process in Maya Prehistory: Studies in Honour of Sir Eric Thompson*, ed. Norman Hammond (1977): 366–403.

73 **long metallurgical tradition:** See Joanne Pillsbury et al., *Golden Kingdoms: Luxury Arts in the Ancient Americas* (2017), in particular the contributions by Joanne Pillsbury (1–13), John W. Hoopes (54–65), Stephen Houston (78–89), James A. Doyle (84).

74 **inhabitants treasured bells:** B. Cockrell et al., "For Whom the Bells Fall: Metals from the Cenote Sagrado, Chichén Itzá," *Archaeometry* 57.6 (2015): 977–95.

74 **People at the top of the society:** Izumi Shimada, "The Late Prehispanic Coastal States," in *The Inca World: The Development of Pre-Columbian Peru, A.D. 1000–1534,* ed. Laura Laurencich Minelli (2000): 49–64, 55–56 (rulers' use of metal), 57–59 (long-distance trade).

74 **inhabitants of North Peru:** Heather Lechtman, *The Central Andes, Metallurgy Without Iron* (1980).

74 **Of varying hues:** Ana Maria Falchetti de Sáenz, "The Darién Gold Pendants of Ancient Colombia and the Isthmus," *Metropolitan Museum of Art Journal* 43 (2008): 39–73, 55–56.

75 **arsenic bronze:** Heather Lechtman, "Arsenic Bronze: Dirty Copper or Chosen Alloy? A View from the Americas," *Journal of Field Archaeology* 23.4 (1996): 477–514.

75 **poisonous fumes:** M. Harper, "Possible Toxic Metal Exposure of Prehistoric Bronze Workers," *British Journal of Industrial Medicine* 44 (1987): 652–56.

75 **axe-moneys:** John Topic, "Exchange on the Equatorial Frontier: A Comparison of Ecuador and Northern Peru," in *Merchants, Market, and Exchange in the Pre-Columbian World*, ed. Kenneth G. Hirth and Joanne Pillsbury (2013): 335–60; Dorothy Hosler, "Ancient West Mexican Metallurgy: South and Central American Origins and West Mexican Transformations," *American Anthropologist*, New Series, 90.4 (1988): 832–55; Christopher Beekman, Anthropology Department, University of Colorado, Denver, email, May 6, 2019.

75 **Wari:** Susan E. Bergh (ed.), *Wari: Lords of the Ancient Andes* (2012).

76 **llama caravans:** Michelle Young, Yale University, email, June 27, 2018.

76 **One computer simulation:** Richard T. Callaghan, "Prehistoric Trade Between Ecuador and West Mexico: A Computer Simulation of Coastal Voyages," *Antiquity* 77 (2003): 796–804.

76 **finds of obsidian:** Finamore and Houston, *Fiery Pool*, Catalog No. 57, 175.

77 **Chichén Itzá began to decline:** Kennett et al., "Development and Disintegration," 788–91.

78 **"when they were brought aboard":** Fernando Colón, *The Life of the Admiral Christopher Columbus by His Son Ferdinand*, trans. Benjamin Keen (1959): 231–32; Edward Wilson-Lee, *The Catalogue of Shipwrecked Books: Young Columbus and the Quest for a Universal Library* (2019): 87–88.

Notes

78 **"small hatchets"**: Fernando Colón, *Historie Del S.D. Fernando Colombo; Nelle quali s'ha particolare, & vera relatione della vita, & de' fatti dell'Ammiraglio D. Christoforo Colombo, suo padre: Et dello scoprimento, ch'egli fece dell'Indie Occidentali, dette Mondo Nuovo, hora possedute dal Sereniss. Re catolico* (1571): 200 (recto); John Florio, *Dictionarie of the Italian and English Tongues* (1611): 297.

Chapter Four: European Slaves

Two colleagues in the Yale History Department provided help early on: Paul Bushkovitch and Francesca Trivellato, who is now at the Institute for Advanced Studies at Princeton. Four colleagues at Oxford suggested important changes: Catherine Holmes, Marek Jankowiak, Jonathan Shepard, and Irina Shingiray. Gunilla Larson met with me in the National Museum of Sweden, Stockholm, March 2015, and in August 2017 Elizabeth Walgenbach very kindly gave me a tour of the National Museum in Iceland and showed me the original manuscript of the Greenlanders' Saga.

81 **Mostly male:** John Fennell, *A History of the Russian Church to 1448* (1995): 4.

81 **the Christian world:** Andreas Kaplony, "The Conversion of the Turks of Central Asia to Islam as Seen by Arabic and Persian Geography: A Comparative Perspective," in *Islamisation de l'Asie Centrale: Processus locaux d'acculturation du VIIe au XIe siècle*, ed. Étienne de la Vaissière (2008): 319–38.

82 **An amalgam of various northern peoples:** *De administrando imperio*, trans. R. J. H. Jenkins (1967): 9, 59 (Rus use of Scandinavian words).

82 **The arrival of the Rus:** Simon Franklin and Jonathan Shepard, *The Emergence of Rus, 750–1200* (1996): 12–13 (Staraya Ladoga tools), 16 (combs), 47 (comparison with eighteenth-century Americas), 114–19 (the 911 and 945 treaties), 135 (Olga's reply to Constantine), 139 (Novgorod kremlin), 145–46 (Sviatoslav and the Byzantines), 155 (Rus pantheon), 230 (limited marriages in 1000s).

84 **Planned towns:** Anders Winroth, *Conversion of Scandinavia: Vikings, Merchants, and Missionaries in the Remaking of Northern Europe* (2012): 3, 30–31 (Cnut), 47–51 (gift giving), 48 (Figure 5 caption: 991 hoard), 95–97, 97 (Figure 18: runestone mentioning Khwarazm), 99–100 (layout of Hedeby), 139–41 (Scandinavian conversions), 146 (political advantages of monotheism), 160, 168 (advantages of conversion).

84 **they gradually formed larger units:** Jonathan Shepard, "Review Article: Back in Old Rus and the USSR: Archaeology, History and Politics," *English Historical Review* 131.549 (2016): 384–405, 393–94 (White Lake settlement), 398 (individual groups).

85 **"strange furs":** Adam of Bremen, *History of the Archbishops of Hamburg-Bremen*, trans. Francis J. Tschan (2002): 190 (slaving), 198–99 (appeal of furs).

85 **Even in warmer climates:** Janet Martin, *Treasure of the Land of Darkness: The Fur Trade and Its Signficance for Medieval Russia* (1986): 1 (fur robes in Arabia), 15 (Rus conquests).

85 **The residents of Constantinople and Baghdad:** Bernard Lewis, *Race and*

Notes

Slavery in the Middle East: An Historical Enquiry (1990): 11; Michael McCormick, *Origins of the European Economy: Communications and Commerce, AD 300–900* (2001): 733–77.

85 **"treat their slaves well"**: Paul Lunde and Caroline Stone, *Ibn Fadlān and the Land of Darkness: Arab Travellers in the Far North* (2012): 126–27; translation slightly modified by Michael Rapoport after comparison with Ibn Rusta, *Kitāb al-Aʿlāq al-nafīsa*, ed. M. J. de Goeje (1891): 145–46.

85 **"Slav"**: See Marek Jankowiak, "From 'Slav' to 'Slave': Tracing a Semantic Shift" (forthcoming).

85 **The Dnieper**: Jonathan Shepard, "Photios' Sermons on the Rus Attack of 860: The Question of His Origins, and of the Route of the Rus," in *Prosopon Rhomaikon: ergänzende Studien zur Prosopographie der mittelbyzantinischen Zeit*, ed. Alexander Beihammer et al. (2017): 111–28, 118.

86 **"slaves in their chains"**: Porphyrogenitos, *De administrando imperio*, 9: 57–63 (slaves and furs).

86 **Saqaliba**: Peter Golden, "al-Ṣaḳāliba," *Encyclopaedia of Islam*, 2nd ed. (2012).

86 **"They carry beaver hides"**: Lunde and Stone, *Ibn Fadlān and the Land of Darkness*, 112 (Ibn Khurradadhbih on the routes of the Rādhānīya and the Rūs c. 830); translation slightly modified by Michael Rapoport after comparison with Ibn Khurradadhbih, *Kitāb al'masālik wa'l-mamālik*, ed. M. J. de Goeje (1889): 149.

86 **They were essential to the Rus ability**: Scott Ashley, "Global Worlds, Local Worlds, Connections and Transformations in the Viking Age," in *Byzantium and the Viking World*, ed. Fedir Androshchuk et al. (2016): 363–87, 376–78.

86 **crucible steel**: Brian Gilmore and Robert Hoyland, "Bīrūnī on Iron," in *Medieval Islamic Swords and Swordmaking: Kindi's Treatise "On Swords and Their Kinds"* (2006): 148–74; James Allan and Brian Gilmour, *Persian Steel: The Tanavoli Collection* (2000): 52 (Figure 4A egg-shaped ingot), 60–63, 75 (al-Biruni description of metalworking).

86 **Ulfberht swords**: Alan Williams, *The Sword and the Crucible: A History of the Metallurgy of European Swords up to the 16th Century* (2012): 24–30 (Arabic sources), 117–22 (genuine and fake swords).

87 **Byzantine traders proffered silks**: Thomas S. Noonan, "European Russia, c. 500–c. 1050," in *The New Cambridge Medieval History*, Volume 3: *c. 900–c. 1204*, ed. Timothy Reuter (1999): 487–513, 490–91 (Cherson), 494–95 (eastern Slav settlements), 506–9 (Rus trade after 900).

87 **the Rus posed as Christians**: Lunde and Stone, *Ibn Fadlān and the Land of Darkness*, 112; Jonathan Shepard, "Byzantine Emissions, not Missions, to Rus', and the Problems of 'False' Christians," in *Rus' in the 9th–12th Centuries: Society, State, Culture*, ed. N. A. Makarov and A. E. Leontiev (2014): 234–42.

88 **religious fertility rite**: Jens Peter Schjødt, "Ibn Fadlan's Account of a Rus Funeral: To What Degree Does It Reflect Nordic Myths," in *Reflections on Old Norse Myths*, ed. Pernille Hermann et al. (2007): 133–48.

88 **Scandinavian funerary practices**: Anne Stalsberg, "Scandinavian

Notes

Viking-Age Boat Graves in Old Rus," *Russian History* 28.1–4 (2001): 359–401.

88 **"I want you to bless me with a rich merchant"**: Aḥmad Ibn Faḍlān, *Mission to the Volga*, trans. James E. Montgomery, in *Two Arabic Travel Books*, ed. Philip F. Kennedy and Shawkat M. Toorawa (2014): 165–266, 243–46 (trader's prayer), 246–47 (Angel of Death), 250–51 (sex with slave girl and her death).

89 **The Rus used containers**: Thomas S. Noonan, "Fluctuations in Islamic Trade with Eastern Europe During the Viking Age," *Harvard Ukrainian Studies* 16 (1992): 237–59, 239–40.

89 **hoard that contained 14,295 coins**: Gunnar Andersson, *Go Beyond the Legend: The Vikings Exhibition* (2016): 37.

90 **the Samanid empire**: Marek Jankowiak, "Dirham Flows into Northern and Eastern Europe and the Rhythms of the Slave Trade with the Islamic World," in *Viking-Age Trade: Silver, Slaves and Gotland*, ed. J. Gruszczyński, M. Jankowiak, and J. Shepard (forthcoming 2020): Chapter 6.

90 **400,000**: Marek Jankowiak proposes the figure of 400,000; the one million is a "sober estimate," Jonathan Shepard, personal communication, October 26, 2018.

90 **one thousand per year**: On October 25, 2018, Marek Jankowiak explained to me his reasons for increasing his earlier estimate given in "Dirhams for Slaves: Investigating the Slavic Slave Trade in the Tenth Century," February 27, 2012; available at academia.edu.

90 **the Danelaw**: F. Donald Logan, *The Vikings in History*, 3rd ed. (2005): 122 (northern region), 153–60 (Viking raids on England, 980–1035).

91 **twenty-four coins from Spain**: Ann Christys, *Vikings in the South: Voyages to Iberia and the Mediterranean* (2015): 7–8.

91 **voyages of the Norse to Sicily**: James M. Powell, "Sicily, Kingdom of," *Dictionary of the Middle Ages*: 11: 263–76.

91 **graffiti**: Krijnie N. Ciggaar, *Western Travellers to Constantinople, The West and Byzantium, 962–1204: Cultural and Political Relations* (1996): 126–27; Sigfús Blöndal, *The Varangians of Byzantium*, trans. Benedikt S. Benedikz (1978): 233.

92 **Ingvar the Far Traveler**: Hermann Pálsson and Paul Edwards (trans.), *Vikings in Russia: Yngvar's Saga and Eymund's Saga* (1989): 44–68, 59; Gunilla Larson, "Early Contacts Between Scandinavia and the Orient," *The Silk Road* 9 (2011): 122–42.

92 **Eventually Ingvar falls ill**: Anders Winroth, *The Age of the Vikings* (2014): 82 (Ingvar), 128 (increasing number of bones from cod).

93 *Russian Primary Chronicle*: Completed in 1113, the *Primary Chronicle* contains a mix of myth and history. See the introduction in Samuel Hazzard Cross and Olgerd P. Sherbowitz-Wetzor (trans.), *The Russian Primary Chronicle: Laurentian Text* (1953): 3–50, 21 (single author of the text), 59 (invitation to the Rurikids), 65–69 (911 treaty), 82 (Constantine's proposal), 93–94 (pre-Christian deities), 110 (Vladimir's decision to wait), 111 (envoys' report), 245n92 (papal envoys to Rus).

93 **Greek fire**: Paolo Squatriti (trans.), *The Complete Works of Liudprand of Cremona* (2007): 180 (Greek fire), 197–98 (king's machines).

Notes

94 **Rus had been baptized as Christians:** Jonathan Shepard, "The Coming of Christianity to Rus," in *Conversion to Christianity: From Late Antiquity to the Modern Age: Considering the Process in Europe, Asia, and the Americas*, ed. Calvin B. Kendall et al. (2009): 195–96.

94 **To avenge her husband:** Shepard, "Back in Old Rus and the USSR," 384–405, 400.

95 **German king Otto I:** Shepard, "Byzantine Emissions," 234–42, 236.

95 **Olga stepped down:** Shepard, "The Coming of Christianity to Rus," 185–222, 194 (Kiev burials), 195 (944 treaty).

95 **Vladimir and an army of Scandinavian mercenaries:** Janet Martin, *Medieval Russia, 980–1584* (1995): 1–11.

96 **Judaism offered the Khazars a middle ground:** Peter Golden, "The Conversion of the Khazars to Judaism," in *The World of the Khazars: New Perspectives: Selected Papers from the Jerusalem 1999 International Khazar Colloquium Hosted by the Ben Zvi Institute*, ed. Peter Golden et al. (2007): 123–62, 152n145, 153 (conversion to Judaism), 156 (dating of conversion).

97 **conversion didn't affect his subjects:** Michael Toch, *The Economic History of the European Jews: Late Antiquity and Early Middle Ages* (2013): 193–204.

97 **three new types of coins:** R. K. Kovalev, "Creating Khazar Identity Through Coins: The Special Issue Dirham of 837/8," in *East Central and Eastern Europe in the Middle Ages*, ed. F. Curta (2005): 220–53, 240–42.

97 **"all of the Khazars are Jews":** Golden, "The Conversion of the Khazars to Judaism," 142; Ibn al-Faqih, *Kitāb al-Buldān*, ed. M. J. de Goeje (1885): 298.

98 **fertility amulets made from hare's feet:** E. E. Kravchenko and A. V. Shamrai, "O gruppe kompleksov s Tsarina gorodishcha v srednem techenii Severskogo Dontsa," in *Problemi zberezhennia i vikoristannia kul'turnoi spadshchini v Ukraini*, ed. P. V. Dobrov and O. V. Kolesnik (2014): 183–92, 185 (amulets); Irina Shingiray, Oxford University, personal communication, October 28, 2018.

98 **Jerusalem wasn't governed by Jews:** Moshe Gil, *A History of Palestine, 634–1099*, trans. Ethel Broido (1992): 51–56 (630s conquest), 364–66 (Fatimids), 409–14 (Seljuks), 839–61 (chronology of the years 610–1153).

98 **"fair woman":** Andrew Rippin, "Ḥourī," *Encyclopaedia of Islam*, 3rd ed. (2016); Maher Jarrar, "Houris," *Encyclopaedia of the Qu'ran* (2002): 2:456–57.

99 **conversation must have been inserted:** Andrzej Poppe, "Two Concepts of the Conversion of Rus in Kievan Writings," *Christian Russia in the Making* (2007): 488–504, 492–93n16 (*Primary Chronicle* date), 495–96 (different Orthodox and Roman fasts).

99 **doesn't present an accurate description:** Fennell, *History of the Russian Church*, 36–37; Paul Bushkovitch, personal communication, July 20, 2016.

99 **Rus ruler named "Vladimir":** Vladimir Minorsky (trans.), *Sharaf al-Zaman tahir Marvazi on China, the Turks, and India: Arabic Text with an English Translation and Commentary* (1942): 36.

99 **Philosopher's Speech:** Alexander Pereswetoff-Morath, *Grin Without a Cat* (2002): 53–57.

Notes

100 **intensive economic and cultural ties:** Christian Raffensperger, *Reimagining Europe: Kievan Rus' in the Medieval World* (2012): 164–66.

102 **Oghuz:** C. Edmund Bosworth, "The Origins of the Seljuqs," in *The Seljuqs: Politics, Society and Culture*, ed. Christian Lange and Songül Mecit (2011): 13–21.

102 **the weather was unusually cold:** Richard W. Bulliet, *Cotton, Climate, and Camels in Early Islamic Iran: A Moment in World History* (2009): 79–81.

102 **"we shall be a small and solitary people":** Omid Safi, *The Politics of Knowledge in Premodern Islam: Negotiating Ideology and Religious Inquiry* (2006): 16; Ernest Wallis Budge, *The Chronography of Bar Hebraeus* (1932): 1: 195.

103 **Vladimir was baptized in 988 or 989:** Because of the problems with the sources, it is not certain where or when Vladimir was baptized.

103 **contact with government officials:** Janet Martin, *Treasure in the Land of Darkness: The Fur Trade and Its Significance for Medieval Russia* (1986): 9.

103 **mid-Dnieper region:** Andrzej Poppe, "The Christianization and Ecclesiastical Structure of Kievan Rus' to 1300," *Harvard Ukrainian Studies* 12–13 (1997): 311–92, 341 (bishops' seats), 344–45 (posthumous baptism).

104 **Western Europe experienced a massive surge of growth:** Angeliki E. Laiou, "Exchange and Trade, Seventh–Twelfth Centuries," in *The Economic History of Byzantium: From the Seventh Through the Fifteenth Century*, ed. Angeliki E Laiou and Charalampos Bouras (2001): 697–770.

104 **Alexandria, Antioch, and Jerusalem came under Muslim rule:** Alfred J. Butler, *The Arab Conquest of Egypt and the Last Thirty Years of Roman Dominion* (1978): xxxviii; "Antioch," *The Oxford Dictionary of Byzantium* (1991): 1: 115–16.

105 **bread leavened with yeast:** Joseph H. Lynch and Philip C. Adamo, *The Medieval Church: A Brief History* (2014): 184–85.

105 **Rejecting the view that Rome and Constantinople were equal:** R. W. Southern, *Western Society and the Church in the Middle Ages* (1970): 67–73.

105 **breach of 1054:** John H. Erickson, "Schisms, Eastern-Western Church," *Dictionary of the Middle Ages*: 11: 44–47.

106 **Venetians were the wealthiest:** Francesca Trivellato, personal communication, August 9, 2017; David Abulafia, *The Great Sea: A Human History of the Mediterranean* (2011): 276 (communes), 278 (eleventh-century Mediterranean campaigns), 293 (twelfth century).

106 **exempted the Venetians:** Experts debate whether the date was 1082 or 1092. See Alain Ducellier, "The Death Throes of Byzantium: 1080–1261," in *The Cambridge Illustrated History of the Middle Ages*, Volume 2: *950–1250*, ed. Robert Fossier (1997): 505 (events of 1082), 507–8 (restoration of Venetian privileges).

107 **The skit had clear racial implications:** Donald M. Nicol, *Byzantium and Venice: A Study in Diplomatic and Cultural Relations* (1988): 87 (mock coronation), 90 (resident foreigners categories), 106–9 (Massacre of the Latins), 115 (Third Crusade).

107 **Venetians went on a rampage:** Thomas F. Madden, *Venice: A New History* (2012): 85–87.

108 **Byzantine emperor Alexios I:** Peter Frankopan, *The First Crusade: The*

Notes

Call from the East (2012): 13–16 (pope and antipope), 19–22 (Urban II), 116 (number of First Crusade participants), 202 (Urban's improved position).

108 **The Pope traveled to Clermont, France:** Thomas F. Madden, *A Concise History of the Crusades*, 3rd ed. (2014): 11 (First Crusades participants), 17–21 (People's Crusade), 98–109 (Fourth Crusade); Barbara H. Rosenwein, *A Short History of the Middle Ages*, 4th ed. (2014): 170–72 (First Crusade), 200–201 (Fourth Crusade).

Chapter Five: The World's Richest Man

Thanks to Roderick McIntosh, Yale Anthropology Department, for giving two information-packed lectures to History 101: Circa 1000, in October 2017; Stephanie Wynne-Jones, York University, for her thorough comments on this chapter; to Matthew Gordon, Miami University, Ohio, for suggesting I read Ibn Butlan; and to Sam Nixon, British Museum, for a most efficient thirty-minute meeting about West African archaeology.

113 **"Muhammadin son of al-Hasan wrote this":** Michael Rapoport modified the translation after comparison with the original. Paolo Fernando de Moraes Farias, "Arabic and Tifinagh Inscriptions," in *Essouk-Tadmekka: An Early Islamic Trans-Saharan Market Town*, ed. Sam Nixon (2017): 41–50 (description and analysis), 48 (Sahelian plain Kufic script), 299–303 (transcriptions). See also De Moraes Farias, "Tadmakkat and the Image of Mecca: Epigraphic Records of the Work of the Imagination in 11th Century West Africa," in *Case Studies in Archaeology and World Religion: The Proceedings of the Cambridge Conference*, ed. Timothy Insoll (1999): 105–15.

114 **modern historians emphatically reject this view:** E. W. Bovill, *The Golden Trade of the Moors* (1968). Sam Nixon of the British Museum is currently working on a broader history of the trade. See also François-Xavier Fauvelle-Aymar, *Golden Rhinoceros: Histories of the African Middle Ages*, trans. Troy Tice (2018).

114 **Some two thirds of the gold:** Andrew M. Watson, "Back to Gold—and Silver," *The Economic History Review* 20.1 (1967): 1–34, 30n1; Bálint Hóman, *Geschichte des ungarischen Mittelalters* (1940): 353.

114 **collection of sailor's tales:** The traditional attribution to Buzurg may be mistaken. See Jean-Charles Ducène, "Une nouvelle source arabe sur l'océan Indien au Xe siècle," *Afriques* (2015), online at: http://journals .openedition.org/afriques/1746.

115 **cost of a slave:** Ralph A. Austen, "The Trans-Saharan Slave Trade: A Tentative Census," in *The Uncommon Market: Essays in the Economic History of the Atlantic Slave Trade,* ed. Henry A. Gemery and Jan S. Hogendorn (1979): 23–73, 31 (Nubian tribute payments in slaves), 44–45 (slave labor in Islamic world), 45 (Zanj rebellion), 52–55 (military slaves), 70 (slave price data).

115 **first abolitionist critics:** David Brion Davis, *The Problem of Slavery in Western Culture* (1967): 484–93.

116 **"as for accompanying you to your ship":** "Buzurg Ibn Shahriyar of

Ramhormuz: A Tenth-Century Slaving Adventure," in *The East African Coast: Select Documents from the First to the Earlier Nineteenth Century*, ed. G. S. P. Freeman-Grenville (1962): 9–13; al-Rāmhurmuzī, *Kitāb ʿAjāʾib al-Hind*, bilingual French and Arabic edition, 1883–1886. Michael Rapoport has corrected the translation after comparison with the Arabic original. Freeman-Grenville translates from the French translation (not the Arabic original), which has many errors.

116 **"rooms as well as shops for slaves"**: Adam Mez, *The Renaissance of Islam*, trans. Salahuddin Khuda Bakhsh and D. S. Margoliouth (1937): 160; al-Yaʿqūbī, *Kitāb al-Buldān*, ed. M. J. de Goeje (1892): 260. See also Matthew S. Gordon, "Abbasid Courtesans and the Question of Social Mobility," in *Concubines and Courtesans: Women and Slavery in Islamic History*, ed. Gordon and Kathryn A. Hain (2017): 27–51, 32.

117 **slaves, gold, ivory, and animal skins**: Shadreck Chirikure et al., *Mapungubwe Reconsidered: A Living Legacy, Exploring Beyond the Rise and Decline of the Mapungubwe State* (2016); Fauvelle-Aymar, *Golden Rhinoceros*, 136–42.

117 **one ton of gold per annum**: Ari Nave, "Gold Trade," *Encyclopedia of Africa* (2010): 1: 525–26.

117 **Tens of thousands of beads**: Peter Garlake, *Great Zimbabwe* (1973): 109 (Chinese ceramics), 132–33 (beads); Bing Zhao, "Chinese-style Ceramics in East Africa from the 9th to 16th Century: A Case of Changing Value and Symbols in the Multi-Partner Global Trade," *L'Afrique orientale et l'océan Indien: connexions, réseaux d'échanges et globalisation* (June 2015). Available online.

118 **rebels posed a significant challenge**: Benjamin Reilly, *Slavery, Agriculture, and Malaria in the Arabian Peninsula* (2015): 130.

118 **Zanj Rebellion**: Alexandre Popovic, *The Revolt of African Slaves in Iraq in the 3rd/9th Century*, trans. Léon King (1998): 136, 141n10.

118 **word *zanj***: Gabriele Tecchiato, "Zanj," *The Oxford Encyclopedia of the Islamic World*, Oxford Islamic Studies Online (2009); E. Savage, "Berbers and Blacks: Ibāḍī Slave Traffic in Eighth-Century North Africa," *Journal of African History* 33.3 (1992): 351–68.

118 **fifteen years of self-rule**: Gwyn Campbell, "East Africa in the Early Indian Ocean World: The Zanj Revolt Reconsidered," in *Early Exchange Between Africa and the Wider Indian Ocean World*, ed. Gwyn Campbell (2016): 275–96, 279 (meaning of Zanj), 281 (Zanj rebel leader), 282 (50,000 rebels), 291, 296 (skepticism about the numbers of East African slaves).

118 **Ibn Butlan**: Floréal Sanagustin, *Médecine et société en Islam médiéval: Ibn Buṭlān ou la connaissance médicale au service de la communauté: le cas de l'esclavage* (2010): 233 (Zanj rhythm), 234–35 (Bagawi slaves), 237 (conclusion). Michael Rapoport did these translations on the basis of the original text, Ibn Buṭlān, *Risāla fī širāʾ al-raqīq wa-taqlīb al-ʿabīd*, in *Nawādir al-makhṭūṭāt*, Volume 1, ed. Hārūn (1973): 374 (Zanj rhythm), 375–76 (Bagawi slaves), 378 (conclusion).

118 **penned a satire**: Joseph Schacht and Max Meyerhof, *The Medico-Philosophical Controversy Between Ibn Butlan of Baghdad and Ibn Ridwan of Cairo* (1937): 18.

119 **Muslim jurists agreed on the basic principles:** Rudolph T. Ware, "Slavery in Islamic Africa, 1400–1800," in *The Cambridge World History of Slavery*, Volume 3: *1420–1804*, ed. David Eltis and Stanley L. Engerman (2011): 47–80.

119 **Although slavery was commonplace:** R. Brunschvig, "ʿAbd," *Encyclopaedia of Islam*, 2nd ed. (2012).

119 **three main sources of slaves:** Maurice Lombard, *The Golden Age of Islam*, trans. Joan Spencer (1975): 2: 194–203, 197 (Slav slaves map), 199 (Turkish slaves map), 202 (African slaves map).

121 **camel:** Richard W. Bulliet, *The Camel and the Wheel* (1975).

121 **600 female slaves:** H. A. R. Gibb (trans.), *The Travels of Ibn Battuta, A.D. 1325–1354* (1994): 4: 975.

121 **slightest mishap:** Paul Lovejoy, *Transformations in Slavery* (2012): 35.

122 **8,700 per year between 900 and 1100:** Austen, "The Trans-Saharan Slave Trade," 37 (Table 2.3 Estimates of the Atlantic Slave Trade, 1450–1600), 40, 66 (Table 2.8 Global Estimate of Trans-Saharan Slave Trade), 67–68.

122 **11.75 million:** For more recent discussions about the Islamic slave trade and the challenges of quantifying it, see Anne Haour, "The Early Medieval Slave Trade of the Central Sahel: Archaeological and Historical Considerations," in *Slavery in Africa: Archaeology and Memory*, ed. Paul J. Lane and Kevin C. MacDonald (2011): 61–78; Roundtable Discussion, "Locating Slavery in Middle Eastern and Islamic History," *International Journal of Middle Eastern Studies* 49.1 (2017): 133–72.

123 **"the common people of his kingdom remained polytheists":** "Al-Bakrī,"in *Corpus of Early Arabic Sources for West African History*, ed. N. Levtzion and J. F. P. Hopkins (1981): 62–87, 64 (red cloth for slaves), 65–66 (Sijilmasa), 68–69 (Awdaghust, dates, and camel armies), 79–81 (Ghana), 81 (Ghiyaru gold mines), 82 (Yarisna), 82–83 (Malal), 83–84 (asbestos), 85 (bald dinars); checked by Michael Rapoport against the original and slightly modified; al-Bakrī, *Kitāb al-Masālik wa-l-mamālik*, eds. van Leeuwen and Ferré (1992): 658, passage 1099 (red cloth for slaves); 835–38, passages 1393–99, 840, 1404 (Sijilmasa), 849–50, passages 1417–20 (Awdaghust, dates, and camel armies); 871–74, passages 1455–61 (Ghana), 874, passage 1460 (Ghiyārū gold mines), 875, passage 1463 (Yarisna), 875–76, passage 1464 (Malal), 878, passage 1469 (asbestos), 880, passage 1472 (bald dinars).

123 **He may have later moved:** Travis Zadeh, *Mapping Frontiers Across Medieval Islam: Geography, Translation, and the ʿAbbāsid Empire* (2011): 17 (biography), 23 (Ibn Khurradadhbih's preface); original Arabic preface in Ibn Khurradādhbih, *al-Masālik wa-l-mamālik*, ed. M. J. de Goeje (1889): 3.

124 **his "routes" provide the travel time:** Marina A. Tolmacheva, "Geography," *Medieval Islamic Civilization: An Encyclopedia*, ed. Josef W. Meri (2006): 1: 284–88.

124 **"Realms" refers to:** André Miquel, *La Géographie humaine du monde Musulman jusqu'au milieu de XIe Siècle*, Volumes 1–4 (1967–1988): 1: 267–85.

Notes

124 **translation from Greek, Latin, Sanskrit, and Persian:** Dmitri Gutas, *Greek Thought, Arab Culture: The Graeco-Arabic Translation Movement in Baghdad and Early Abbasid Society (2nd–4th/8th–10th centuries)* (1998).

124 **factories in Baghdad:** Jonathan Bloom, *Paper Before Print: The History and Impact of Paper in the Islamic World* (2001).

125 **"caliph" means "successor":** Hugh Kennedy, *Caliphate: The History of an Idea* (2016): 1–31.

125 **Kharijites:** Fred M. Donner, *Muhammad and the Believers at the Origins of Islam* (2012): 163–70.

126 **first two centuries of Muslim rule:** Richard W. Bulliet, "Conversion to Islam and the Emergence of a Muslim Society in Iran," in *Conversion to Islam,* ed. Nehemia Levtzion (1979): 30–51; Elton L. Daniel, "Conversion ii: Of Iranians to Islam," *Encyclopædia Iranica* (2011).

126 **governor of Fustat:** Michael Bonner, "The Waning of Empire, 861–945," in *The New Cambridge History of Islam,* Volume 1: *The Formation of the Islamic World, Sixth to Eleventh Centuries,* ed. Chase F. Robinson (2010): 305–59.

127 **collecting taxes for all of Egypt:** Thierry Banquis, "Autonomous Egypt from Ibn Ṭūlūn to Kāfūr, 868–969," in *The Cambridge History of Egypt, Volume 1: Islamic Egypt, 640–1517,* ed. Carl F. Petry (1998): 86–119, 91–92 (Ibn Ṭūlūn's background), 98 (composition of his army), 103 (anti-Christian riots).

127 **"Greeks," a blanket term:** Michael Brett, "Egypt," in Robinson, ed., *The New Cambridge History of Islam,* Volume 1: 541–80, 558–59.

127 **Buyid ruler imprisoned the caliph:** Hugh Kennedy, "The late ʿAbbāsid Pattern, 945–1050," in Robinson, *The New Cambridge History of Islam,* Volume 1: 360–93, 361 (shared traditions), 361–62 (failed Zoroastrian revival), 365 (events of 945), 387 (Muslim commonwealth), 387–93 (Sunni-Shi'ite divisions).

128 **"the Victorious":** Jonathan M. Bloom, *Arts of the City Victorious: Islamic Art and Architecture in Fatimid North Africa and Egypt* (2007): 54–59.

128 **the reigning Fatimid caliph, al-Hakim:** Matthieu Tillier, "Droit et messianisme chez les Fatimides de l'an 1000," unpublished conference paper delivered at the conference Histoires de l'an mil, Fondation des Treilles, France, September 9–14, 2019; Jonathan Bloom, "Nāṣir Khusraw's Description of Jerusalem," in *No Tapping Around Philology: A Festschrift in Honor of Wheeler McIntosh Thackston Jr.'s 70th Birthday,* ed. Alireza Korangy and Daniel J. Sheffield (2014): 395–406; Paul E. Walker, *The Caliph of Cairo: Al-Hakim bi-Amr Allah, 996–1021* (2009): 200–204, 260–61.

129 **condolence notes:** S. D. Goitein, "Slaves and Slavegirls in the Cairo Geniza Records," *Arabica* 9.1 (1962): 1–20.

129 **population around 500,000:** Jonathan P. Berkey, "Culture and Society During the Late Middle Ages," in Petry, *The Cambridge History of Egypt,* Volume 1: 379–80.

130 **beautifully carved ivory boxes:** Sarah M. Guérin, "The Tusk," in *The Salerno Ivories: Objects, Histories, Contexts,* ed. Francesca dell'Aqua (2016): 21–28.

130 **rioted against the Amalfi merchants:** Yaacov Y. Lev, "The Fatimid

267

Notes

State and Egypt's Mediterranean Trade, 10th–12th Centuries," in *East and West: Essays on Byzantine and Arab Worlds in the Middle Ages*, ed. Juan Pedro Monferrer-Sala et al. (2009): 121–25, 123; S. D. Goitein, *Letters of Medieval Jewish Traders* (1973): 39–44; S. D. Goitein, *A Mediterranean Society: The Jewish Communities of the Arab World as Portrayed in the Documents of the Cairo Geniza*, Volume 1 (1967): 46, 49; Claude Cahen, "Un text peu connu relative au commerce oriental d'Amalfi au Xe siècle," *Archivio Storico per le Province Napoletane, n.s.* 34 (1953–1954): 3–8.

130 **fire on May 5 that destroyed:** An alternative source says the fire occurred on May 16 and destroyed five ships. Obviously one of these accounts is wrong, but no one knows which one.

131 **"sorcerers of these people":** Al-Bakrī gives the distance as 6 Arabic *mīl*, a unit about 2 km in length. See Muhammad Ismail Marcinkowski, *Measures and Weights in the Islamic World: An English translation of Walther Hinz's Handbook Islamische Masse und Gewichte* (2002): 92.

132 **multiple capitals:** Conrad Leyser, Naomi Standen, and Stephanie Wynne-Jones, "Settlement, Landscape and Narrative: What Really Happened in History," in *The Global Middle Ages*, ed. Catherine Holmes and Naomi Standen, *Past and Present*, Supplement 13 (2018): 232–60, 237. See also R. A. Mauny, "The Question of Ghana," *Africa: Journal of the International African Institute* 24.3 (1954): 200–13, 205–7.

132 **Ghiyaru:** Nehemia Levtzion, *Ancient Ghana and Mali* (1973): 26 (Niger River burials), 43–47 (decline of Ghana), 132 (peak of gold trade), 155 (location of gold fields).

132 **Nile River:** Nehemia Levtzion and Jay Spaulding (eds.), *Medieval West Africa: Views from Arab Scholars and Merchants* (2003): xi.

132 **bend in the Niger River:** Levtzion and Hopkins, ed., *Corpus of Early Arabic Sources for West African History*, 387n53.

133 **100,000 imported glass and carnelian beads:** Thurston Shaw, *Unearthing Igbo-Ukwu: Archaeological Discoveries in Eastern Nigeria* (1977): 42–43 (storehouse objects), 58–59 (burial chamber objects); Thurston Shaw, *Igbo-Ukwu: An Account of Archaeological Discoveries in Eastern Nigeria*, Volumes 1–2 (1970): 1: 237–39.

133 **raw materials . . . new trade routes:** Frank Willett, "Who Taught the Smiths of Igbo Ukwu?," *New Scientist* (April 14, 1983): 65–68; Paul T. Craddock et al., "Metal Sources and the Bronzes from Igbo-Ukwu," *Journal of Field Archaeology* 24.4 (1997): 405–29.

133 **Only a large population:** Roderick McIntosh, "Jenne-Jeno, Year 1000: Yale's Explorations Along the Niger," lecture in History 101: Circa 1000, Yale University, October 9, 2017.

134 **as a spice, not as a sweetener:** Paul Freedman, *Out of the East: Spices and the Medieval Imagination* (2008): 12–13.

134 **Major commercial and agricultural centers:** Levtzion and Hopkins, ed., *Corpus of Early Arabic Sources for West African History*, 62–63.

134 **one third of their property:** E. Ann McDougall, "The View from Awdaghust: War, Trade and Social Change in the Southwestern Sahara, from the Eighth to the Fifteenth Century," *Journal of African History* 26.1 (1985): 1–31, 17.

Notes

134   **reduced the influence of the Kharijite Muslims:** Ousmane Oumar Kane, *Beyond Timbuktu: An Intellectual History of Muslim West Africa* (2016): 46.

135   **carried the gold and slaves to the north:** Ronald A. Messier and James A. Miller, *The Last Civilized Place: Sijilmasa and Its Saharan Destiny* (2015): 110 (triangle trade), 110 (3–4 tons of gold/year for Almoravids and Saladin's dynasty), 111–15 (Almoravid coins); Jean Devisse, "Or d'Afrique," *Arabica* 43 (1996): 234–43.

135   **molds used to cast such gold coins:** Sam Nixon and Thilo Rehren, "Gold Processing Remains," in Sam Nixon, ed., *Essouk-Tadmekka*, 174–87, 176 (Figure 15.2: coin mold), 185–87 (Al-Bakri).

135   **brass rods:** T. Monod, "Le «Maᶜaden Ijâfen»: une épave caravanière ancienne dans la Majâbat al-Koubrâ," *Actes du 1er Colloque International d'Archéologie Africaine* (1967): 286–320.

135   **West African demand for goods:** A.C. Christie and Anne Haour, "The 'Lost Caravan' of the Ma'den Ijafen Revisited: Re-appraising Its Cargo of Cowries, a Medieval Global Commodity," *Journal of African Archaeology* 16.2 (2018): 125–44.

136   **Charlemagne:** James E. Alleman and Brooke T. Mossman, "Asbestos Revisited," *Scientific American* 277.1 (1997): 70–75.

136   **Herodotus:** Timothy F. Garrard, "Myth and Metrology: The Early Trans-Saharan Gold Trade," *Journal of African History* 23.4 (1982): 443–61.

136   **"There is perfect honesty on both sides":** Herodotus, *The Histories*, trans. Aubrey de Sélincourt (1996): 4: 277.

137   **"desired an increase":** al-Masᶜūdī in Levtzion and Hopkins, ed., *Corpus of Early Arabic Sources for West African History*, 32; al-Masᶜūdī, *Murūj al-dhahhab*, Volume 2, ed. ᶜAbd al-Ḥamīd (1958): 261.

137   **Writers who hadn't seen the actual trade:** P. F. de Moraes Farias, "Silent Trade: Myth and Historical Evidence," *History in Africa* 1 (1974): 9–24.

137   **myth about the silent trade:** Yāqūt, in Levtzion and Hopkins, ed., *Corpus of Early Arabic Sources for West African History*, 11.

137   **climate change:** Sebastian Lüning et al., "Hydroclimate in Africa During the Medieval Climate Anomaly," *Palaeogeography, Palaeoclimatology, Palaeoecology* 495 (2018): 309–22; George E. Brooks, "A Provisional Historical Schema for Western Africa Based on Seven Climate Periods (ca. 9000 B.C. to the 19th Century)," *Cahiers d'Études Africaines* 101.2 (1986): 43–62.

137   **growing number of horses:** Roderick J. McIntosh, *Ancient Middle Niger: Urbanism and the Self-Organizing Landscape* (2005): 177.

138   **3 or 4 tons of gold:** Ari Nave, "Gold Trade," *Encyclopedia of Africa* (2010): 1: 525–26.

138   **price of gold in Cairo:** Al-ᶜUmarī, in Levtzion and Hopkins, ed., *Corpus of Early Arabic Sources for West African History*, 262 (al-Dukkali on gold mining), 269 (100 cart loads), 271 (gold price falls), 272 (gold mining). Translation updated by Michael Rapoport after comparison with the original text al-ᶜUmarī, *Mamlakat Mālī*, ed. Ṣalāḥ al-Dīn al-Munajjid (1963), 45–67.

138   **13 and 18 tons of gold:** These estimates are based on accounts saying that Mansa Musa traveled with 80–100 loads of gold, each equal to 336 pounds (152.4 kg). The gold in the staffs of his 500 slaves weighed an additional

English ton (.9 metric ton). Michael Gomez, *African Dominion: A New History of Empire in Early and Medieval West Africa* (2018): 106.

140 **Torrid Zone:** Peter Russell, *Prince Henry the Navigator* (2001): 109–34 (Cape Bojador voyages), 256 (1444 procession of slaves), 258 (number of African slaves before 1460).

140 **El Mina:** Ivor Wilks, *Forests of Gold: Essays on the Akan and the Kingdom of Assante* (1993); Peter L. Bernstein, *The Power of Gold: The History of an Obsession* (2012): 118.

140 **price fluctuations:** Pierre Vilar, *A History of Gold and Money, 1450–1920*, trans. Judith White (1976): 19 (8-cubic-meter cube), 56 (gold exports to Europe 1500–1520).

141 **Wangara:** Ivor Wilks, "Wangara, Akan and Portuguese in the Fifteenth and Sixteenth Centuries," *Journal of African History* 23.3 (1982): 333–49; Wilks translates the original, P. de Cenival and Th. Monod, *Description de la Côte d'Afrique de Ceuta au Sénégal par Valentim Fernandes (1506–1507)* (1938): 84–87.

141 **Atlantic slave trade:** Lovejoy, *Transformations in Slavery*, 36–37 (Table 2.3 Estimates of the Atlantic Slave Trade, 1450–1600), 40 (Atlantic trade).

Chapter Six: Central Asia Splits in Two

Thanks to Arezou Azad (University of Birmingham), George E. Malagaris (Oxford), Lance Pursey (University of Birmingham), Irina Shingiray (Oxford), and Naomi Standen (University of Birmingham) for their help with this chapter.

143 **Only after 1500:** Hugh Kennedy, *Mongols, Huns, and Vikings: Nomads at War* (2002): 208–11.

143 **around 15 miles per day:** John Masson Smith, Jr., "From Pasture to Manger: The Evolution of Mongol Cavalry Logistics in Yuan China and Its Consequences," in *Pferde in Asien: Geschichte, Handel und Kultur*, ed. Bert G. Fragner et al. (2009): 63–73; "ʿAyn Jālūt," *Harvard Journal of Asiatic Studies* 44.2 (1984): 307–45, 335 (rates of travel), 336 (consumption of fresh grass); Martón Ver, a postdoctoral scholar at the Turfanforschung, Berlin-Brandenburg Academy of Sciences and Humanities, email, September 21, 2018. See also Ashleigh N. Deluca, "World's Toughest Horse Race Retraces Genghis Khan's Postal Route," *National Geographic News* (August 7, 2014).

147 **600,000 silver coins:** Peter B. Golden, "The Karakhanids and Early Islam," in *The Cambridge History of Early Inner Asia* (1990): 347; Ibn Khurradādhbih, *Kitab al-Masalik wa-l-mamālik*, ed. M. J. de Goeje (1889): 37, 39.

147 **to train military slaves:** Peter B. Golden, *Central Asia in World History* (2011): 66.

147 **Persian:** Michael Bonner, "The Waning of Empire, 861–945," in *The New Cambridge History of Islam*, Volume 1: *The Formation of the Islamic World, Sixth to Eleventh Centuries*, ed. Chase F. Robinson (2010): 305–59, 344 (Samanid slaving), 345 (use of Persian), 346 (Sunni beliefs of the Samanids).

Notes

147 *The Limits of the World*: V. Minorsky, Ḥudūd al-ʿĀlam, *"The Regions of the World," A Persian Geography, 372 A.H.—982 A.D.* (1937): 3–44.

147 the growing popularity of the language: David Durand-Guédy, "Une 'mutation de l'An mil' en Iran?," unpublished conference paper delivered at the conference Histoires de l'an mil, Fondation des Treilles, France, September 9–14, 2019.

147 two years in Bukhara: C. Edmund Bosworth, "Bīrūnī, Abū Rayḥān i. Life," *Encyclopædia Iranica* (1989).

148 Syriac Christians in India: David Pingree, "Āṯār al-bāqīa," *Encyclopædia Iranica* (2011).

148 His prose is dense but methodical: The most recent full translation, done in 1879, captures the complex style of the original. Al-Biruni, *The Chronology of Ancient Nations,* trans. and ed. C. Edward Sachau (1879): 5 (length of day), 13 (Jewish calendar), 312 (Syriac Christians).

149 Muslims used a solar calendar: Reza Abdollahy, "Calendars, ii. in the Islamic Period," *Encyclopædia Iranica* (1990).

149 madrasa: Marshall G. S. Hodgson, *The Venture of Islam: Conscience and History in a World Civilization,* Volume 2, *The Expansion of Islam in the Middle Periods* (1974): 3–61, 255–92.

149 seventy-three different madrasas: J. Pederson et al., "Madrasa," *Encyclopaedia of Islam,* 2nd ed. (2012).

150 Multiple female scholars: Ruth Roded, *Women in the Islamic Biographical Collections: From Ibn Saʿd to Who's Who* (1994): 3 (Table 1), 12.

150 Samanid rule was a fiction: Elton L. Daniel, "The Islamic East," in Robinson, ed., *The New Cambridge History of Islam,* 1: 448–505, 503–4.

151 "right hand of the dynasty": C. E. Bosworth, *The Ghaznavids: Their Empire in Afghanistan and Eastern Iran, 994–1040* (1963): 46 (Abbasid caliph's titles for Mahmud), 126–28 (army size).

151 personal odor of the giver: Finbarr B. Flood, *Objects of Translation: Material Culture and Medieval "Hindu-Muslim" Encounter* (2009): 76–77.

151 Mahmud retained power: H. Amedroz and D. S. Margoliouth, *The Eclipse of the ʿAbbasid Caliphate* (1920–1921): II: 328–29; Hugh Kennedy "The Late ʿAbbāsid Pattern," in Robinson, ed., *The New Cambridge History of Islam,* 1: 390.

151 Mahmud championed the use of Persian: Viola Allegranzi, *Aux sources de la poésie ghaznévide. Les inscriptions persanes de Ghazni* (2 vols.) (2019): 1: 207–18.

151 campaigns against non-Muslim peoples: C. Edmund Bosworth, "Asfījāb," *Encyclopædia Iranica* (2011).

151 Ghaznavids' main target: David Morgan, *Medieval Persia, 1040–1797* (1988): 22.

152 loot cities with Muslim populations: Kennedy, "The Late ʿAbbāsid Pattern," 360–93, 370–73 (Sunni beliefs of the Ghaznavids), 376–77 (Somnath).

152 several different Hindu kings: Flood, *Objects of Translation,* 4 (Hindus in Mahmud's army), 78–79 (Hindu quarter in Ghazna), 79–86 (alliances with Hindu rulers).

Notes

152 **only in the 1200s:** Abū l-Faḍl Bayhaqī, *The* History *of Beyhaqi (The History of Sultan Masʿud of Ghazna, 1030–1040)*, trans. C. E. Bosworth (2011): I: 8–9.

152 **shrine to Shiva at Somnath:** André Wink, *Al-Hind: The Making of the Indo-Islamic World*, Volume 2: *The Slave Kings and the Islamic Conquest, 11th–13th Centuries* (1997): 294–333, 294 (conversions outside Mahmud's territory), 327–28.

152 **among the most controversial sackings:** Romila Thapar, *Somanatha, The Many Voices of a History* (2004).

152 **destroyed the main image of Shiva:** Al-Bīrūnī, *Alberuni's India*, trans. Edward Sachau (1887): 2: 103–4.

153 **Lashkar-i Bazaar:** Finbarr Barry Flood, "Painting, Monumental and Frescoes," in *Medieval Islamic Civilization: An Encyclopedia*, ed. Joseph W. Meri (2006): 586–89; Daniel Schlumberger, *Lashkari Bazar: une résidence royale ghaznévide et ghoride* (*Mémoires de la Délégation archéologique française en Afghanistan*, Volume 18, Part 1) (1983); Martina Rugiadi, "The Ghaznavid Marble Architectural Decoration: An Overview," available at web.mit.edu.

153 **Karakhanids:** Since surviving documents refer to "kara khans," or "black leaders," they are known as the Karakhanids. Peter Golden, "The Origins of the Karakhanids," in *The Cambridge History of Early Inner Asia*, ed. Denis Sinor (1990): 354 (name of the Karakhanids), 363 (conquest of Khwarazm).

153 **Satuq Bughra Khan:** Michal Biran, "The Qarakhanids' Eastern Exchange: Preliminary Notes on the Silk Roads in the Eleventh and Twelfth Centuries," in *Complexity of Interaction Along the Eurasian Steppe Zone in the First Millennium CE*," ed. Jan Bemmann (2015): 575–96, 578.

153 **Khotan:** Valerie Hansen, *The Silk Road: A New History with Documents* (2016): 368–71; William Samolin, *East Turkistan to the Twelfth Century: A Brief Political Survey* (1964): 81.

154 **"We came down on them":** Maḥmūd al-KāšＴarī *Compendium of the Turkic Dialects*, ed. and trans. Robert Dankoff and James Kelly, Volume 1 (1982): 270.

154 **centuries-long struggle:** Abolqasem Ferdowsi, *Shahnameh: The Persian Book of Kings*, trans. Dick Davis (2016).

155 **ancient enemies of the rulers of Iran:** C. E. Bosworth, "Barbarian Invasions: The Coming of the Turks into the Islamic World," in *Islamic Civilisation, 950–1150*, ed. D. S. Richards (1973): 1–16.

155 **satire deeply critical of Mahmud:** Djalal Khaleghi-Motlagh, "Ferdowsi, Abu'l-Qāsem, i.Life" *Encyclopædia Iranica* (2012).

155 **Avicenna:** William E. Gohlman, *The Life of Ibn Sina: A Critical Edition and Annotated Translation* (1974): 41.

155 **married his daughter:** Valerie Hansen, "International Gifting and the Kitan World, 907–1125," *Journal of Song-Yuan Studies* 43 (2013): 273–302, 288–89.

156 **Buddhist tenets:** Lothar Ledderose, "Changing the Audience: A Pivotal Period in the Great Sutra Carving Project at Cloud Dwelling Monastery Near Beijing," in *Religion and Chinese Society*, ed. John Lagerwey, Volume 1 (2004): 385–409.

156 **Abaoji backdated the start of his reign:** Denis Twitchett, "The Liao's Changing Perceptions of Its T'ang Heritage," in *The Historian, His Readers, and the Passage of Time: The Fu Ssu-nien Memorial Lectures, 1996* (1997): 31–54.

156 **"tanistry":** Joseph Fletcher, "The Mongols: Ecological and Social Perspectives," *Harvard Journal of Asiatic Studies* 46.1 (1988): 11–50, 17.

157 **different groups came together in Liao society:** Pamela Crossley, "Outside In: Power, Identity, and the Han Lineage of Jizhou," *Journal of Song-Yuan Studies* 43 (2013): 51–89.

157 **partially deciphered:** Daniel Kane, "Introduction, Part 2: An Update on Deciphering the Kitan Language and Scripts," *Journal of Song-Yuan Studies* 43 (2013): 11–25.

158 **Treaty of Chanyuan:** Nap-Yin Lau, "Waging War for Peace? The Peace Accord Between the Song and the Liao in AD 1005," in *Warfare in Chinese History*, ed. Hans van de Ven (2000): 183–221, 213.

158 **100,000 Chinese ounces of silver:** The Chinese ounce (*liang*) weighed 37.3 metric grams, one third more than an ounce in the English system of measurement, which is equal to 28 metric grams. In 1042, the payments were increased to 200,000 Chinese ounces of silver and 300,000 bolts of silk.

158 **2,000 ingots:** Hsueh-man Shen (ed.), *Gilded Splendor: Treasures of China's Liao Empire (907–1125)* (2006): 363; Brian Thomas Vivier, "Chinese Foreign Trade, 960–1276," PhD thesis, Yale University (2008): Figure 1.2.

159 **Fukuoka:** Richard von Glahn, "The Ningbo-Hakata Merchant Network and the Reorientation of East Asian Maritime Trade, 1150–1350," *Harvard Journal of Asiatic Studies* 74.2 (2014): 249–79; Bruce L. Batten, *Gateway to Japan: Hakata in War and Peace, 500–1300* (2006): 40; Yiwen Li, email, December 18, 2018.

160 **gifts to the Liao royal family:** Hansen, "International Gifting and the Kitan World, 907–1125," 273–302.

160 **artisans (often Chinese):** Zou Tong, personal communication, May 9, 2009, at the Shangjing Museum.

160 **pinelike fragrance:** Jenny F. So, "Scented Trails: Amber as Aromatic in Medieval China," *Journal of the Royal Asiatic Society*, 3rd Series, 23.1 (2013): 85–101, 94–95.

160 **"Slavonic sea":** Vladimir Minorsky (trans.), *Sharah al-Zaman Tahir: Marvazi on China, the Turks, and India: Arabic Text with an English Translation and Commentary* (1942): 16–17 (imports to China), 19–21 (translation of letters), 78 (Turkic as language of diplomacy).

160 **originated in the Baltic region:** Curt W. Beck and Edith C. Stout, "Amber from Liaoning Province and Liao Amber Artifacts," in *Adornment for the Body and Soul: Ancient Chinese Ornaments from the Mengdiexuan Collection*, ed. E. C. Bunker et al. (1999): 167–72; Xu Xiaodong, *Zhongguo gudai hupo yishu* (2011).

160 **trade resumed:** Sem Vermeersch, *A Chinese Traveler in Medieval Korea: Xu Jing's Illustrated Account of the Xuanhe Embassy to Koryŏ* (2016): 14–39.

160 **Liao princess:** Biran, "The Qarakhanids' Eastern Exchange," 578.

161 **Uighurs:** There were two Uighur kingdoms at this time; it seems more likely that the Uighurs based in Turfan had the resources to send an envoy all the way to Afghanistan. (The other Uighur state, in Ganzhou, was invaded and destroyed in 1028.) See Minorsky, *Marvazi*, 77–78.

161 *khutu:* Anya King, "Early Islamic Sources on the Kitan Liao: The Role of Trade," *Journal of Song-Yuan Studies* 43 (2013): 253–71, 262–63.

161 **"of his excellence in bravery and courage":** The translation provided here is by Michael Rapoport, who has updated Minorsky's translation on the basis of the original Arabic.

161 **musk:** Anya H. King, *Scent from the Garden of Paradise: Musk and the Medieval Islamic World* (2017); James Cave, "You Don't Even Want to Know Where Musk Comes From," *HuffPost*, February 24, 2016.

163 **one might expect them to have converted to Islam:** Andreas Kaplony, "The Conversion of the Turks of Central Asia to Islam as Seen by Arabic and Persian Geography: A Comparative Perspective," in Étienne de la Vaissière, *Islamisation de l'Asie Centrale: processus locaux d'acculturation du VIIe au XIe siècle* (2008): 319–38; Michal Biran, *The Empire of the Qara Khitai in Eurasian History: Between China and the Islamic World* (2005): 196–201.

163 **"with seven years remaining":** This is Mimi Yiengpruksawan's translation, and I have substituted English names for the Buddhist eras. Mimi Yiengpruksawan, "Countdown to 1051," in *Texts and Transformations: Essays in Honor of the 75th Birthday of Victor Mair*, ed. Haun Saussy (2018): 369–434, 376 (Kyoto disasters), 379–80 (Buddhist monastery in Fangshan district, Beijing), 380 (Northern Pagoda translations), 386–94 (different calendars), 394 (Kitan envoy at Goryeo court), 402–4 (Japan-Liao contacts), 406 (eclipse).

164 **offerings in a repository:** D. Max Moerman, "The Archeology of Anxiety: An Underground History of Heian Religion," in *Heian Japan, Centers and Peripheries*, ed. Mikael Adolphson et al. (2007): 245–71.

164 **including pearls:** Liaoning sheng wenwu kaogu yanjiu suo and Chaoyang shi beita bowuguan (eds.), *Chaoyang Beita: Kaogu fajue yu weixiu gongcheng baogao* (2007): plate 48.

165 **ruled until 1058:** William H. McCullough, "The Heian Court, 795–1070," in *The Cambridge History of Japan*, Volume 2: *Heian Japan*, ed. William H. McCullough and Donald H. Shively (1999): 20–96, 67–80.

165 **fifteen Buddhist texts:** Yiwen Li, "Networks of Profit and Faith: Spanning the Sea of Japan and the East China Sea, 838–1403," PhD thesis, Yale University (2017): 80, 85–86 (Fujiwara no Michinaga), 112–13 (Liao sutra containers).

165 **unofficial trading zone:** Yiwen Li, "Chinese Objects Recovered from Sutra Mounds in Japan, 1000–1300," in *Visual and Material Cultures in Middle Period China*, ed. Patricia Buckley Ebrey and Shih-shan Susan Huang (2017): 284–318.

166 **Korean calendrical experts:** Yannick Bruneton, "Astrologues et devins du Koryŏ (918–1392): une analyse de l'histoire officielle," *Extrême-Orient Extrême-Occident*, no. 35 (2013): 45–81.

166 **unusual metal ornamentation:** Mimi Yiengpruksawan, "A Pavilion for

the Amitabha," in *Buddhist Transformations and Interactions*, ed. Victor H. Mair (2017): 401–516, 447–52.

167 **gave a larger share of the plunder:** Igor de Rachewiltz, *The Secret History of the Mongols: A Mongolian Epic Chronicle of the Thirteenth Century* (2004).

168 **history of the world:** Janet Abu-Lughod, *Before European Hegemony: The World System A.D. 1250–1350* (1989).

168 **Black Death:** James Belich, "The Black Death and the Spread of Europe," in *The Prospect of Global History*, ed. James Belich et al. (2016).

Chapter Seven: Surprising Journeys

The following scholars have helped me with this chapter by providing materials, discussing questions, and critiquing drafts: Haydon Cherry, Northwestern University History Department; Jan Wisseman Christie, professor emerita at the Centre for South-East Asia Studies, University of Hull; David Ludden, NYU History Department; R. I. Moore, professor emeritus of History at University of Newcastle; Himanshu Prabha Ray, Oxford Centre for Hindu Studies; and Charles Wheeler, AcademicEditorial.com.

171 **monsoon winds:** Himanshu Prabha Ray, "Seafaring in the Bay of Bengal in the Early Centuries AD," *Studies in History* 6.1 (1990): 1–14.

171 **Eurasia heats up:** Sunil S. Amrith, *Crossing the Bay of Bengal: The Furies of Nature and the Fortunes of Migrants* (2013): 10–13.

171 **voyaging across the open ocean:** Gwyn Campbell, "Africa and the Early Indian Ocean World Exchange System in the Context of Human-Environment Interaction," in *Early Exchange Between Africa and the Wider Indian Ocean World*, ed. Gwyn Campbell (2016): 3. See also Sunil Gupta's essay about contacts between Africa and India.

172 **language of the islands, Malagasy:** Claude Allibert, "Austronesian Migration and the Establishment of the Malagasy Civilization," *Diogenes* 55.2 (2008): 7–16; Ann Kumar, "'The Single Most Astonishing Fact of Human Geography': Indonesia's Far West Colony," *Indonesia* 92 (2011): 59–96.

172 **all the way to Madagascar:** Peter Bellwood, *First Islanders: Prehistory and Human Migration in Island Southeast Asia* (2017): 231; Peter Bellwood, "The Austronesians in History: Common Origins and Diverse Transformations," in *The Austronesians: Historical and Comparative Perspectives,* ed. Peter Bellwood, James J. Fox, and Darrell Tryon (1995): 1–16.

173 **2,433 charred seeds:** Alison Crowther et al., "Ancient Crops Provide First Archaeological Signature of the Westward Austronesian Expansion," *Proceedings of the National Academy of the Sciences* 113.24 (June 14, 2016): 6635–40.

173 **heavy rice diet:** Nicole Boivin et al., "East Africa and Madagascar in the Indian Ocean World," *Journal of World Prehistory* 26.3 (2013): 213–81.

173 **Tupaia:** Anne Salmond, *The Trial of the Cannibal Dog: Captain Cook in the South Seas* (2003): 38, 110.

173 **Pierre-Yves Manguin:** "Austronesian Shipping in the Indian Ocean:

Notes

From Outrigger Boats to Trading Ships," in Campbell, ed., *Early Exchange*, 51–76, 59–60 (Cirebon wreck), 62 (lashed-lug technique), 65 (locations of excavated ships).

174 **Phanom Surin shipwreck:** Lisa Niziolek et al., "Revisiting the Date of the Java Sea Shipwreck from Indonesia," *Journal of Archaeological Science: Reports* 19 (May 2018): 781–90; Horst Hubertus Liebner, "The Siren of Cirebon: A Tenth-Century Trading Vessel Lost in the Java Sea," PhD thesis, University of Leeds (2014).

174 **disparity between long and short chronologies:** Janet M. Wilmshurst et al., "High-Precision Radiocarbon Dating Shows Recent and Rapid Initial Human Colonization of East Polynesia," *Proceedings of the National Academy of Sciences* 108.5 (February 1, 2011): 1815–20.

176 **traditions that had died out:** Ben Finney, *Voyage of Rediscovery: A Cultural Odyssey Through Polynesia* (1994).

176 **Using no navigational instruments at all:** Steve Thomas, *The Last Navigator: A Young Man, an Ancient Mariner, the Secrets of the Sea* (1997).

178 **Population density was low:** Anthony Reid, "Low Population Growth and Its Causes in Pre-Colonial Southeast Asia," in *Death and Disease in Southeast Asia: Explorations in Social, Medical and Demographic History*, ed. Norman G. Owen (1987): 33–47, 36.

179 **accustomed to moving from place to place:** M. C. Ricklefs (ed.), *A New History of Southeast Asia* (2010): 8–10 (early social structures), 21 (Indian inscriptions), 30, 61–64 (Srivijaya), 40–42 (Angkor), 43 (temple state model).

179 **chakravartin ideal:** John E. Cort, *Open Boundaries: Jain Communities and Cultures in Indian History* (1998): 98.

180 **balloon:** The image of a balloon state draws on Burton Stein's model of the segmentary state from his *History of India* (1998): 20, as well as O. W. Wolters's concept of the mandala state from his *History, Culture and Region in Southeast Asian Perspectives* (1999): 27–28.

180 **Cholas on the tip of South India:** Jan Wisseman Christie, "The Medieval Tamil-Language Inscriptions in Southeast Asia and China," in *Southeast Asian Archaeology, 1994*, ed. Pierre-Yves Manguin (1998): 241 (rise of Cholas), 244 (883 inscription), 244–45 (shift in trading destinations), 246 (changing composition of merchant community), 249 (economic downturn), 254 (Chola raids in Southeast Asia).

181 **Esoteric Buddhism:** Andrea Acri, "Introduction: Esoteric Buddhist Networks Along the Maritime Silk Routes, 7th–13th Century AD," in *Esoteric Buddhism in Mediaeval Maritime Asia*, ed. Andrea Acri (2016): 1–25, 4 (Esoteric Buddhist practices), 7 (Yijing), 16 (Map 1.1: Paths traveled by the monks); Koichi Shinohara, *Spells, Images, and Maṇḍalas: Tracing the Evolution of Esoteric Buddhist Rituals* (2014): 194–204.

181 **dynastic history of the Song:** *Songshi* 489: 14088.

181 **monopoly on frankincense and sandalwood:** Zhu Yu, *Pingzhou ketan*, Song Yuan biji congshu series (1989): 1: 2.

182 **fleet of 1,000 vessels:** O. W. Wolters, "Studying Śrīvijaya," in *Early Southeast Asia: Selected Essays*, ed. Craig J. Reynolds (2008): 77–108, 92–94;

"Restudying Some Chinese Writings on Sriwijaya," 109–47, in the same volume.

182 **shipbuilding centers for dhows:** Hyunhee Park, *Mapping the Chinese and Islamic Worlds: Cross-Cultural Exchange in Pre-modern Asia* (2013): 30–31 (dhows), 69–70, 219n58 (Huang Chao rebellion).

182 **Phanom Surin shipwreck:** John Guy, "The Phanom Surin Shipwreck, a Pahlavi Inscription, and Their Significance for the History of Early Lower Central Thailand," *Journal of the Siam Society* 105 (2017): 179–96.

182 **exhibition about the wreck:** Michael Flecker, "The Ethics, Politics, and Realities of Maritime Archaeology in Southeast Asia," *International Journal of Nautical Archaeology* 31.1 (2002): 12–24; Michael Flecker, "A Ninth-Century AD Arab or Indian Shipwreck in Indonesia: First Evidence for Direct Trade with China," *World Archaeology* 32.3 (2001): 335–54.

182 **Belitung ship:** Regina Krahl (ed.), *Shipwrecked: Tang Treasures and Monsoon Winds* (2011): 36; available online.

183 **Abbasid ceramics as models:** John W. Chaffee, *The Muslim Merchants of Premodern China: The History of an Asian Maritime Trade Diaspora, 750–1400* (2018): 29.

183 **Chinese ceramics as superior:** Arthur Lane, *Early Islamic Pottery: Mesopotamia, Egypt, and Persia* (1947): 31.

183 **In response to the threat of Chinese imports:** Robert B. J. Mason, *Shine Like the Sun: Lustre-Painted and Associated Pottery from the Medieval Middle East* (2004): 2 (how to make lusterware); 31 (750, the date of earliest Basra ceramics that copy Chinese models); 158 (after 800 Basra lusterware excavated from East African coast and tip of Africa).

183 **gifts from the Tang emperor:** François Louis, "Metal Objects on the Belitung Shipwreck," in Krahl, ed., *Shipwrecked*, 85–91.

184 **Stone reliefs of merchant ships:** John N. Miksic, *Borobudur: Majestic, Mysterious, Magnificent* (2010).

184 **Shailendra kings:** Kenneth R. Hall, *History of Early Southeast Asia: Maritime Trade and Societal Development, 100–1500* (2011): 125–26.

184 **volcanic explosion or earthquake:** Jan Wisseman Christie, "Revisiting Early Mataram," in *Fruits of Inspiration: Studies in Honour of Prof. J. G. de Casparis*, ed. M. J. Klokke and K. R. van Kooij (2001): 25–56, 47.

185 **the Buddha saves a ship:** August Johan Bernet Kempers, *Ageless Borobudur: Buddhist Mystery in Stone, Decay and Restoration, Mendut and Pawon, Folklife in Ancient Java* (1976): 109–19, plates 32, 79, 201 (depictions of ships); Himanshu Ray, personal communication, October 24, 2018.

185 **more female vendors:** Jan Wisseman Christie, "Javanese Markets and the Asian Sea Trade Boom of the Tenth to Thirteenth Centuries A.D.,"*Journal of the Economic and Social History of the Orient*, 41.3 (1998): 344–81, 348 (merchant guilds), 350 (market officials), 352–53 (black pepper and safflower), 356 (potters), 360 (women vendors), 360 (Chinese coin imports and copies).

186 **no evidence of a long-distance trade in slaves:** Jan Wisseman Christie, email, December 10, 2018. See her "Preliminary Notes on Debt and Credit in Early Island Southeast Asia," in *Credit and Debt in Indonesia, 860–*

1930: From Peonage to Pawnshop, from Kongsi to Cooperative, ed. D. Henley and P. Boomgaard (2009): 41–60, 178–190.

186 **no conflict between the two religions:** Anthony Reid, personal communication, March 30, 2018.

187 **ultimate end-users:** G. F. Hourani, *Arab Seafaring in the Indian Ocean in Ancient and Early Medieval Times* (1951, 1995): 89–105.

187 **one group harvested a certain product:** Dato Dr Nik Hassan Shuhaimi Nik Abdul Rahman (ed.), *The Encyclopedia of Malaysia: Early History*, Volume 4 (1998): 76.

188 **trade throughout the entire region slowed down:** Geoff Wade, "An Early Age of Commerce in Southeast Asia, 900–1300 CE," *Journal of Southeast Asian Studies* 40.2 (2009): 221–65.

188 **number of foreigners killed:** John W. Chaffee strongly questions these figures in *Muslim Merchants of Premodern China*, 48. See also Howard Levy, *Biography of Huang Ch'ao*, Chinese Dynastic History Translations 5 (1961): 109–21 (Arabic sources); Valerie Hansen, *The Silk Road: A New History with Documents* (2016): 266–67.

188 **Muslim traders pulled out of China:** Chaffee, *The Muslim Merchants of Premodern China,* 52.

188 **most important trading partners:** O. W. Wolters, "Tambralinga," *Bulletin of the School of Oriental and African Studies* 21.3 (1958): 587–607, 605; *Song Huiyao*, Fanyi 7:20b (Shanghai guji chubanshe edition, 2014), Volume 16: 9948.

189 **They had much less control:** David Ludden, *Peasant History in South India* (1985).

189 **far-flung states:** Gokul Seshadri, "New Perspectives on Nagapattinam," in *Nagapattinam to Suvanadwipa: Reflections on the Chola Naval Expeditions to Southeast Asia*, ed. Hermann Kulke et al. (2009): 121–28; Peter Schalk (ed.), *Buddhism Among Tamils in Pre-Colonial Tamilakam and Ilam*, Volume 2 (2002): 513–670, 596.

189 **Rajaraja I invaded:** George W. Spencer, *The Politics of Expansion: The Chola Conquest of Sri Lanka and Srivijaya* (1983): 5–6 (results of conquest), 34 (Rajaraja I conquests), 44 (Rajendra's Ganges campaign), 60 (commercial taxes), 64 (withdrawal from Sri Lanka), 144–45 (ties to other countries).

190 **"The Cholas seized the Mahesi":** Spencer, *The Politics of Expansion*, 54–56, translating an original passage from the historical chronicle of Sri Lanka titled *Cūlavaṃsa* 55.16–22.

191 **Cholas as a powerful state:** Hermann Kulke, "The Naval Expeditions of the Cholas in the Context of Asian History," in Kulke et al, ed., *Nagapattinam to Suvarnadwipa*, and the essays by Noboru Karashima and Tansen Sen.

191 **"Rajendra having dispatched many ships":** Spencer, *Politics of Expansion*, 138–39, citing the translation given in K. A. Nilakanta Sastri, *Sri Vijiya*, 80.

191 **persuaded the Chola ruler to give up Hinduism:** Kulke et al., ed., *Nagapattinam to Suvanadwipa*, 12.

Notes

191 **detailed knowledge of Rajendra's scribes:** A. Meenakshisundararajan, "Rajendra Chola's Naval Expedition and the Chola Trade with Southeast Asia," in Kulke et al., ed., *Nagapattinam to Suvanadwipa*, 168–77, 170. See also the map on the flyleaf of that volume.

192 **inscription from Mysore:** Burton Stein, "Coromandel Trade in Medieval India," in *Merchants & Scholars: Essays in the History of Exploration and Trade Collected in Memory of James Ford Bell*, ed. John Parker (1965): 49–62; N. A. Nilakanta Sastri, "A Tamil Merchant-guild in Sumatra," *Tijdschrift voor Indische taal-, land-, en volkenkunde* 72 (1932): 314–27, 322–24.

192 **"like the elephant":** John Guy, "Tamil Merchant Guilds and the Quanzhou Trade," in *The Emporium of the World: Maritime Quanzhou, 1000–1400*, ed. Angela Schottenhammer (2001): 283–308, 291 (early Tamil inscriptions Southeast Asia), 293 (Baros, Sumatra guild), 294 (hiring of mercenaries), 295–96 (Quanzhou Tamil inscription), 296–302 (temple remains).

193 **downgrade the Cholas:** Tansen Sen, *Buddhism, Diplomacy, and Trade: The Realignment of Sino-Indian Relations, 600–1400* (2003): 224.

194 **The king's subjects made offerings:** Michael D. Coe and Damian Evans, *Angkor and the Khmer Civilization* (2003, 2018): 11 (dimensions of the site), 116 (traits of Classic Angkor civilization), 163 (Third Gallery dimensions), 188 (Zhou Daguan on imports and exports), 189 (kingfisher hunting), 209 (imported Chinese ceramics), 212–14 (textiles and dress), 239 (traits of post-Classic).

194 **lidar:** Julia Wallace, "Cambodia's Hidden Cities: Aerial Laser Imaging," *New York Times* (September 20, 2016): D1, D5.

194 **dwellings packed together:** Roland Fletcher et al., "Angkor Wat: An Introduction," *Antiquity* 89.348 (2015): 1388–1401, 1396.

195 **Angkor Wat's population:** Damian Evans and Roland Fletcher, "The Landscape of Angkor Wat Redefined," *Antiquity* 89.348 (2015): 1402–19, 1410–11.

195 **earliest Muslim graves:** M. C. Ricklefs, *Mystic Synthesis in Java: A History of Islamicization from the Fourteenth to the Early Nineteenth Centuries* (2006): 12–21.

195 **Minister Zhou:** Zhou Daguan, *Zhenla Fengtu ji jiaozhu* (Zhonghua shuju edition, 2000): 141–42 (local products), 148 (Chinese goods); Zhou Daguan, *The Customs of Cambodia*, trans. Michael Smithies (2001): 59–60 (local products), 63 (Chinese goods).

196 **Located on a major trade route:** Li Tana, "A View from the Sea: Perspectives on the Northern and Central Vietnamese Coast," *Journal of Southeast Asian Studies* 37.1 (2006): 83–102, 95–96; Momoki Shiro, "Dai Viet and the South China Sea Trade: From the 10th to the 15th Century," *Crossroads* 12.1 (1998): 1–34, 20.

196 **Van Don:** John K. Whitmore, "Vân Đồn, the 'Mạc Gap,' and the End of the Jiaozhi Ocean System," in *The Tongking Gulf Through History*, ed. Nola Cooke et al. (2011): 101–16.

197 **office near Van Don to collect pearls:** John K. Whitmore, *Vietnam, Hồ Quý Ly, and the Ming (1371–1421)* (1985): 112.

Notes

197 A contemporary source describes the facility: Tatsuro Yamamoto, "Van-don: A Trade Port in Vietnam," *Memoirs of the Research Department of the Toyo Bunko* 39 (1981): 1–32, 5 (Chinese clothing, food, and drink), 10 (pearl-fishing compound). This is the translation of a Japanese-language article from *Tōhō Gakuhō* 9 (1939): 277–309; the original passage appears in Chen Weiwen (ed.) *Qinding Yueshi tongjian gangmu* (Taipei Central Library edition, 1969): 13: 1549–50.

Chapter Eight: The Most Globalized Place on Earth

Thanks to Anna Shields (Princeton) and Robert Hymes (Columbia) for giving me a chance to present an early draft of this chapter at Princeton University at their conference about the Tang-Song transition in 2018. Ari Levine, the editor of the Journal of the Song-Yuan Studies, *sent a draft of the article to two anonymous reviewers who offered many helpful suggestions, as did Yuan Julian Chen (Yale), Yiwen Li (City University of Hong Kong), David Porter (Yale), and Helen Wang (British Museum).*

199 Some of the goods the Chinese purchased: Angela Schottenhammer, "China's Emergence as a Maritime Power," in *The Cambridge History of China*, Volume 5, Part 2: *Sung China, 960–1279*, ed. John W. Chaffee and Denis Twitchett (2015): 437–525, 512–18.

199 woven rattan mats: Dato Dr Nik Hassan Shuhaimi Nik Abdul Rahman (ed.), *The Encyclopedia of Malaysia*, Volume 4: *Early History* (1998): 87.

199 aloeswood: Paul Wheatley, "Geographical Notes on Some Commodities Involved in Sung Maritime Trade," *Journal of the Malayan Branch of the Royal Asiatic Society* 32.2 (1959): 3–139, 22–23 (changing rates of taxes on fine and coarse goods), 25–26 (appointment of trade superintendants), 69–72 (aloeswood).

200 recipes for perfume: Yang Zhishui, "L'Encens sous les Song (960–1279) and les Yuan (1279–1368)," in *Parfums de Chine: la culture de l'encens au temps des empereurs,* ed. Éric Lefebvre (2018): 68–75.

200 *The Tale of Genji*: Ivan Morris, *The World of the Shining Prince: Court Life in Ancient Japan* (1964); Dennis Washburn (trans.), Murasaki Shikibu, *The Tale of Genji* (2017): 407 (lingering fragrance), 608–13 (incense contest).

200 aromatics originated: Tanaka Fumio, *Kokusai kōeki to kodai Nihon* (2012): 180.

201 a contest for the best fragrance: Melissa McCormick, *The Tale of Genji: A Visual Companion* (2018): 149–51.

201 would have varied with the season: Dennis Washburn, professor of Asian Societies, Cultures, and Literatures, Dartmouth College, email, October 2, 2019.

202 furniture and storage containers made from fragrant woods: Joseph Needham, "Constituents of Incense, and Other Aromatics," in *Science and Civilisation in China*, Volume 5: *Chemistry and Chemical Technology, Part II, Spagyrical Discovery and Invention: Magisteries of Gold and Immortality* (1974):

Notes

(Table 94); Olivia Milburn, "Aromas, Scents, and Spices: Olfactory Culture in China Before the Arrival of Buddhism," *Journal of the American Oriental Society* 136.3 (2016): 441–64; Frédéric Obringer, "Dans L'empire de fous de parfums. Une introduction au monde des senteurs en Chine impériale," in Lefebvre (ed.), *Parfums de Chine*, 10–24.

202 **musk:** Anya H. King, *Scent from the Garden of Paradise: Musk and the Medieval Islamic World* (2017); Paul Freedman, *Out of the East: Spices and the Medieval Imagination* (2008): 15–16.

202 **frankincense and myrrh:** Jenny F. So, "Scented Trails: Amber as Aromatic in Medieval China," *Journal of the Royal Asiatic Society*, 3rd Series, 23.1 (2013): 85–101, 90; Edward Schafer, *Golden Peaches of Samarkand* (1963): 155.

203 **Persian Gulf ports:** John Chaffee, *The Muslim Merchants of Premodern China: The History of a Maritime Asian Trade Diaspora, 750–1400* (2018): 27–28.

203 **"The people of this country":** Duan Chengshi, *Youyang zazu* 4: 25, Sibu congkan edition, accessed through the Zhongguo jiben gujiku database; Carrie E. Reed, "Motivation and Meaning of a 'Hodge-podge': Duan Chengshi's 'Youyang zazu,'" *Journal of the American Oriental Society* 123.1 (2003): 121–45.

203 **Some fictional tales:** Julie Wilensky, "The Magical Kunlun and 'Devil Slaves': Chinese Perceptions of Dark-Skinned People and Africa Before 1500," *Sino-Platonic Papers* 122 (2002): 1–51.

203 **customs duties in Guangzhou:** Wang Gungwu, "The Nanhai Trade: A Study of the Early History of Chinese Trade in the South China Sea," *Journal of the Malayan Branch of the Royal Asiatic Society* 31.2 (1958): 1–135; Hugh R. Clark, *Community, Trade, and Networks: Southern Fujian Province from the Third to the Thirteenth Century* (1991): 49.

204 **Tang trade policy:** Huang Chunyan, *Songdai haiwai maoyi* (2003), 129–32; Abū Zayd al-Sīrāfī, *Accounts of China and India*, trans. Tim McIntosh-Smith (2017): 17.

204 **One lashed-lug vessel:** Michael Flecker, *The Archaeological Excavation of the Tenth Century Intan Shipwreck, Java Sea, Indonesia*, BAR International Series S1047 (2002); Michael Flecker, "Treasure from the Java Sea: The Tenth-Century Intan Shipwreck," *Heritage Asia Magazine* 2.2 (2004–2005), available online.

204 **inscriptions on the silver ingots:** Denis Twitchett and Janice Stargardt, "Chinese Silver Bullion in a Tenth-Century Indonesian Wreck," *Asia Major* 15.1 (2002): 23–72, 25 (value of silver), 41 (nature of payment).

204 **Cirebon:** Horst Hubertus Liebner, "The Siren of Cirebon: A Tenth-Century Trading Vessel Lost in the Java Sea," PhD thesis, University of Leeds (2014): 85 (tonnage), 304 (quantities of ceramics carried by different sunken ships).

205 **shipboard compass:** Robert K. G. Temple, *The Genius of China: 3,000 Years of Science, Discovery, and Invention* (1986): 148–57.

205 **Chinese boatbuilders:** Chaffee, *Muslim Merchants*, 81–83.

205 **company of several concubines:** H. A. R. Gibb (trans.), *The Travels of Ibn Battuta, A.D. 1325–1354* (1994): 4: 813–14.

205 **Song envoys armed with fill-in-the-blank forms:** *Song Huiyao*, Zhiguan
44: 2 (Shanghai guji chubanshe edition, 2014), Volume 7: 4204; Derek
Heng, *Sino-Malay Trade and Diplomacy from the Tenth Through the Fourteenth
Century* (2009): 73.

206 **tribute voyages came to a temporary halt:** Chaffee, *Muslim Merchants*,
65–75.

207 **in 995:** *Song Huiyao*, Zhiguan 44: 3 (Shanghai guji chubanshe edition,
2014), Volume 7: 4204.

207 **raised the direct confiscation to 40 percent:** Concerning the year 1141,
see *Song Huiyao*, Zhiguan 44:25 (Shanghai guji chubanshe edition, 2014),
Volume 7: 4216.

207 **Treaty of Chanyuan:** Nap-Yin Lau, "Waging War for Peace? The Peace
Accord Between the Song and the Liao in AD 1005," in *Warfare in Chinese
History*, ed. Hans van de Ven (2000): 183–221, 213.

207 **Horses, whose sale the Liao forbade:** Shiba Yoshinobu, "Sung Foreign
Trade: Its Scope and Organization," in *China Among Equals: The Middle
Kingdom and Its Neighbors, 10th–14th Centuries*, ed. Morris Rossabi (1983):
89–115, 98; Brian Thomas Vivier, "Chinese Foreign Trade, 960–1276,"
PhD thesis, Yale University (2008).

208 **paper money:** Richard von Glahn, "The Origins of Paper Money in
China," in *The Origins of Value: The Financial Innovations That Created Modern Capital Markets*, ed. William N. Goetzmann and K. Geert Rouwen-
horst (2005): 65–89.

208 **Horses were the most important overland import:** Paul J. Smith, *Taxing
Heaven's Storehouse: Horses, Bureaucrats, and the Destruction of the Sichuan Tea
Industry, 1074–1224* (1991).

208 **South Indians financed a Buddhist temple:** Friedrich Hirth and W. W.
Rockhill (trans.), *Chau Ju-kua, His Work on the Chinese and Arab Trade in
the Twelfth and Thirteenth Centuries, Entitled Chu-fan-chi* (1911): 111; Zhao
Rukuo, *Zhufan zhi jiaoshi* (1996): 86; Wu Wenliang and Wu Youxiong,
Quanzhou zongjiao shike (2005).

209 **Mosque of the Prophet's Companions:** Nancy Shatzman Steinhardt,
China's Early Mosques (2015): 38–52.

209 **China's largest foreign community:** Chaffee, *Muslim Merchants*, 80–81
(summarizing Heng—shift from luxury to bulk commodity trade), 141–42
(Arabic tombstones found in Quanzhou).

209 **This level of contact:** Clark, *Community, Trade, and Networks*, 32–37 (origins of Quanzhou trade), 129 (unusually high number of foreign residents).

209 **"there were two types of foreigners":** *Fangyu shenglan*, preface dated
1239, 12:6a, Siku quanshu edition, accessed through the Zhongguo jiben
gujiku database.

209 **"The sea-going merchant vessels":** Chao Buzhi (1053–1110), *Jileji* 70:
370. Sibu congkan edition, accessed through the Zhongguo jiben gujiku
database; Huang, *Songdai haiwai maoyi*, 185n1.

209 **first Superintendent of Maritime Trade:** Huang, *Songdai haiwai maoyi*,
101–3 (Chinese investment in ships), 103 (Chinese woman investor), 120–
21 (main street where foreign merchants lived), 147, 162–63 (wholesaler

and direct purchases of cargo), 186 (trade superintendent for Quanzhou), 223–24 (Quanzhou surpassing Guangzhou).

209 **port of Fukuoka:** Yiwen Li, "Networks of Profit and Faith: Spanning the Sea of Japan and the East China Sea, 838–1403," PhD thesis, Yale University (2017).

209 **Zhu Yu:** Don J. Wyatt, *The Blacks of Premodern China*, 43 (Guangzhou), 48–60 (Zhu Yu).

210 **Zhu Yu is the only writer:** The book was entitled *Pingzhou ketan* (Conversational topics from Pingzhou) because Zhu Yu retired to Pingzhou, which is located in modern Huanggan, Hubei. See the Song Yuan biji congshu edition (1989): 2: 25 (ships' arrival, popularity of drinks), 2: 26 (compass). See also Derek Heng, "Shipping, Customs Procedures, and the Foreign Community: The 'Pingzhou Ketan' on Aspects of China's Maritime Economy in the Late Eleventh Century," *Journal of Song-Yuan Studies* 38 (2008): 1–38.

210 **"the foreign slaves are good at swimming":** Zhu, *Pingzhou ketan*, 2: 26.

210 **"Their hair is curly as well as yellow":** Zhu, *Pingzhou ketan*, 2: 28, 56.

210 **kwashiorkor:** See the discussion of kwashiorkor on healthline.com. Thanks to John Southworth for this excellent suggestion.

211 **"every day that he was in his office":** Ouyang Xiu, *Guitian lu* 2: 10b. Baihai edition, Ming imprint accessed through the Zhongguo jiben gujiku database.

212 **Wartime made it difficult to collect taxes:** William Guanglin Liu, "The Making of a Fiscal State in Song China, 960–1279," *Economic History Review* 68.1 (2014): 48–78.

212 **"The profits from overseas trade":** *Song Huiyao,* Zhiguan 44: 20 (Shanghai guji chubanshe edition, 2014), Volume 7: 4213–14; John Chaffee, "The Song Dynasty and the Multi-State and Commercial World of East Asia," *Crossroads: Studies on the History of Exchange Relations in the East Asian World* 1 (2010), available online.

213 **about 5 percent:** Jung-Pang Lo, "The Emergence of China as a Sea Power During the Late Sung and Early Yuan Periods," *Far Eastern Quarterly* 14.4 (1955): 489–503, especially 499n37; Li Xinchuan, *Jianyan yilai chaoye zaji*, Part 1, juan 15, p. 211; Yuhai 1883 edition 186: 11.

213 **aloeswood was the main ingredient:** Lefebvre (ed.), *Parfums de Chine*, 72–73, illustration 4 (gift for courtiers), 75 (first incense sticks).

214 **Even the poorest consumers:** Huang, *Songdai haiwai maoyi*, 210, citing *Dongjing menghua lu* and *Mengliang lu.*

214 **set prices artificially high:** Robert Hartwell, "Foreign Trade, Monetary Policy and Chinese 'Mercantilism,'" in *Liu Tzu-chien hakushi shoshū kinen Sōshi kenkyū ronshū,* ed. Kinugawa Tsuyoshi (1988): 456, dubs this uprising "The Frankincense Rebellion," but the sources (Zhu Xi's *xingzhuang* biography in *Hui'an xiansheng Zhu Wengong wenji*, 97.4a; *Songshi* 185: 4358) give no specifics.

214 **druggists prescribed:** Hartwell, "Foreign Trade," 477–80 (Appendix, Table IV, "Medical Use of Foreign Commodities for Specific Syndromes of Symptoms, Tang, N. Song, S. Song").

Notes

214 **first public pharmacy:** Asaf Goldschmidt, *The Evolution of Chinese Medicine; Song Dynasty, 960–1200* (2009): 123–36.

214 *Mr. Chen's Guide to Incense:* Hartwell, "Foreign Trade," 480 (Appendix, Table V, "Number and Percentage of Foreign Commodities Contained in a Sample of 300 Recipes for Incense"); Chen Jing, *Chenshi xiangpu,* Siku quanshu zhenben edition.

215 **boat built entirely from Chinese cedar:** Zhou Mi, *Guixin zashi* (1988): xuji, Part 2, 197.

215 **all stood to make a handsome profit:** Fu Zongwen, "Houzhu guchuan: Song ji nanwai zongshi haiwai jingshang de wuzheng," *Haiwai jiaotong yanjiu* 2 (1989): 77–83.

215 **The aromatics trade was so lucrative:** The imperial clan included "all patrilineal descendants of the Song founders," John Chaffee, *Branches of Heaven: A History of the Imperial Clan of Sung China* (1999): 11–12.

215 **deeply involved in the aromatics trade:** Ma Duanlin, *Wenxian tongkao* (2011): 259: 7066; Clark, *Community, Trade, and Networks,* 140.

215 **The city's population:** In 1080, Quanzhou prefecture had 201,406 households; in 1241–52, 255,758 households. Clark, *Community, Trade, and Networks,* 77. For Baghdad, see Maya Shatzmiller, *Labour in the Medieval Islamic World* (1994): 62. For Kaifeng and Hangzhou, see Bao Weimin, *Songdai Chengshi Yanjiu* (2014): 304–5.

216 **And some made salt:** Clark, *Community, Trade, and Networks,* 158–63 (population involved in growing agricultural crops), 163–67 (workers in nonagricultural sectors).

216 **ceramics industry:** So Kee Long, "The Trade Ceramics Industry in Southern Fukien During the Sung," *Journal of Song-Yuan Studies* 24 (1994): 1–19, 13 (estimated number of vessels per firing), 14 (percentage of the population working in ceramics trade). Professor So's estimate of three million for the population of Fujian is too low. It was much closer to five million in the opinion of Professor Lu Xiqi, History Department, Wuhan University (April 21, 2019, email), whose estimate is based on the population figure of 6,214,195 for 1283–1285 as given in *Yuanshi* 26: 1504.

217 **de facto currency:** Richard von Glahn, "Cycles of Silver in Chinese Monetary History," in *The Economy of Lower Yangzi Delta in Late Imperial China: Connecting Money, Markets, and Institutions,* ed. Billy K. L. So (2013): 18–25; "The Ningbo-Hakata Merchant Network and the Reorientation of East Asian Maritime Trade, 1150–1350," *Harvard Journal of Asiatic Studies* 74.2 (2014): 249–79, 252 (Chinese policies about paper money), 258 (Japanese use of Chinese coins).

217 **"mica and frankincense":** Shiba Yoshinobu, *Commerce and Society in Sung China,* trans. Mark Elvin, Michigan Abstracts of Chinese and Japanese Works on Chinese History (1970): 160 (translation of the account of the Shaoxing market in *Jiatai Kuaiji zhi* 7: 9b), 162–63 (translation about the Chengdu market from Du Zheng, *Xingshang tanggao,* juan 1).

217 **Zhao Rukuo:** For Zhao's epitaph see *Kaogu* 19 (1987): 956–57; German translation, Angela Schottenhammer, *Grabinschriften in der Song-Dynastie* (1995): 172–74.

217 *Record of Various Foreign Peoples*: Friedrich Hirth and W. W. Rockhill (trans.), *Chau Ju-kua, His Work on the Chinese and Arab Trade in the Twelfth and Thirteenth Centuries, Entitled Chu-fan-chi* (1911): 111; Zhao Rukuo, *Zhufan zhi jiaoshi* (1996).

217 **Earlier trade superintendents:** Huang, *Songdai haiwai maoyi*, 115–16.

218 **black-and-white detail from Qingming scroll furniture store:** Yang Zhishui, *Gushiwen mingwu xinzheng* (2004): 1: 115–16; Valerie Hansen, "The Beijing Qingming Scroll and Its Significance for the Study of Chinese History," *Journal of Song-Yuan Studies* (1996): Section 25.

218 **former trade superintendent's office:** The Daoist deity, the Emperor of the Dark Heavens (Xuantian shangdi), is named Marshal Tian Du of the Palace of Water Immortals (Shuixian gong Tian Du yuanshuai).

218 **distinguish between higher- and lower-quality goods:** Heng, *Sino-Malay Trade*, 136.

219 **"In the West there is an island":** Hirth and Rockhill, *Chau Ju-kua*, 149; Zhao, *Zhufanzhi jiaoshi*, 127.

219 **"People don't dare get close":** Hirth and Rockhill, *Chau Ju-kua*, 232; Zhao, *Zhufanzhi jiaoshi*, 207.

220 **"Assume that there is a sea-going junk":** Qin Jiushao, *Shushu jiuzhang* 17: 119–20; Shiba, *Commerce and Society*, 32; Ulrich Libbrecht, *Chinese Mathematics in the Thirteenth Century* (1973): 152–62.

220 **A ship that sank just outside Quanzhou:** Jeremy Green, "The Song Dynasty Shipwreck at Quanzhou, Fujian Province, People's Republic of China," *International Journal of Nautical Archaeology and Underwater Exploration* 12.3 (1983): 253–61. The initial Chinese-language reports about the shipwreck were published in *Wenwu* (1975): 1–34, and an updated, Chinese-English version of the report has now appeared: Fujian Sheng Quanzhou haiwai jiaotong shi bowuguan (ed.), *Quanzhou wan Songdai haichuan fajue yu yanjiu* (2017): 16–18, 99–100 (keel decoration); 26–31, 105–6 (aromatics); 32–36, 106–7 (wooden cargo labels); 83–87, 148–52 (how the boat sank). I also visited the Quanzhou Shipwreck Museum located on the grounds of Kaiyuansi in Quanzhou several times in fall 2016.

221 **repairs using the lashed-lug technique:** Janice Stargardt, "Behind the Shadows: Archaeological Data on Two-Way Sea-Trade Between Quanzhou and Satingpra, South Thailand, 10th–14th Century," in *The Emporium of the World: Maritime Quanzhou, 1000–1400*, ed. Angela Schottenhammer (2001): 309–93, 373 (evidence of repairs), 375 (scuttling hypothesis).

221 **"southern family":** Fu Zongwen, "Houzhu guchuan: Song ji nanwai zongshi haiwai jingshang de wuzheng," *Haiwai jiaotong yanjiu* 2 (1989): 77–83.

224 **Pu Shougeng:** John W. Chaffee, "Pu Shougeng Reconsidered: Pu, His Family, and Their Role in the Maritime Trade of Quanzhou," in *Beyond the Silk Roads: New Discourses on China's Role in East Asian Maritime History*, ed. Robert J. Antony and Angela Schottenhammer (2017): 63–75; Kuwabara Jitsuzō, "On P'u Shou-keng," *Memoirs of the Research Department of the Tōyō Bunko* 2 (1928): 1–79; 7 (1935): 1–104, 57–59.

Notes

222 **pacification commissioner:** Billy K. L. So, *Prosperity, Region, and Institutions in Maritime China: The South Fukien Pattern, 946–1368* (2000): 107–14, 302–5.

222 **Pu switched his allegiance:** John Chaffee, "The Impact of the Song Imperial Clan on the Overseas Trade of Quanzhou," in Schottenhammer, ed., *The Emporium of the World*, 34–35.

222 **"The total amount of traffic":** Ronald Latham (trans.), *The Travels of Marco Polo* (1958): 237.

223 **"beautiful" and "cheap" porcelain:** Latham, *The Travels of Marco Polo*, 237–38.

223 **Ibn Battuta:** H. A. R. Gibb (trans.), *The Travels of Ibn Battuta, A.D. 1325–1354* (1994): 4: 813–14.

223 **Guangzhou gazetteer:** *Dade nanhaizhi* 7:17b, Song Yuan difangzhi congshu xubian edition, p. 1412; Shiba, "Sung Foreign Trade," 105.

223 **South China Sea:** Heng, *Sino-Malay Trade*, 136 (grading system), 138 (Guangzhou gazetteer); *Dade nanhai zhi*. Song Yuan difangzhi congkan xubian edition (1990): 7:19a–20b.

224 **"still farther east [of Java]":** Hirth and Rockhill, *Chau Ju-kua*, 75, 79n2; Zhao, *Zhufan zhi*, 54–55.

224 **"Of all the waters of the world":** Burton Watson, *Chuang Tzu: Basic Writings* (1964): 97.

224 **Kuroshio Current:** Huang Chunyan, *Zao chuanye shiye xia de Songdai shehui* (2017): 216–17; Joseph Needham, *Science and Civilisation in China*, Volume 4: *Physics and Physical Technology, Part III: Civil Engineering and Nautics* (1971): 549.

224 **"If they catch a gust of wind":** Zhou Qufei, *Lingwai daida jiaozhu* (1999): 36–37; Matthew Torck, "The Unimaginable and Immeasurable? China's Visions of the Pacific—Needham's Views Re-examined," in *The Perception of Maritime Space in Traditional Chinese Sources,* ed. Angela Schottenhammer and Roderich Ptak (2006): 141–52, 146.

225 **Ming dynasty:** Roderich Ptak, "Ming Maritime Trade to Southeast Asia," in *From the Mediterranean to the China Sea: Miscellaneous Notes,* ed. Claude Guillot et al. (1998): 157–91, 164; *Ming Shilu*, 201:3008; Geoff Wade, *The Ming Shi-lu*, 2: 133.

225 **An imperial fleet of 317 ships:** G. F. Hourani, *Arab Seafaring in the Indian Ocean in Ancient and Early Medieval Times* (1951): 61.

225 **Chinese-language inscriptions:** J. V. G. Mills, *Ying yai sheng lan: "The Overall Survey of the Ocean's Shores,"* [1433] (1970): 6, 11, 12, 49, 59, 138.

225 **covering 8,000 miles** Luke Stanek used Google Earth Pro software to calculate these distances.

225 **Portuguese concentrated on exporting gold:** Pierre Vilar, *A History of Gold and Money, 1450–1920*, trans. Judith White (1976): 57.

Notes

Epilogue

227 **malaria:** Daniel Headrick, *The Tools of Empire: Technology and European Imperialism in the Nineteenth Century* (1981): 58–79.

228 **Malemo Cana:** One source gives his name as Cana, the other as Canaca. Sanjay Subrahmanyam, *The Career and Legend of Vasco da Gama* (1997): 119–28.

228 **Malinché:** Stuart B. Schwartz and Tatiana Seijas, *Victors and Vanquished: Spanish and Nahua Views of the Fall of the Mexica Empire*, 2nd ed. (2018): 38.

229 **massive outbreaks of disease:** Noble David Cook, *Demographic Collapse: Indian Peru, 1520–1620* (1981): 94; Michael E. Smith, *The Aztecs* (1996): 62.

229 **Squanto:** Neal Salisbury, "Squanto: Last of the Patuxets," in *Struggle and Survival in Early America*, ed. David G. Smith and Gary B. Nash (1982): 228–46.

230 **"I want to take sulfur":** Shaykh Mushrifuddin Sa'di of Shiraz, *The Gulistan (Rose Garden) of Sa'di*, trans. Wheeler M. Thackston (2008): 85; Benedikt Koehler, *Early Islam and the Birth of Capitalism* (2014): 185.

232 **China needed machines that used less cotton:** Mark Elvin, "The High-Level Equilibrium Trap," in *Another History: Essays on China from a European Perspective*, ed. Mark Elvin (1996): 38.

232 **Only after 1800:** Kenneth Pomeranz, *The Great Divergence: China, Europe, and the Making of the World Economy* (2000).

Illustration and Photograph Credits

Illustration and Photograph Credits

17. Mansa Musa: Alamy Stock Photo Image ID PWCGDH.
18. Bost Palace: Alamy Stock Photo Image ID A47C10.
19. Mahmud of Ghazna: Mahmud b. Sebüktigin receiving a robe from caliph al-Qadir from the album Jami al-tawarikh, University of Edinburgh Library.
20. Amber hand grip: Inner Mongolian Institute of Cultural Relics and Archaeology and Zhelimu League Museum, Tomb of the Princess of State Chen (Beijing: 1993). Color Plate 30: no. 1. Cultural Relics Publishing House.
21. Mounted warrior: *Stag Hunt*. Attributed to Huang Zongdao. Edward Elliott Family Collection, Purchase, The Dillon Fund Gift, 1982. Accession number: 1982.3.1. Metropolitan Museum of Art.
22. Borobudur Buddhas: Alamy Stock Photo Image ID EDKXHN.
23. Borobudur boat bas-relief: Alamy Stock Photo Image ID C95YNM.
24. Double canoe: *A canoe of the Sandwich Islands, the rowers masked, Series.* Rex Nan Kivell Collection (NK1224/15), *Pictures Collection of the National Library of Australia. ID no.* 1789062.
25. Two Persian vessels: The Louvre, accession nos. Mao S 2488 and 524. © RMN-Grand Palais/Art Resource NY.
26. Genji: *The Plum Tree Branch (Umegae), Illustration to Chapter 32 of* The Tale of Genji *(Genji monogatari)* by Tosa Mitsunobu, datable to 1509–10. Rendition Number: 75054A; Accession Number: 1985.352.32.A. Harvard Art Museums/Arthur M. Sackler Museum, Bequest of the Hofer Collection of the Arts of Asia.
27. Haeinsa Library: Geoff Steven; Our Place World Heritage Collection.
28. Byodoin: Alamy Image ID: A4ATPR

Interior

48 Inuit carving: Drawing by Amelia Sargent.
51 Icelandic map: Royal Danish Library, GKS 2881 kvart, The Skálholt Map.
103 Bluetooth logo: Drawing by Amelia Sargent.
218 Qingming scroll furniture store: Zhang Zeduan, *Qingming shanghetu*, Beijing Palace Museum copy, section 25 of 26 photographs, near the end of the painting. Cultural Relics Press, China.
221 Quanzhou shipwreck: The Maritime Museum of Quanzhou, Fujian (Fujian sheng Quanzhou haiwai jiaotongshi bowuguan) (ed.), *Quanzhouwan Songdai haichuan fajue yu yanjiu* (1987): 191, photo no. 7.

Index

Index

Index

Index

Index

Index

Index

Index

Kitan peoples *(cont.)*
    Song dynasty's war and later peace
        with, 158–59, 160, 212
    tanistry system and, 156–57
Kolodny, Annette, 37–38
Korea, 158–59, 166
Koumbi Saleh, Ghana empire, 131, 137
Kyoto, Japan, 164, 166, 200–1

Labrador, 27, 36, 40–41, 46, 60–61
Labrador Current, 21
Landa, Diego de, 71, 77
L'Anse aux Meadows, Newfoundland,
    40–44, 52
    archeological evidence of Norse
        settlement of, 43, 44
    Dorset objects found in, 35
    Ingstads' research on structures and
        objects at, 40–42, 57
    lack of grapes at as contradiction to
        Vinland identification of, 42–43
    Norse abandonment of, 44–45
    Norse settlement of, 40–44, 49, 57
    range of indigenous groups at, 35
    Vinland sagas' information as guide
        to, 35, 44
Lapland, 31
Las Monjas, Chichén Itzá, Mexico, 58
Late Woodland peoples, 61
Latin America. *See also specific countries*
    maritime trade with, 76
Latin Empire, 110
Latin sources and texts, 14, 16, 18, 30, 39,
    49, 50, 105, 124, 200
Leif Erikson, 21, 44
    Erik the Red's Saga on, 30
    Helluland landing of, 27, 40
    Markland landing of, 27, 40
    naming of Vinland by, 27, 42
    shipwrecked sailors rescued by, 47, 59
    Vinland landing of, 27–28, 40, 42–43,
        46
    voyage to Americas by, 27–28, 81
Leifsbudir, Vinland, 27, 28, 29, 42–43, 44
Liao dynasty, East Asia, 157, 158–61
    Buddhism and, 162, 163–65
    capitals used by nomadic rule of, 158–59
    founding of, 157
    Japan's contact with, 159, 164, 165
    Jurchen invasion and, 212
    negotiations between Mahmud and
        the Ghaznavids and, 160–63

Northern Pagoda built by, 163–64
Princess of Chen tomb artifacts in,
    159–60
Song ban on export of coins to,
    207–8
Song dynasty's war and later peace
    with, 158–59, 160
trading contacts of, 159, 164
treaty on trade limits between Song
    dynasty and, 158, 165, 207, 208
Limits of the World, The (Persian
    geographic work), 147
Lindisfarne, Northumberland, United
    Kingdom, 31
Liudprand of Cremona, 93

Madagascar, 172–73, 174, 177, 184, 219
madrasas, 149, 231
Mahmud of Ghazna, 158
    attack on Hindu temple in India for
        gold by, 151–52
    dynastic succession after death of, 166
    Firdawsi's satire on, 155
    Ghaznavid rule in Central Asia and,
        150–53
    Khwarazm conquered by, 154
    negotiations between Liao dynasty
        and, 160–63
    North India raids of, 151–52, 158
    peace between the Karakhanids and
        Ghaznavids achieved by, 155–56
Maine
    archeological research in, 60
    Norse presence in, 44, 46
Malacca Strait, 180–81, 186, 203, 225
Malagasy language, 172
Malal, king of, 122–23, 125, 134
Malaya, 19, 192
Malayo-Polynesian languages, 172–73
Malayo-Polynesian routes, 177–78
Malay Peninsula, 172–73, 174, 177, 188,
    191, 192, 204
Malaysia, 199
Malinché, 228–29, 230
Mamluk dynasty, Egypt, 137
Manguin, Pierre-Yves, 173–74, 177
Mansa Musa, of Mali, 138–39, 152
Mansur, caliph, 124
maps
    African trade routes, 112
    of Afro-Eurasia by Cresque (1375),
        139

Index

Index

Index

Index

Index

Princess of Chen tomb, Kitan
   peoples, artifacts and, 159–60
Rus confederation in Eastern Europe
   for, 81–82, 84
Rus routes in, 87–88, 90
Sacred Cenote, Chichén Itzá, artifacts
   and, 73, 74
slaves and. *See* slave trade
trading centers of Americas, 54 (map)
treaty limits on Song dynasty and the
   Liao in, 158, 165, 207, 208
Venetian merchants in Byzantine
   empire and, 106–7
Vietnam and, 196
Vinland sagas' information on, 35, 38
Wabanaki Alliance and, 36
translation of texts, and technological
   transfer, 124–25
Treaty of Chanyuan (1005), 158, 160,
   161, 165, 167, 207, 208, 212, 213
Turkey, slaves from, 121
Turkic language, 151
Turkic mercenary soldiers, 126, 127
Turkic slaves, 126, 127, 150
Turkic tribes. *See also* Oghuz; *specific
   tribes*, 102, 147, 155–56, 163
Tyrkir the Southerner, 42–43

Ulfberht swords, 86–87
Ultimate Drain belief, 224–25, 231
Urban II, Pope, 108, 110
Uighurs, 157, 161–62
Uzbekistan, 92, 144, 146, 147

Varangian Russians, 91, 93
Venetian galleys, 78
Venetian merchants, and tensions in
   Constantinople, 106–7, 110, 234
Vietnam, 24, 178, 196–97, 203, 217, 224
Vikings, 27–52, 231. *See also* Norse
Adam of Bremen's history on voyages
   of, 40
boats and ships used by, 31–33
burial practices of, 32
in Chichén Itzá, possible presence,
   55–58
earliest voyages and raids of, 31
England and, 92
importance of voyages across the
   Atlantic by, 51–52
Ingstads' research on voyages of, 40–41
as key player in the year 1000, 2

L'Anse aux Meadows settlement by,
   40–44
Leif Erikson's voyage and, 27–28
map (1590) showing understanding
   of Americas by, 50–51
meaning of "viking," 31
Mediterranean activities of, 91
navigation techniques of, 24, 32
North American exploration of, 26
   (map)
range of voyages and trade of, 32
reasons for exploratory voyages of,
   30–31
reliability of Vinland sagas'
   information about, 34, 35, 37
slaves on voyages of, 29, 43, 45–46
slave trade and, 85
Thorvald Erikson's voyage to, 28, 30
three separate voyages to Americas
   by, 27
use of term in book, 31
Vinland sagas' description of life of,
   before Christianity, 30–31
Viking Ship Hall, Bygdoy, Norway, 32
Vinland
Adam of Bremen's history on, 40, 49, 50
lack of grapes on Newfoundland as
   contradiction to name of, 42–43
L'Anse aux Meadows settlement and,
   40–44
later European knowledge of, after
   Norse departure, 49, 50
Leif Erikson's landing on, 27–29, 40,
   42–43
Leifsbudir settlement on, 27, 28, 29,
   42–43, 44
map (1590) showing, 50–51
naming of, 27, 42–43
Norse decision to abandon
   settlements in, 47, 50
possible locations for, 40–41, 44, 45
   (map)
reliability of sagas' information on,
   34, 37
Thorfinn Karlsefni's description of
   indigenous people on, 28–29,
   38–39
Vinland sagas' information on, 44
Vinland sagas, 39–40, 49. *See also Erik the
   Red's Saga; Greenlanders' Saga*
anecdote soup theory on
   composition of, 34–35

Index